Word

for the

Day

KATHY BARKER

ISBN 978-1-0980-8590-2 (paperback)
ISBN 978-1-0980-8591-9 (digital)

Christian Faith Publishing, Inc.
832 Park Avenue
Meadville, PA 16335
www.christianfaithpublishing.com

Printed in the United States of America

To my family who captures my heart, I am blessed to share life with you! I send special thanks to each person who has prayed over our family, sent a card, worked alongside of us, and supported us. To a special couple who loaned their camper, we will never forget your acts of love and friendship you have graciously shown our children. Prayer partners, you are a God-send! You know who you are, and I cherish our bond! I give special recognition to The First Pentecostal Holiness Church family (Goldsboro, North Carolina) and to Samaritan's Purse. We are forever grateful!

INTRODUCTION

The date was September 14, 2018. Hurricane Florence made landfall on North Carolina's coast. The storm slowed to a crawl, dumping over thirty inches of rain. Storm surge and rain totals produced record-breaking floods in the coastal areas. My son and daughter-in-law were hunkered down at the grandparents' house, listening to the howling winds and watching the yard disappear into inches of rain. They had just bought their first home a few miles from there. Living a couple of hours inland, my husband and I witnessed the outer bands of the storm, but the greatest concern was our children. Were they okay? What about their new property? Our communication was limited since we had lost power and had to conserve cell phone usage. Our first inkling of what was to come was the news that the Reserves had been sent to my children's neighborhood. I was so grateful my children had decided to evacuate the day before the storm arrived. Days passed before the storm moved. A couple more days passed before they could venture out to see if their new home had incurred damage.

I will never forget the day my son called to tell us they lost everything. The house flooded. The grief was suffocating. Yes, I was very grateful that my children were safe, but I also understood the depth of their loss. They had invested all they had to get a home. Now they were tied to a thirty-year mortgage on a home that was no longer livable. News like this hits a parent's gut. We had prayed about this house. We felt the Lord gave them this house. I continually reassured them that the Lord wouldn't allow what He had just given them to be taken from them. Never have His words created a more teachable moment for me: "'My thoughts are nothing like your thoughts,' says the LORD. 'And my ways are far beyond anything you could imagine'" (Isaiah 55:8 NLT).

For *days* I walked in a *daze*. I had no words. The Lord allowed me some time to process my grief. Then He spoke into my spirit and encouraged me to get up and get going. There was much to do. My children were going to need me more than ever now. Help was on the way, and I needed to prepare them for it. I remember reaching for my phone and calling them to share the words the Lord placed in my spirit. "Help is on the way. Get ready for it. Allow people to help you. The Lord is sending them."

My pastor was one of the first to reach them. He went with words of love, compassion, and encouragement, assuring them their church family would walk through this ordeal with them all the way. We will be forever grateful for the day he pulled up in the driveway where my children stood, staring at their home in disbelief. My pastor came with more than words. He handed them cash to help meet their immediate needs. My church family followed. A group drove down and spent a couple of days mucking out the house. The stench and the heat were suffocating, but the volunteers didn't complain. The work they completed was incredible, but the love they showed was priceless! The outpouring of gifts has continued throughout this twenty-one-month journey. I cannot name every person or organization that has come to our rescue, but my heavenly Father can and will reward each one graciously!

Shortly after the cleanup began, my Father started speaking words into my spirit to help me encourage my children. As I dove into His Word, He would give me a word. As I read the Scriptures, it seemed as though a word would jump out at me. Through this rebuilding journey, I have shared my "Word for the Day" with my children and anyone who would read my daily posts. According to 2 Corinthians 1:4 (NLT), "He comforts us in all our troubles so that we can comfort others. When they are troubled, we will be able to give them the same comfort God has given us." We all have our troubles. Yours may be different from mine, but God has a word—His Word—that heals, encourages, teaches, and prepares us. My "Word for the Day" came from diving into His Word. At a time when my words became empty, He replaced them with His. I'm so honored to share His Word with you.

Word for the Day

PRACTICAL

One of the things I love about the Bible is that it's the perfect life lesson book. Our Creator cared about us before we were ever born, and He's made provisions for us to live with Him in heaven someday. He also cares deeply about what's going on today, what we're facing next week, and the choices we make. His Word addresses truths for *practical* living.

When we obey these truths, we find success in every aspect of living: physically, financially, emotionally, relationally—as well as spiritually. Our heavenly Father created the whole person—each layer of our being. Each layer is divinely connected. Each part is impacted when one part is suffering or neglected.

The Bible is loaded with *practical* truths. Proverbs is a great book filled with nuggets of wisdom. Ephesians chapters 5 and 6 contain valuable life lessons. Paul tells us to imitate God. He's the perfect role model. He provides *practical* life lessons for successful family living. Wives must respect their husbands and acknowledge them as head of the family. Husbands must love their wives as Christ loved the church—a sacrificial love that puts her needs first. Children are instructed to obey their parents because it's the right thing to do. Workers and leaders alike are encouraged to respect each other, working as though what we do is for the Lord.

When heeded, God's Word brings blessings. Success hinges on our willingness to put life lessons into practice. Knowing His truth is one thing. Living it makes all the difference!

Word for the Day

INHERITANCE

Have you ever wondered what you might *inherit* from family? Maybe it's Grandmama's corner table you've always loved, or the quilt your mother made, or the knife that's been passed from one generation to another. But more importantly, have you thought about what you will pass on?

The Gospels share the account of Jesus's trial and crucifixion. Pilate, the Roman governor, found no fault in Jesus and desired to release Him. The mob cried louder to crucify Jesus. As many politicians often do, Pilate gave in to the rioting crowd, but he washed his hands before them to symbolize his innocence in murdering Jesus. The people yelled, "We will take responsibility for his [Jesus] death—we and our children!" (Matthew 27:25 NLT). I shudder when I read this verse. How could these people lay this horrific sin on their children?

Our sins don't just hurt us, but those closest to us. How we live our lives—who we live for—will impact our children. Deuteronomy 30:19–20 is one of many scripture passages that compel us to make righteous choices so that our children will be blessed. Father, help me to leave a great *inheritance* to my children and their children in wisdom, godliness, fruitfulness, and wholeness that will bless them for their entire lives.

ARTIST

I love how some people can take a piece of "nothing" and make it so beautiful. That's talent! Our heavenly Father is the master *artist*! What He works with is far more valuable than a commodity or substance. He works with people.

I love the book of Ruth. This Moabite woman wasn't a Jew; she was an outsider. She didn't carry the credentials of God's chosen people. She left her family, hometown, and lifestyle to accompany her mother-in-law to Bethlehem. Fast-forwarding to the end of the book, God chooses Ruth to birth the grandfather of David, His chosen king and leader for Israel. God has a way of taking our "nothingness" and making something beautiful, something meaningful, out of it.

Perhaps you know someone who just can't get it together—someone who seems to be helpless and hopeless. We may look on with pity and even give up on them, but not God! The master *artist* goes to work and creates stunning beauty! Perhaps a small scar remains to tell the story of redemption.

Father, thank You for bringing value and purpose to our existence. Help me to visualize every soul as a piece of artwork in Your hands. As long as there is breath, no one is too far removed from You. Like Ruth, we may not hold prestigious credentials, but our story of redemption gives us "beauty for ashes" and glorifies the master *artist* (Isaiah 61:1–3).

ATTITUDE

Are you wearing an *attitude*? We all are. I have a closet full of *attitude*! Some of it needs to be trashed—not even valuable enough for yard sale or donation. I can assure you the *attitude* stored in my closet that speaks encouragement, models compassion, and works alongside others comes directly from Christ, my Savior. I would love to get rid of the rest of my *attitudes*, but you know how it is. The enemy displays the clearance rack, and I buy into the cheap stuff!

The character of God comes at a higher cost. Encouragement and compassion come by trials. Working with others requires the fruit of the Spirit working in us. Philippians 2:5–7 (NLT) says, "You must have the same attitude that Christ Jesus had. Though he was God, he did not think of equality with God… Instead, he gave up his divine privileges." I love that! Jesus gave up His divine privileges for us!

Sometimes we have to lay aside our entitlements to serve. Sometimes this entails suffering so that God the Father can work through us to model comfort, courage, and faith to a hopeless world. This generation has a closet full of *attitude*, but it's the things of God that truly make us beautiful. I need to get into the Word and add more of His character to my closet!

Word for the Day

HOME

Being the great teacher, Jesus often used stories to expose truth. He told the story of a prodigal son in Luke 15. The story goes like this: A man had two sons. The younger one wanted his inheritance immediately, so he could move out and do his own thing. The young son left home with his portion and lived it up until there was nothing left. His precarious lifestyle left him destitute and stripped of all the comforts and security he had once known. The young man came to his senses and realized he was living far below the living conditions of the servants in his father's house. The young man returned *home* to ask his dad to take him back as a servant, for he no longer felt worthy of sonship. The father saw him coming, long before he ever reached the house. I can imagine the father ran with all his strength to meet his son. The young man was welcomed with the finest clothing and a celebration feast.

Romans 3:23 says we all have sinned and fall short of God's glory; but when we come *home*, we find the Father eagerly waiting for us. He celebrates our return and clothes us with His glorious righteousness! We become royal sons and daughters of the King! Have you come *home*? Your Father is looking for you!

TRAINING

I was never good in sports. In elementary school, I was usually the last one picked to play on a team. When I was a freshman in college, I joined an intramural baseball team for girls. We were called the "Classic Collection." Our team was composed of girls who had never played sports. This was my kind of team! In case you're wondering, we never won any games, but I did enjoy wearing the baseball t-shirt!

Looking back, I think there were two things I lacked in being athletically competitive: interest and *training*. It takes both to be successful. In 1 Timothy 4:8 (NLT), Paul says, "Physical training is good, but training for godliness is much better, promising benefits in this life and in the life to come." I believe God wants us to take care of our bodies—inside and out. The spiritual condition, however, must be first and foremost. When we *train* for spiritual fitness, we benefit wholly—emotionally, physically, financially, relationally, and spiritually. Not only do we enjoy the benefits today, but we have a secure future filled with glorious benefits that cannot be fully described or imagined.

At my age, I recognize the importance and benefits of physical *training*. It can make the difference in my quality of life. At my age, I'm absolutely convinced *training* in godliness is priority. It can make the difference in life and death!

Word for the Day

MIRACULOUS

What better word describes our Lord and Savior? Mark 5 tells how a couple of guys returned from a long night of fishing without catching a thing. (Sound familiar, guys?) Jesus asked to use their boat, and Simon Peter launched it for Him. Afterward, Jesus instructed Peter to take the boat out a bit deeper and cast his nets again. Peter was exhausted from the long night's work and disappointed that he had come up empty-handed, but this time was different. The "Fisherman" was onboard! Jesus created the fish and strategically placed them to fill Peter's nets that morning.

Often our best efforts are just not enough, but what God can do surpasses explanation or imitation. He is *miraculous*! We must not dismiss the *miracles* that God is doing in our lives. He will move heaven and earth for His children! "For the eyes of the LORD run to and fro throughout the whole earth, to show Himself strong on behalf of those whose heart is loyal to Him" (2 Chronicles 16:9 NKJV).

Word for the Day

YES!

One day Jesus met a man, at the pool of Bethesda, who had been sick for thirty-eight years. Crowds of diseased people camped around the pool as they waited for the water to be stirred. The scripture says whoever entered the pool first, once the water was stirred, was healed. Jesus knew this man had been sick for a long time, so He asked the man if he wanted to be made well. You would think the man would have eagerly responded, "*Yes, yes, oh yes!* Will you help me?" Instead, he proceeded to tell Jesus his sad story. "'I can't, sir,' the sick man said, 'for I have no one to put me into the pool when the water bubbles up. Someone else always gets there ahead of me'" (John 5:7 NLT). This man didn't have a clue that he was talking to the Healer—the one who sent the angel to stir the water.

Sometimes we are required to wait on the Lord. The length of the wait can blur our vision, cloud our faith. Consequently, our expectations dwindle, and we settle for where we are—just camping out by the pool. Father, Your promises are for me and are forever! Teach me how to live in the miracle, not the moment. May my faith unequivocally say *yes*.

> "Therefore do not cast away your confidence, which has great reward" (Hebrews 10:35 NKJV).

PURIM

According to the book of Esther, the Festival of *Purim* was established for the Jews to remember and celebrate the intervention of God against a plot to annihilate them. The man responsible for this scheme was Haman. He convinced the king to issue a decree to destroy the Jews. The date of annihilation was determined by casting lots (called *Purim*).

All the while, God was looking out for His people. He placed Esther (a Jew) into the palace as the queen to King Xerxes. God gave her favor with the king. Esther's guardian, Mordecai, tells her, "Who knows if perhaps you were made queen for just such a time as this?" (Esther 4:14 NLT).

Once the decree was issued, Esther risked her own life, revealing her nationality to the king and her desire to save her people. While his decree could not be revoked, the king issued a second one, permitting the Jews to defend themselves. God favored the Jews. Haman and all their enemies were destroyed.

Perhaps the enemy has scheduled an attack for you. Our Warrior God already knows the dates and times. Sometimes He chooses to stop the attack before it starts, and we are totally unaware of the battle. Other times, our Father allows the battle to come, but we are never left to fight it alone. The battle has purpose: it teaches, strengthens, and matures us. We too can celebrate *Purim*. Whatever time—day or night—the enemy chooses, our Warrior God is already a step ahead! "In your strength I can crush an army; with my God I can scale any wall" (2 Samuel 22:30 NLT).

ABANDON

I am guilty of starting projects I never finish. Of course, I have plenty of reasons. Perhaps a more fitting word is "excuses!" Sometimes the inspiration dwindles, or distractions take me in a different direction. Other times I may get tired when I don't see the end in sight. In any case, whatever was important at one time loses its value, and the project is *abandoned*.

Chapters 11 and 12 of 2 Samuel describe a major downfall in the life of David—a man who had fought battle after battle and won victory after victory for the Israelites. In the spring of the year when kings normally went out to war, King David sent his army, but this time, he stayed home. Perhaps he was tired, or maybe the "good life" distracted him. Whatever caused him to *abandon* his duty as commander was a major mistake for David. Had he continued in the pursuit of battle, he would not have been walking on the palace roof and seen a married lady bathing. Instead of thinking about the pleasure this woman could bring, he would have been thinking about the enemy and how to win another victory for his kingdom. In the process, David not only *abandoned* his soldiers, but he *abandoned* his conscience, his soul, his favor with God.

Whatever causes us to stray from our convictions will eventually cause us to *abandon* our walk with God. When we back away from our daily personal time with the Lord, our inspiration can dwindle, distractions may take us elsewhere, and weariness can cause us to lower our guard. Make no mistake—the enemy is on it!

Father, there are so many things to do and never enough time to do them. Help me to prioritize what's important to You. Reveal those things that can pull me away from You. Teach me to *abandon* those things, not our time, not our relationship. "Search me, O God, and know my heart… And see if there is any wicked way in me, And lead me in the way everlasting" (Psalm 139:23–24 NKJV).

STOP

There is so much to learn about David. He was a courageous young man. He was talented. He was a great warrior. He went from leading sheep to leading the nation of Israel. He was a man after God's own heart! But in chapters 11 and 12 of 2 Samuel, the Scriptures show David was in the wrong place at the wrong time.

Have you ever been there? David yielded to temptation and had sexual relations with a married woman. His attempt to hide his sin only catapulted David into one sinful dilemma after another, leading him to murdering a loyal soldier in his own army. Eventually, his sins led to the death of his own innocent child. That's what sin does—destroys everything and everyone we love.

The devil will say you've already messed up, there's no going back. He will try to convince you to cover things up. And if you fall for that, he may even convince you it's okay, you're justified in what you're doing. Sin rarely ends with one action, but it can! All we have to do is *stop* and ask for forgiveness. First John 1:9 (NLT) says, "If we confess our sins to him, he is faithful and just to forgive." Had David initially repented, he would not have lost so much.

Father, when I take a wrong step, give me the courage to *stop* in my tracks and confess my wrong. Thank You for being faithful to forgive. Thank You for saving me from continuing a destructive path.

Word for the Day

WHY

I imagine we all ask the question, *"Why?"* I have asked this question many times. Sometimes the answer has come swiftly, and some answers are yet to be revealed. In Judges 6, the angel of the LORD told Gideon He was with him. "Gideon replied, 'if the LORD is with us, why has all this happened to us? And where are all the miracles'" (Judges 6:13 NLT).

Have you ever felt this way? Sometimes the answer is disobedience, as it was in the case of Gideon and the Israelites. Sometimes the answer is that God may be glorified, that we be matured and prepared to serve. Other times, we continue to wait for revelation. Our Father understands there are times when people like Gideon, you, and I reach a crossroad where we feel we have been abandoned.

When Jesus was hanging on the cross for us, He asked God, "Why have You forsaken Me?" Perhaps Jesus said this, knowing hurting people could relate and be assured that God is still our Father and He is working all things for good. The crossroad doesn't have to shake our devotion to Him or destroy our faith in Him. And the hurt that the Father sees in our eyes does not offend Him. The hurt in His eyes reveals His complete compassion for us. You may be searching for answers. That's okay with God, but until the answers come, just trust Him for all the *whys* in your life.

Word for the Day

BELIEVE

The word *believe* is common and used frequently, but I'm not sure many of us recognize its power. No, I'm not talking about a Christmas Hallmark movie! I'm talking about the unlimited power of God!

In Judges 6, God told Gideon to destroy the Midianites and that He would be with him. Just like most of us, Gideon wanted a sign; he wanted proof. He asked for a supernatural sign, and God granted it. But then Gideon wanted another sign, just in case the first one was a coincidence. I confess I can be like that too! If I ask for a miracle and God grants it, sometimes I'm slow to share it. I'm afraid others may not *believe*. Perhaps there is a seed of doubt in my own mind. I find myself explaining the miracle away.

Today, standing in the middle of much needed miracles, I unequivocally proclaim that I *believe*! Either we *believe* the Word, or we don't. It's all the way or nothing! I'm all in today! I *believe*! Jesus said, "If you can believe, all things are possible to him who believes" (Mark 9:23 NKJV).

DONKEY

I have the desire to be an artsy, crafty person; however, my artwork says I'm just average. People look at things I make and say, "You made that, didn't you?" (It's not a compliment, okay!) Their response is gracious, but it really implies that it doesn't look professional or made with skilled hands. You might describe me as one who does a lot of things but nothing extraordinary. The mentality of comparison can impact our Christian service. If we're not careful, we may pass up opportunities to work for the Lord because others are better at it.

God seldom chooses the extraordinary. In Numbers 22, the Lord used a *donkey* to change the mind-set of Balaam. He took an ordinary animal and gave him the ability to speak! The Gospels do not detail the transportation Joseph and Mary used to get to Bethlehem, but tradition portrays Mary and the unborn Son of God riding on a *donkey*. In Matthew 21, Jesus fulfilled the prophecy of riding a *donkey* through Jerusalem as the people shouted, "Hosanna to the Son of David!" (Matthew 21:9 NKJV).

Let me get to the point: God made man in His image and gave us the responsibility to care for the rest of His creation on earth. If the Lord can use a *donkey*—to speak man's language—to carry the very Son of God on his back, perhaps He can use me! The qualifications are few: know Him, be willing, have a teachable spirit, prepare ourselves in the Word, and just "let God." As 2 Corinthians 4:7 (NLT) says, "We now have this light shining in our hearts, but we ourselves are like fragile clay jars containing this great treasure. This makes it clear that our great power is from God, not from ourselves."

Word for the Day

HOME

Exodus 13 describes how the children of Israel were instructed to establish a tradition in their *homes* to celebrate and commemorate the day the Lord brought them out of Egypt. Moses said, "In the future, your children will ask you, 'What does all this mean?'" (Exodus 13:14 NLT). "This ceremony will be like a mark branded on your hand or your forehead. It is a reminder that the power of the LORD's mighty hand brought us out of Egypt" (Exodus 13:16 NLT).

From the Scripture, we can see how important it is for devotions to be established in the *home*. The time we invest in teaching our children about Jesus will be their greatest treasure. Toys, trips, allowances, and cars will come and go, but the Word of God will last a lifetime.

Your children may have strayed. They may not be serving God, but the Word you have planted in their hearts will never depart (Proverbs 22:6). They may run to the far corners of the world, but the Word is implanted within. They take it with them. The Word of God is not void but accomplishes what the Lord desires (Isaiah 55:11). Perhaps you failed to make that connection while your children were at *home*. Now they are grown and gone. It's never too late, friend! God does not want anyone to perish. Your prayers, your tears, move the heart of God, so keep praying and keep believing. Your child may just be one prayer away from receiving salvation!

EYES

My siblings and I have one common facial feature that makes us resemble each other—our *eyes*. We have those small, squinty *eyes* that look like our ponytails were pulled too tight!

In Numbers chapter 13 and 14, there were twelve sets of *eyes* that explored the land of Canaan. Ten sets of *eyes* saw the giants, but two sets of *eyes* saw God's Promised Land flowing with milk and honey—theirs for the taking.

Father, You made us all in Your image. As Your child, I pray that I take on more of Your likeness each day. Teach me to see by Your Word, for it is a lamp to my feet and a light to my path (Psalm 119:105). Though there be giants, help me to see the promises of Your Word. When I cannot see, teach me to trust in You, knowing You will not let me slip (Psalm 121:3). As I grow in You, may others see Your resemblance in me—recognizing I have my Father's *eyes*.

GAP

In Genesis 18, the Lord tells Abraham that the sins of Sodom and Gomorrah have come to His attention. Abraham asks the Lord if He were to find fifty righteous people living there, would He spare the city. When the Lord's response was favorable, Abraham asked the same question—this time reducing the number of righteous people to forty-five. He continued to repeat the question until he asked the Lord if He would spare the entire city for the sake of ten righteous people. Each time the Lord responded with a favorable reply.

Our Father loves us that much! He doesn't want anyone to perish (2 Peter 3:9). God loved you so much that He would have sent His Son to the cross if you were the only person on earth. Let me encourage you to stand in the *gap* for your family, your neighbors, your community, your fellowman. Your prayer may be the one that opens their eyes to the loving Savior.

Word for the Day

PROVISION

Building the family tree has become quite popular. We are all interested in discovering our family story. However, we don't have to purchase ancestry software to learn about our very beginnings—it's recorded for us in Genesis. The Godhead made human beings in their image and designated man to take care of creation. God provided everything we would need to live well and to live forever.

The Garden of Eden had docile animals, beautiful trees and delicious fruit, pure rivers, gold and other fine gems. In the middle of the garden the Lord placed a tree of life, providing fruit whereby Adam and Eve could live forever. Their disobedience changed their lives and ours, but the love of our Creator continued to make *provision*. He established a covenant relationship with a people who would worship Him, and He would be their father who nurtures, *provides*, and protects them. Mankind continued to fail, but God reached out with mercy and made the ultimate *provision*: He sacrificed His only Son, Jesus Christ, to die for mankind's sin debt—once and for all.

This *provision* makes it possible for mankind to return, at God's appointed time, to the life He originally designed for us. We will live forever in peace and harmony and health. "No longer will there be a curse upon anything… And there will be no night there—no need for lamps or sun—for the Lord God will shine on them. And they will reign forever and ever" (Revelation 22:3, 5 NLT).

HOLE

Adam and Eve changed the course of mankind. From the moment they chose to disobey God, our birth nature changed. Sometimes we say there are good people and bad people in this world, but the truth is we are all born with a nature to do wrong. We are all born with a *hole* in our heart, deep within our soul. Sadly, many spend their lifetimes trying to fill the *hole*. We look for purpose and fulfillment in possessions, pleasure, relationships, good deeds, and even religion.

The God-sized *hole* can never be filled by anyone or anything except Jesus Christ. We who know Christ as Lord and Savior have an incredible opportunity to share the good news with a helpless and hopeless world. This world is not about who is good and who is bad. But for the grace of God, my life would be horribly different. What about yours?

Father, I desire to make a difference in someone's life, a home, a community, the world. How can I not share the good news, knowing it fills the God-sized *hole* deep within the soul? I can't change people—that's Your job—but help me see beyond their hardened exterior. Help me look past their sin and see the *hole* deep within that can only be healed by You. May I never become too busy or too backward to share the good news.

"Proclaim the good news of His salvation
from day to day" (Psalm 96:2 NKJV).

26

Word for the Day

LIGHT

Ever find a small *light* annoying when trying to sleep? In the day-time, it's rarely noticed because the *light* is so insignificant. It's only when darkness fills the room that this tiny *light* seems to stare right through you!

Matthew 5:14–15 says we are *light* to the world. The *light* is not meant to be hidden. The *light* of God's love is to be shared with a dark world. The *light* reveals sin, and to some, that is annoying. The *light* also reveals a better way and draws those who are searching for change.

In Acts 9, Paul shares his testimony of how a bright *light* changed his life. The *light* converted him from a raving-mad terrorist to a Spirit-filled apostle of Jesus Christ. The enemy may try to convince us that our *light* is insignificant, but as the childhood jingle goes, "This little *light* of mine, I'm gonna let it shine. Let it shine! Let it shine! Let is shine!"

Father, I pray my *light* shines in this dark world. I desire courage and confidence to stand for truth when I'm surrounded by the lies of darkness. Remind me, Lord, that You have many *light*-bearers. Together, we shine, not only by profession, but by our actions.

> "Let your light so shine before men, that
> they may see your good works and glorify your
> Father in heaven" (Matthew 5:16 NKJV).

LIFT

How long can you extend your arms without getting tired? For me, it's just a few minutes! Exodus 17 describes a battle where it was crucial for Moses to keep his staff *lifted* so that the Israelites would have strategic advantage against their enemy. As long as Moses held up the staff, the Israelites prevailed in battle. Moses found himself getting tired and unable to keep the staff *lifted*. Consequently, the Amalekites would gain advantage, so a couple of guys stood on each side of Moses to keep his hands raised. By sunset, the enemy was totally destroyed, and there is no record of Amalekite inhabitants today.

What can we learn from this passage? We need to *lift* up each other. Victory is contingent on our faith. Sometimes we need the support of prayer partners who will stand with us. The waiting can get long and tiresome. I'm so grateful for Christian friends who will agree to *lift* my needs to the Father. We don't always know what others are facing or will face, but our heavenly Father often brings them to mind.

Father, help me to hear Your whisper of a friend's name or face. May I drop to my knees for them, encourage them, and be there for them. I thank You for every prayer partner and encourager You send my way.

> "Pray for each other so that you may be healed. The earnest prayer of a righteous person has great power and produces wonderful results" (James 5:16 NLT).

Word for the Day

MANNA

While the children of Israel were wandering in the wilderness, the Lord provided *manna* to sustain them. Exodus 16:31 (NKJV) says that the *manna* tasted like "wafers made with honey." We who have a sweet tooth would probably find *manna* appealing. My pastor would probably say it resembles Krispy Kreme doughnuts!

Shortly after the Israelites entered Canaan, Joshua reestablished the covenant ceremonies that God set in place for them. Joshua 5:10–12 (NLT) says they celebrated Passover. "The very next day they began to eat unleavened bread and roasted grain harvested from the land. No manna appeared on the day they first ate from the crops of the land, and it was never seen again."

Our Father is always with us, but He's closest when we are being tested. In our times of trial, our compassionate Father is feeding us spiritual *manna* to sustain us through these times. No one likes to struggle, but the hard times bring nurturing and a refining process that is life-changing. You may be walking through one of those times today. Know the Lord is offering all the *manna* you can eat. There's nothing comparable to the sweet comfort of our loving Father.

Word for the Day

FAMILY

Missionary work doesn't have to take us across country or even across town. We can be missionaries within our own home. I am so grateful for my Christian heritage! In my growing up years, we never had to decide if we were going to church. We didn't take a vote, didn't think about how tired we were, or if we had the time. We just did! We gathered around the table and knelt in prayer before each meal—everyday. Let me be transparent. We certainly had our problems. Most of them were due to my siblings of course! The stories I could tell. Seriously, the love of God was lived in front of us kids and carries great influence in our lives today.

We are living in the last days, and our *families* are under attack. There's no amount of discipline or tolerance that will restore the *family* unit. Only God can! What can we do? Let the words of Joshua become our resolve: "But as for me and my family, we will serve the LORD." (Joshua 24:15 NLT). Consecrating our *family* to God is His will, and "this is the confidence that we have in Him, that if we ask anything according to His will, He hears us" (1 John 5:14 NKJV).

Some of the hardest missionary work may be done right within our own walls. As Jesus says in Mark 12:30 (NKJV), "Love the LORD your God will all your heart, with all your soul, with all your mind, and with all your strength." When we love God with all our hearts, our *family* members will see Christ in us; they will know us at our best! Then we are loving our *families* with the love God gives us. His love reaches further than ours ever will. Never underestimate the love of God!

GARMENT

Second Samuel 6 describes King David and the house of Israel celebrating and worshipping God as the Ark of the Lord was being transported home. David took off his royal robe, put on a linen ephod, and danced before the Lord with all his might. The ephod was a worship *garment* often worn by the priests. Perhaps David wore the worship *garment* as an act of reverence. Maybe the royal attire was heavy and would have prevented David from dancing with vigor. In any case, this made me think: what keeps us from worshipping with all our might?

Is it the *garment* of busyness? Our lives are filled with too much stuff, and there's never enough time. Being overloaded, we consequently find ourselves dressed in the *garment* of weariness. Mind and body being depleted, we go through the mechanical process of worship but fail to connect with the heart. How about the *garment* of worry? A similar *garment* is sure to follow: doubt—making it hard to see the miracle for the moment. Perhaps some of us wear the *garment* of pride—always worrying about what others think. I must confess I have these *garments* in my closet, and I have worn them all at one time or another.

My desire is to lay these heavy *garments* aside and put on the *garment* of praise. When we do that, we receive the abundance Christ has provided: "A crown of beauty for ashes, a joyous blessing instead of mourning, festive praise instead of despair" (Isaiah 61:3 NLT). Never underestimate the power of praise. It gets the attention of God and brings us into His presence.

FEET

Am I the only one who wonders where time goes? I didn't think so! Our mind has a way of rehearsing all the things we need to do, cluttering our thought process. When I get overwhelmed, I engage in a two-minute exercise to clean the clutter! Starting the timer, I begin writing down everything I need to do as quickly as I can. Usually I empty my brain before the two-minute buzzer alarms. To my surprise, my task list is not as big as my brain suggests!

The Gospels describe a woman named Martha who may have benefited from my two-minute exercise. Jesus came to visit Martha and her sister, Mary. Martha had dinner to prepare, and she found herself frustrated that Mary was just sitting at the *feet* of Jesus. I imagine Martha was mumbling to herself as she was peeling the potatoes. Frustration peaking, Martha says to Jesus, "'Lord, doesn't it seem unfair to you that my sister sits here while I do all the work? Tell her to come and help me.' But the Lord said to her, 'My dear Martha, you are worried and upset over all these details! There is only one thing worth being concerned about. Mary has discovered it, and it will not be taken away from her'" (Luke 10:40–42 NLT).

The time we spend going here and there, doing this and that, may consume our day with little gain, but the time we spend sitting at the *feet* of Jesus is never wasteful. "Seek the Kingdom of God above all else, and live righteously, and he will give you everything you need" (Matthew 6:33 NLT).

Word for the Day

ABIDE

While reading John 15, I had a flashback of my shortest career. It lasted an entire day! My sister talked me into hoeing weeds from a watermelon field. While neither of us knew anything about working in a field, she persuaded me to take the job saying it would be easy money and we would get lots of sun. Within a couple of hours, we knew we were not cut out for this. I probably chopped down as many watermelon plants as I did weeds. Needless to say, we didn't go back for a second day, and I imagine the farmer was relieved. Had we continued to work, we may have wiped out his entire crop of watermelons!

Jesus says in John 15:4 (NLT) that a "branch cannot produce fruit if it is severed from the vine." When I read this, I can't help but think of all those watermelon plants I chopped! In verse 5 (NKJV), Jesus says, "I am the vine, you are the branches. He who abides in Me, and I in him, bears much fruit; for without Me you can do nothing."

Our Father breathes life into our soul. He says no one can snatch us from His hand (John 10:28–29). If we become severed, it is of our own choosing. If we choose to *abide* in Him, this is His promise to us: "If you abide in Me, and My words abide in you, you will ask what you desire, and it shall be done for you" (John 15:7 NKJV).

DO

Peter is one of my favorite disciples. As much as I admire him, Peter was loud and always speaking out of turn. I've made as many mistakes as Peter did, but I tend to hang out in the shadows where my blunders aren't as public!

Acts 2 records a gospel sermon preached by a mighty man of God who spoke with authority and conviction. This single sermon brought three thousand people to the Lord! The mighty man of God was Peter—the same Peter who jumped out of the boat to walk on water and then became frightened and began to sink. This is the same Peter who attempted to correct Jesus's theology on feet washing. I'm talking about Peter who totally denied knowing Jesus after He was arrested. How could a man like this become the great evangelist?

What change came about that made such a difference in Peter? The Holy Spirit changed Peter from the inside out—empowering his testimony with a freshly added dimension of truth and boldness. God's Holy Spirit can *do* the same thing in us! The Spirit greatly enriches our lives, but He comes with purpose. The Spirit stirs us within, but He brings more than a feeling—He has come to help us *do* Kingdom work. The Spirit of God within us can *do* all things (Philippians 4:13).

There's an old chorus I grew up singing that goes like this: *"Holy Spirit, flow through me. Holy Spirit, flow through me, and make my life what it ought to be. Holy Spirit, flow through me."*

Holy Spirit, *do* in me what I cannot *do* for myself. *Do* through me what glorifies You, the Son, and the Father.

SOURCE

I prefer fixing something—finding the solution instead of "Band-Aiding" it. My motto is "Fix it now, fix it right, so you don't touch it a second time." Doing just enough to get by only means the problem will return. I admit it's not always feasible, but when we can, it's worth fixing it right the first time.

What makes us try to Band-Aid our lives with alternatives instead of heading straight to the *source*? The world does this because they don't know the *source*, but as born-again children of God, perhaps we should ask ourselves this question. I believe the Lord has given us the body and mind to put a roof over our heads. Ecclesiastes 3:13 (NKJV) says, "Every man should eat and drink and enjoy the good of all his labor—it is the gift of God."

We must remind ourselves, however, that our Creator is the *source* that gives us the ability and the strength to do for ourselves. He is also the *source* to do in us and for us what we cannot do for ourselves.

Psalm 43:4 says God is our *source* of joy.

Psalm 119:114 says the Lord is our *source* of hope.

Isaiah 45:24 says the Lord is the *source* of our righteousness and strength.

Micah 5:5 says the Lord will be our *source* of peace.

First Corinthians 12:4 says the Spirit is the *source* of our spiritual gifts.

Second Corinthians 1:3 says God is our *source* of comfort.

Hebrews 5:9 says Jesus is our *source* of eternal salvation.

As my dad often says, "Do what you can for yourselves, and let the Lord do the rest." Don't overlook the *source*!

STRONGHOLD

Proverbs 18:10 (NLT) is one of my all-time scripture favorites. "The name of the LORD is a strong fortress; the godly run to him and are safe."

One dictionary refers to a fortress as a military *stronghold*. I often think of a *stronghold* as some type of bondage that the devil holds over us, but do you know the name of Jesus carries a *stronghold* over the believer? How powerful is that? If we run to Him, we are safe from any attack the devil can launch at us. The name of Jesus strongly defends our faith!

Romans 8:37 (NKJV) says, "We are more than conquerors through Him who loved us." The New Living Translation (NLT) version says, "Overwhelming victory is ours." We don't have to live as though we are barely escaping—we can stand with boldness, arms folded, wearing a hallelujah grin, as we camp under the shadow of the Almighty. We have the name of Jesus, and His name sends the devil running!

FRAGRANCE

My sniffer doesn't take in as much as some. It seems like I'm just getting a whiff when others are doused! This may be a good thing, because what smells sweet to one may smell the opposite to another.

Paul says in 2 Corinthians 2:14–15 (NLT), "Now he uses us to spread the knowledge of Christ everywhere, like a sweet perfume. Our lives are a Christ-like fragrance rising up to God. But this fragrance is perceived differently by those who are being saved and by those who are perishing."

Everyone will not accept Christ, but thank God for those who will! Our *fragrance* may not entice every person who crosses our paths. We must remember sharing the gospel is our part. The rest is up to the Lord and the will of each individual. I love how the NLT version describes us as giving off a "Christ-like *fragrance*" to God. Jesus paid our sin debt on the cross, so the stench of our sin never reaches the Father. Purified by the blood of Jesus and drenched in the heavenly aroma of the Holy Spirit, we become like His Son. I could never wash myself clean enough or do enough good to rid myself of sin's stench. As one song says, *"I couldn't earn it. I don't deserve it."*

Father, thank You for cleaning me inside out. I pray the *fragrance* of Your Son, Jesus, never leaves my soul and You are blessed daily by His aroma. I pray my testimony will spread to others like a sweet perfume and they too will experience a life-changing transformation.

WISDOM

The *wisdom* of God rested on the shoulders of His Son, Jesus, at an early age. When Jesus was only twelve years old, He was in the temple sitting among religious teachers, listening, and asking questions. Those who heard His words were amazed at His understanding. The Bible says He grew in *wisdom* and favor with God (Luke 2:41–52).

The Word also tells us that our Father's *wisdom* is available to us for the asking. His *wisdom* will connect us to His will. His *wisdom* is divine and is always appropriate. His *wisdom* cuts straight to the heart of man. His *wisdom* can speak a thousand words in a moment of silence.

Father, I seek Your *wisdom* in every life choice I make. Your *wisdom* will spark life and freedom, confidence and newness in the days ahead.

> "If any of you lacks wisdom, let him ask of God, who gives to all liberally and without reproach, and it will be given to him" (James 1:5 NKJV).

OVERCOMER

After Jesus was baptized, the Scriptures say the Spirit led Him to the wilderness where He fasted for forty days. There the devil met Him, appealing to His hunger, His kingship, and His power (Luke 4:1–13).

In each case, Jesus responded with the Word of God. He could have chosen a different method, but I believe He modeled the only way you and I can effectively deal with the enemy. The devil doesn't flinch at our words and is ready to argue with us all day long. The Word of God, however, draws a line that the devil knows he can't cross.

If we deposit the Word into our hearts and minds daily, we can be prepared for the attacks that will surely come. A healthy dose of the Word will grow our faith, our confidence, and elevate our praise game. The Word will make us *overcomers*!

> "Guide my steps by your word, so I will not
> be overcome by evil" (Psalm 119:133 NLT).

WORSHIP

Matthew 21:12–13 says Jesus entered the temple and began driving out all the people who had turned it into a marketplace. The temple was to be a house of prayer. First Corinthians 6:19 says we are the temple of God and that our body is the temple of the Holy Spirit.

This leads me to ask myself some very important questions: How does my temple look before the Lord? Have I turned my temple into something other than what God designed it to be? *Worship* is more than attending a church service. It's more than a song. It's not confined to one day a week. Rather it's my everyday living—everything I live and breathe, everything I make time for, what I do in the good times and what I do in the bad.

Father, may my *worship* align with Your design. "Let the words of my mouth and the meditation of my heart Be acceptable in Your sight, O LORD, my strength and my Redeemer" (Psalm 19:14 NKJV).

Word for the Day

LOVE

This word has been used so frequently and has become so common that we often miss its magnitude. The *love* of God is a priceless treasure that cannot be purchased or earned, stolen or consumed. It is God's gift to whomever will receive it.

Scriptures tell us that God's perfect *love* casts out fear. And if you've ever felt the grip of fear, you know just how powerful that is. But just think: God's *love* is more powerful than fear! "God is love, and all who live in love live in God, and God lives in them. And as we live in God, our love grows more perfect… Such love has no fear, because perfect love expels all fear. If we are afraid, it is for fear of punishment, and this shows that we have not fully experienced his perfect love" (1 John 4:16–18 NLT).

Living somewhere between fearless and fearful, I strive to grasp the *love* of God in its fullness. Then and only then will I live in complete freedom and abundance through Christ.

Father, open my eyes to embrace the magnitude of Your *love* and forever be changed.

Word for the Day

COMPASSION

John 11 tells the story of two sisters who mourned the loss of their brother, Lazarus. They had sent for Jesus, believing He could heal Lazarus, but Jesus did not arrive in time. Grieving, both sisters told the Lord that if only He had been there, their brother would not have died. Scriptures say Jesus wept at the burial site, and He became deeply troubled. One version says He was angry. His anger was not directed at Mary or Martha, rather the satanic powers that held Lazarus in their grip.

Our Father is raised with indignation when the enemy strikes at us—much like the mama or papa bear instinct that surges when our children are attacked. His *compassion* for us is fiercely strong! Our Father's *compassion* spurs a quick and sure defense, for He will not allow the enemy to have us. Aren't you glad He's your Father?

> "Through the LORD's mercies we are not consumed, Because His compassions fail not. They are new every morning; Great is Your faithfulness" (Lamentations 3:22–23 NKJV).

DEPENDENCE

The Gospels share an account of Jesus feeding five thousand men plus women and children. The day was getting late, and the disciples asked Jesus to send the crowd home so they could get food for themselves. Instead Jesus said, "You feed them." (Great topic to address another time.)

The disciples knew they didn't have the means to feed a crowd such as this. Jesus knew that also, but He wanted the disciples to experience what He could do. The disciples had only five loaves and two fish. At best, their most creative stew, the disciples would surely have disappointed the crowd. When they allowed Jesus to take charge, everyone had all they could eat, and twelve baskets were left over.

God has called us to be His hands and feet in a hopeless and helpless world. At best we can impact a few. Our days are short, so we must *depend* on God—His power, His wisdom, His resources—to get the work done. Our talents, our programs, nor our facilities will ever be enough. "Unless the LORD builds the house, They labor in vain who build it" (Psalm 127:1 NKJV).

Our Father doesn't expect us to accomplish His work within ourselves. He delights to do great things when we declare our *dependence* solely in Him.

Word for the Day

CALLED

First Corinthians 12 says a spiritual gift is given to each of us to help one another. The Spirit decides which gift each person should have. Every believer, however, is *called* to do two things: love God with everything we have and love our neighbor as ourselves.

Jesus defines the term "neighbor" as He tells a story about a man beaten, robbed, and left to die along a roadside. In His story, a priest and a temple assistant ignore the dying man lying helplessly by the road. Perhaps they felt they were too busy doing church work. Certainly, the spiritual gifts of these leaders were important, but church work was never designed to replace our duty to love God first and serve our neighbor.

So who is our neighbor? Not just the person next door or our circle of friends. It's whoever God places in our path on any given day.

Father, teach me to love my neighbor as I want to be loved. When I am loving my neighbor, I am loving You (Luke 10:30–37).

Word for the Day

LIGHT

John 9 tells how Jesus healed a man who had been blind from birth. The Pharisees downplayed the miracle by questioning whether the man had really been blind all his life. When they could not discredit his story, the Pharisees attempted to convince the man that God should get the glory and not this man, Jesus, whom they called a sinner. "'I don't know whether he is a sinner,' the man replied. 'But I know this: I was blind, and now I can see!'" (John 9:25 NLT).

Spiritual blindness covers much of the world. Truth has become whatever one desires it to be. Our Father knew our fleshly desires would steer us the wrong way, so He gave us His Word. The Word of God is a lamp to our feet and a *light* to our path (Psalm 119:105).

It's not what I think; it's not what you think. Our life choices should be solely based on the truth of God's Word. It's always relevant, true, powerful, and life-changing! "The entrance of Your words gives light; It gives understanding to the simple" (Psalm 119:130 NKJV). So go ahead—dig into the Word and dig out of the darkness!

MATURING

The Gospels share many stories about the disciples. My favorite disciple is Peter—the impulsive one, quick to speak, always ready to act, passionate, and sometimes requiring correction. Sound like anyone you know?

At the Last Supper, Jesus told the disciples that one of them would betray Him and they all would desert Him. Peter emphatically declared his loyalty, but Jesus told Peter he would deny Him three times before the rooster crowed twice. Peter did just that—he denied knowing Jesus as predicted. Hearing the rooster crow, he remembered the Lord's words and wept.

After Jesus was resurrected, the angel instructed the ladies at the tomb to go tell the disciples, including Peter, that Jesus would meet them in Galilee (Mark 16:7). I love that verse because the angel specifically names Peter, wanting him to know the Lord still loved him and had plans for him. Peter went on to be a great evangelist, winning around three thousand converts in his very first sermon.

Our Father knows our failures, yet He still loves us. He has plans for our future. He doesn't give up on us when we mess up. He keeps loving on us and *maturing* us.

Father, grow my faith and Your character in me. Thank you for being faithful to forgive. Keep writing my story. May I do everything I can—while I can. Make every moment count for You.

Word for the Day

HOPE

I imagine every Christian knows someone who needs God. We pray for them day after day, week after week, year after year. And we may get discouraged sometimes, wondering if our loved ones and friends will ever accept Christ's saving grace.

Acts describes the conversion of one of the great New Testament preachers. Saul was passionately against Jesus Christ and His followers. His mission was to imprison every Christian he could capture. But Jesus changed his story—gave him a complete makeover. Saul's mission to destroy the followers of Christ was replaced with passion to win people to Christ.

Know God loves every individual as much as He loves His own Son, Jesus. Never underestimate the power of God's grace, and never give up *hope* for your loved ones.

"I wait for the LORD, my soul waits, And in His word I do hope" (Psalms 130:5 NKJV).

MIRACLE

Acts 12 shares the account of Peter's *miraculous* rescue from prison. Though he was guarded by soldiers and shackled in chains, Peter didn't need a SWAT team to move in. The Lord sent one angel. The angel woke up Peter and told him to get dressed. The chains fell off his wrists, and Peter followed the angel right past the guard posts. The iron gate to the city opened up all by itself. All this time, Peter thought he was experiencing a vision. Once he was through the gate and walking down the street, the angel disappeared, and Peter came to his senses. The Lord had *miraculously* rescued him!

Miracles still happen today! Believe in them. Expect them. Don't try to explain them away. Know God is your Warrior God.

> "For the eyes of the LORD run to and fro throughout the whole earth, to show Himself strong on behalf of those whose heart is loyal to Him" (2 Chronicles 16:9 NKJV).

Word for the Day

WITNESS

In Acts 16, Paul and Silas find themselves in prison for delivering a demon-possessed woman. They were stripped, beaten, and chained to the innermost part of the dungeon to ensure they didn't escape. The other prisoners were watching. At midnight, Paul and Silas had worship service! The prisoners heard their prayers and songs as they lavished praise to the Almighty God. Suddenly there was a massive earthquake. Prison doors opened, and the chains of every prisoner fell off! When the jailer woke and discovered the doors were wide open, he drew his sword to kill himself. Paul shouted out to let the jailer know all were accounted for—no one had left the prison. The jailer asked what he could do to be saved.

What an amazing *witness*! Paul and Silas could have felt sorry for themselves and sang the blues. They could have run out of prison when the doors opened, but their actions brought the jailor to Christ—perhaps other prisoners. It's easy to be a *witness* when all is going well, but our light actually shines brighter when we are in a dark place.

Father, teach me how to comfort those with the comfort You have shown me. May Your character shine brightly through me in difficult times (2 Corinthians 1:4).

SERVANTHOOD

The Gospels give the account of Jesus and the disciples sharing the last Passover meal together. Jesus stood up from the table, took off His robe, and began to wash the disciples' feet. He was modeling *servanthood*. Jesus told the disciples that one of them would betray Him. (Had I been sitting around the table, my face would have turned red, and my heart would have knocked inside my chest. Perhaps that's because I know my own weaknesses. But for God's grace, I realize I could be just one choice away from making the biggest mistake of my life.)

Luke 22 says the disciples began to argue among themselves as to who would be greatest. Jesus, The Teacher, began telling them that a leader's heart is not to be lord but to be *servant*. Our culture may align leadership to position, title, rank, and status. But godly leadership *serves* and motivates others to follow.

Father, teach me how to *serve* in Your Kingdom. Give me a humble heart and a teachable spirit. May I approach every task You place in my path with gladness, understanding everything I do is for You (Matthew 25:35–40).

Word for the Day

LABORER

In Luke 19, Jesus was in Jericho and spotted a man sitting in a tree. Jesus called the man by name (Zacchaeus) and told him to come down so He could go home with him. Zacchaeus was thrilled that Jesus noticed him in the crowd. He never dreamt that Jesus would see him, much less ask to go home with him!

Zacchaeus wasn't a friend of the people. He was a tax collector who had prospered by unfairly taking from others. There was something about Jesus. Zacchaeus just had to see. His short stature prevented him from getting a roadside view. Certainly no one was going to be neighborly and offer Zacchaeus front-row accommodations, so he climbed a tree. And then Jesus saw him! Zacchaeus's life was changed that day—he became a new man. Salvation came to his house!

People are seeking for God and may not even know it. Father, show me the Zacchaeuses in my path—those who need You most. Open my eyes that I may see them; open my ears to their faint cries for help. Forgive me for being focused on myself, being so busy that I walk right past them. Give me another chance to be a *laborer* in Your harvest—make a difference in a life.

> "The harvest truly is plentiful, but the laborers are few" (Matthew 9:37 NKJV).

Word for the Day

TRUST

The Gospels describe an evening where Jesus and the disciples encounter a fierce storm as they cross a lake. The waves are breaking into the boat, and it begins to fill with water. Being fisherman and sailors by trade, the disciples' panic clearly defines the severity of the storm. All this time, Jesus is napping! The violent tossing of the boat does not disturb Him. He is not awakened by the howling of the winds or the fierce waves that threaten to sink the boat. The disciples are terrified, for they do not understand the master of the winds is onboard. They wake Jesus, shouting, "Teacher, don't you care that we're going to drown?" (Mark 4:38 NLT).

When crisis hits, we sometimes wonder if Jesus cares. But our Lord is not caught off guard. He knows about our tests, trials, and seasons long before we encounter them.

Father, help me to understand You are my Warrior God. Your outstretched hand covers me, and You are in control. Help me grasp the magnitude of Your love and compassion—Your power and faithfulness. When I fully grasp these things, I will fully *trust* (Psalm 91).

SLEEP

The Old and New Testaments describe two different events where there is a fierce storm on the water and boat passengers fear for their lives. In each event, there is one man aboard who is *sleeping*, while all the other passengers are desperately clinging for life. One man is Jesus; the other man is Jonah.

In both instances, those who are frightened wake up the one who is *sleeping* and ask how he can *sleep* at a time like this. The difference between the two men is this: Jesus *slept* because He was at total peace. He was (and is) the peacemaker. While circumstances were dire, He was always in complete control—having authority to suppress the wind and waves. Jonah *slept* because he was trying to escape the call of God. He knew he had disobeyed God, and the storm was his fault.

When we make wrong choices, we often know deep down. Instead of quickly repenting and getting back on track, sometimes we choose to ignore the warnings. We lull ourselves to *sleep* so that we can simply ignore the Holy Spirit and go our own way.

Father, I pray that when my head hits the pillow tonight, my *sleep* will be sweet—knowing all is well between You and me. "Create in me a clean heart, O God, And renew a steadfast spirit within me" (Psalm 51:10 NKJV).

Word for the Day

CONNECTIONS

D aniel 6 sources the infamous account of Daniel being thrown into a lion's den. What an amazing account of God's intervention and power! There is also a subtle truth that we can extract from this passage, modeling what our work ethics should mirror. The Scriptures say King Darius appointed Daniel to a significant supervisory position in his kingdom. Daniel's work ethics placed him head-and-shoulders above the others—so much that the king planned to place him over the entire empire. You could say Daniel had *connections*.

So what's new in the workplace, right? We've all seen it—people who get selected, promoted, and handed the top job just for who they know or dazzle to get there. But this is what you need to understand: Daniel's *connections* exceeded the throne of King Darius. His *connections* went straight to the top: the Lord God Almighty! His *connections* not only shaped his spiritual-man but impacted his everyday living-man. He worked hard, and he worked with integrity.

It isn't always popular (as this is why Daniel came to be thrown into the lion's den), but it's how we bring glory to God. Our *connections* to the Almighty may not always land us the highest position, but it will always bring the highest praise!

> "Let your light so shine before men, that
> they may see your good works and glorify your
> Father in heaven" (Matthew 5:16 NKJV).

PRESSURE

As a child, I was raised in a very conservative home and sheltered from ungodly culture. Much of my play time involved playing "church." My siblings and I played it big time because, in most of our childhood years, we lived next door to a church house—my father being the pastor.

In contrast, I look at the environment our kids have today. We're frustrated that our schools are failing and feel like all is out of control. Families don't look like families anymore. People murder just for kicks. Protests run rampant. The flag is disrespected. We have strayed so far from truth that we have lost our freedom. We no longer live as the "United" States of America. With that being said, our country still has been blessed for much of its existence. We now join other countries in reaping the chaos we have sown in these latter years.

Chaos was also common in biblical times. Daniel 3 describes the *pressure* imposed in Babylon to worship a gold statue. Three Jews (Shadrach, Meshach, and Abednego) refused to bow to the idol. When questioned by the king, they stood for their rights to serve the Almighty God! Their resolve landed them in a blazing furnace. They believed God would save them (and He did), but they were ready to die.

Father, I want to be a part of this generation who is taking a stand for truth. Make my testimony strong and compelling to the world. I don't want to bow to the *pressure* of society or to Your enemies. Teach me how to stand for Your Word in a way that honors You—with godly boldness, courage, wisdom, and love.

> "Be on guard. Stand firm in the faith. Be courageous. Be strong. And do everything with love" (1 Corinthians 16:13–14 NLT).

Word for the Day

PRAISE

Do you ever think about stepping up your *praise* game? We're taught to thank God for our food. We're encouraged to offer *praise* in worship service. We're directed to *praise* in the hard times as well as the good.

Why is *praise* so crucial? Allow me to share an example from 2 Chronicles 20. King Jehoshaphat learns that multiple armies have joined forces to invade Israel. Terrified, King Jehoshaphat orders everyone to fast. The Lord hears their cries and tells them not to be discouraged by this vast army—He will do the fighting for them. On the day of battle, Jehoshaphat marches his army toward their enemies. He tells them if they will believe in the Lord their God, they will be able to stand. Second Chronicles 20:21 (NLT) says Jehoshaphat appoints singers to walk ahead of the army, singing, "Give thanks to the Lord; his faithful love endures forever!" (You know, the song we sometimes sing in worship.) At the moment they begin to sing, the armies who had joined forces against the children of Israel charge. The crazy thing is they are not fighting the children of Israel; rather, they are fighting each other! By the time Jehoshaphat and his army reach them, the invasion is over. Not a single soldier is alive—their opposing armies have killed each other!

This is one of many accounts the Scriptures give to show us what *praise* can do. Statistics say for every negative thought we have, it takes ten positive thoughts to wipe out the bad one. Can I challenge you to try it? Get your *praise* game on by responding with the Word! A psalm or a scripture of promise is a wonderful place to start. Thank God for who He is and begin naming all the things He has blessed you with. Sing a song of *praise*! Then sing another one! The devil will soon realize he's just helping you step up your *praise* game every time he hurls a negative thought your way. When you get intentional with your *praise*, the Lord shows up and the enemy flees!

Word for the Day

SHEPHERD

In the Old Testament, God made leaders out of *shepherds*—people like Abraham, Moses, and David. I would hardly consider the role of a *shepherd* a glamour job. The work entailed long, hard, selfless hours.

In the New Testament, Jesus refers to Himself as the Good *Shepherd*. He temporarily laid down His royalty to take on the role of a *shepherd*. Never before or again in the history of mankind will the *shepherd* become the Sacrificial Lamb. Once and for all, He made the ultimate sacrifice by dying on the cross for us. The Lamb of God was the only one who was pure enough, perfect enough, to redeem every human being. Jesus says no one is able to snatch us out of His hand (John 10:27–30). We are His sheep. He provides shelter, food, community, protection, and personal, one-on-one care (Matthew 6:25–33). He's always watching (2 Chronicles 16:9). Our *shepherd* desires to lead us, restore us, protect us, anoint us, and keep us! (Psalm 23).

He desires to be your *shepherd*. All you have to do is pray this prayer from your heart: Jesus, I believe You laid down Your life for mine. You dealt with the sins of mankind once and for all. That includes my sins. Jesus, forgive me of my sins and live in my heart from this moment forward. I want You to be my *shepherd*, and I want to live under Your protective, loving care.

Word for the Day

HEALING

Can you imagine what it feels like to have a doctor look at you or a family member and say you're going to die? Perhaps you can—you've already walked this journey. In 2 Kings 20, Isaiah visits King Hezekiah and gives him a death message from God. The news is heartbreaking, and the king begins to weep. He reminds God that he has served Him with all his heart. God is moved by his prayer. Before Isaiah can exit the middle courtyard, God instructs Isaiah to return to Hezekiah and let him know that his tears have been seen and his prayers have been heard. God adds fifteen years to his life!

Jesus's blood was shed for our sins and His body was broken for our *healing*. The price for redemption is beyond what you and I can grasp. Calvary covers it all—*healing* for soul, body, and mind. It is for you, it is for me—for all who will believe. I am going to trust God for complete wholeness!

Father, I accept the *healing* that Your Son sacrificially provided on the cross—*healing* for my soul, body, and mind. Jesus paid a precious price—the ultimate price for it—and I receive *healing* with overwhelming gratitude.

> "He was wounded for our transgressions, He was bruised for our iniquities; The chastisement for our peace was upon Him, And by His stripes we are healed" (Isaiah 53:5 NKJV).

Word for the Day

SHARE

Second Kings 7 describes how four lepers walk into an enemy's camp to find it abandoned. They march into the camp with intentions to be taken captive. They felt their fate—be it life or death—would be no worse than starvation; for a terrible famine had struck Samaria. As they head toward the camp, the Lord caused the Aramean army (the enemy) to hear what sounded like an invasion of mighty armies. Terrified, the soldiers fled, leaving all they had behind. The invasion was simply four leper men.

How amazing is that? But there's more to learn from this passage. The lepers began to eat and drink and take valuables from the tents. Finally, they realized it would not be right for them to hoard all the goods, so they returned to the city and *shared* the good news. Our heavenly Father brings good news: whoever believes in Him can have everlasting life (John 3:16). Those of us who have accepted Him now enjoy the countless blessings He provides. Now we must *share* the gospel with everyone God places in our path. This is our calling—our purpose.

What does it look like to *share*? It's more than words. It's our words put into action—loving, giving, mentoring, praying, encouraging, teaching, forgiving, and supporting.

Father, help me *share* the gracious blessings You have given me. You have called us all to *share* the Good News with a helpless and hopeless world. Teach me to *share*: to be *s*elfless in *h*elping those *a*round me, *r*eaching out to *e*veryone You place in my path (*share*). May I do what I can to meet physical and emotional needs so that I have an opportunity to address spiritual needs with the Good News (2 Corinthians 9:8–10).

PURPOSE

According to 2 Kings 5, the Aramean army invaded Israel. Among the captives was a young girl who was given to the commanding officer to serve his wife. The Scriptures don't tell us much about the young girl but implies that she was treated fairly because she spoke freely to her mistress. She wanted her master to go see the prophet Elisha from her hometown. She believed that the God of Elisha could heal her master. Naaman, the commanding officer, listened to the young girl and made arrangements to see the prophet. After following Elisha's instructions, Naaman was healed from his leprosy.

That's a great story within itself and will follow this devotional. But I'm intrigued by the young girl. She was taken from her homeland, forced to live in a strange community, and isolated from those she loved. In all her struggles, God had *purpose* for her life. *Purpose* doesn't always bring comfort or convenience, but it brings fulfillment and glory to God. Because of this young girl, Naaman met The Healer and confessed, "Now I know that there is no God in all the world except in Israel" (2 Kings 5:15 NLT).

Father, I desire Your *purpose* to be fulfilled in my life. The cost may be more than I can grasp at the moment, but I know Your will for me will far outweigh my struggles. What I can do on my own will never turn a head, but what You can do through me can make a difference in a soul, in a family, in a community.

"But indeed for this purpose I have raised you up, that I may show My power in you, and that My name may be declared in all the earth" (Exodus 9:16 NKJV).

HUMBLE

This devotional continues in the book of 2 Kings 5. The Scriptures describe how Naaman came to meet the prophet Elisha. Naaman and his wife had a slave who was taken captive from Israel, and this young girl witnessed to her master about the prophet Elisha's God. She told Naaman how Elisha could heal his leprosy. With hope for a cure, Naaman made arrangements to visit the prophet. Understand Naaman was the commanding officer of the entire Aramean army—a man of prestige and power. I imagine he expected the prophet to be honored at his coming.

Waiting at the door of the prophet's home, Naaman must have been surprised (and offended) when the prophet didn't even come to the door. Instead Elisha sent out a messenger and told Naaman to go wash himself in the Jordan River seven times. This was not the way he was usually treated! And the Jordan River! Really? Naaman left angry, but his officers convinced him to listen to the prophet. Reluctantly he did as Elisha instructed and dipped himself seven times in the Jordan River. The leprosy disappeared! Naaman returned to the prophet with new skin and a new heart! He promised Elisha that he would never worship another god.

Father, forgive me of my prideful ways. I lay them before You even if it takes me doing so every day for the rest of my life. I desire to have a *humble* and teachable spirit. I won't always understand Your ways, but I trust in Your Sovereignty over my own pitiful, pious wisdom.

"Humble yourselves in the sight of the Lord,
and He will lift you up" (James 4:10 NKJV).

Word for the Day

FOLLOW

My patience tends to run thin with people who prolong making a decision, like the people who get in front of me at the drive-thru. I mean, really, how many questions can one person ask about a burger? I confess intolerance is a character flaw. Certainly, there is benefit in exercising caution when making decisions. I will also confess I'm even more annoyed with people who keep changing their minds.

Living with the children of Israel in biblical times would have been a challenge for me because of their inconsistency in serving God. (I say that with all sarcasm because I recognize my own inconsistencies and must confess, I am more like them than I desire to be.) According to 1 Kings 18, Elijah appeared to be frustrated with the people of Israel, as he said, "How much longer will you waver, hobbling between two opinions? If the LORD is God, follow him!" (1 Kings 18:21 NLT).

This passage hit me in the gut today! Elijah and the prophets of Baal demonstrated a "showdown" to prove, once and for all, the true God. Of course, Elijah's God showed up miraculously! The fire of God flashed down from heaven and burned up the sacrifice that had been drenched in water. Everything was consumed. The fire even licked up all the water standing in the trench! This was not the first miracle the children of Israel saw, nor the last. And unfortunately, this was not the last time they wavered in their beliefs. Let me be real here. Sometimes I find myself on a "high" when God miraculously intervenes. Before I can give Him the praise He deserves, I find myself in another struggle—struggling to obey His Word.

Father, You *are* God! Forgive me when I fail to *follow* You. My thinking will never get me to heaven, but Your Word will! May it be seared into my soul, body, mind, and spirit so that Your Word takes charge of my everyday living.

"My soul follows close behind You; Your right hand upholds me" (Psalm 63:8 NKJV).

STRENGTH

After God showed up big time at Mount Carmel, you would think Elijah would be strutting his stuff! But as I mentioned in my previous devotional, struggles often follow victory—and so it did with Elijah. When Jezebel learned what Elijah had done to the prophets of Baal, she came after Elijah. Frightened, he fled to the wilderness. He was tired of running for his life and exhausted from the journey, so much that he asked God to let him die. He fell asleep and was later awakened by an angel who told Elijah to get up and eat. He ate the food the angel provided and fell back asleep. Once again, the angel woke him and instructed him to eat more, for he would need it for the journey ahead. The food gave Elijah enough *strength* to travel forty days and nights to Mt. Sinai.

Just when our *strength* depletes, the Lord steps in! God didn't scold Elijah for being downcast and feeling alone. Our compassionate God met Elijah in his despair and *strengthened* him for the journey. He sent an angel to fix a meal and a prophet-in-training to assist him. Our Father knows exactly what we need to *strengthen* our Christian walk. He may send a friend, a word, a song, a card, an angel. Be assured He will be your *strength* and you are never alone.

> "My flesh and my heart fail; But God is the strength of my heart and my portion forever" (Psalm 73:26 NKJV).

FRIENDSHIP

The value of *friendship*. There's nothing like it! I'm so grateful for people whom the Lord has placed in my life. Some are there for a season, and others are there for a lifetime. I believe the Lord puts people in our lives for a specific time and purpose. We were never created to live independently from one another. We are His sheep and are designed to be at our best when we are living life together.

In 1 Samuel 20, the Scriptures describe a model *friendship* between Jonathan and David. There were circumstances that promoted competition, jealousy, and rivalry between the two. Jonathan was King Saul's son and in line to inherit the throne. David was a mighty warrior who had won the respect of the kingdom. King Saul felt threatened by David's favor with God and with the people. Saul's jealousy birthed a hatred for David. Jonathan made a secret pact with David and helped him escape from the hands of his father. He put his loyalty to David above the flesh-and-blood bond.

I don't believe God divides us, but it is our enemy and the circumstances he creates that brings division. For this reason, I believe we must always love everyone, understanding our real enemy is not human. Our enemy is the enemy of God—the rulers of the darkness of this age (Ephesians 6:12).

Father, I want to take time out today to thank you for the people you have placed in my life. I am a blessed woman and cherish every *friendship*—past, present, and future. I desire to be a *friend* that others will cherish. Whether it be for a season or longer, teach me how to be a *friend* like Jonathan.

Word for the Day

TESTIMONY

First Samuel 20 describes how Jonathan helped his friend David escape from the hands of his father. Jonathan knew his father, King Saul, was a great man. Great as he was, Jonathan also witnessed a decline in his father's favor with God as he says, "May the Lord be with you [talking to David] as he used to be with my father" (1 Samuel 20:13 NLT).

Those words pierced my heart today. The world is watching us. When we choose to act in ways that do not mirror God's character, we hurt our *testimony*. We misrepresent the character of God. I realize just how easy it is—in one moment of frustration, one moment of temptation, one moment of disobedience—to step out of God's character. We don't always recognize the impact we have on our circle of friends, our community, but we may just be the pivotal light that leads them to Jesus.

Father, help me to remember people are watching in the grocery store. People are watching on Facebook. People are watching at the workplace. My family is watching the way I conduct myself at home. People are watching *me*!

> "Become blameless and harmless, children of God without fault in the midst of a crooked and perverse generation, among whom you shine as lights in the world" (Philippians 2:15 NKJV).

UNSHAKABLE

The battle of David and Goliath is one of the most popular writings in the Old Testament. It's recorded in 1 Samuel 17. Who doesn't like a story where the "underdog" becomes the hero? According to the Scriptures, Goliath was over nine feet tall, and his armor weighed more than some adults (okay, not me)!

When King Saul and his army looked at the stature of Goliath and heard the taunts of this giant, they were terrified and deeply shaken. Our enemy can hurl situations at us for which we feel we are totally unprepared. Everything could have been fine yesterday, but today is a different day. Who would have ever thought a calamity such as this would visit my house today!

Perhaps a tsunami of events has flooded your household. You are shaking in your shoes. You don't even know how to process what's just happened, much less resolve it.

Multiple times in this passage of Scripture, David refers to the Israelite army as the "armies of the living God." What made this army different from all the others? The Israelites served the living God—the God of heaven and earth—the same God you and I serve! Our heavenly Father has already told us that we cannot defeat the enemy on our own (Ephesians 6), but He has equipped us with His power to stand our ground. The Lord will do the fighting for us (Deuteronomy 3:22). Take on the armor of God and become *unshakable*!

WHOLE

I will call my next few devotionals a *series* since they are connected in theme. As we approach the return of Christ, we'd better get prepared for enemy attacks. Perhaps you need to know how to stand your ground. God has given us specific instructions on how to stand when the enemy attacks. We must be aware of them and intentionally put these instructions in place. The Scriptures, in Ephesians 6, refer to it as taking on the *whole* armor of God.

Today I place emphasis on the *whole* armor—all of it. When we leave one piece off, we open up an area of our life that becomes vulnerable. Think of it as going outside on a freezing cold, blustery day. Who would layer up with scarf, gloves, and coat, but leave off shoes?

God didn't save us to let us be defeated! He gives us power, strength, and endurance through His Word. He gives us the formula for success: putting on the *whole* armor of God. And just in case the thought has not occurred to you, this means there will be battles—there will be struggles. We wouldn't need armor if there were no battles. Know you are not alone. You are not being punished. You are not being singled out! You are a child of God, and that makes you satan's target. Remember, "We are more than conquerors through Him who loved us" (Romans 8:37 NKJV).

TRUTH

The devotional prior to this one addresses the need to wear the whole armor of God so that we can stand our ground when the enemy attacks. Let's begin to dissect the pieces of armor, beginning with *truth*. Ephesians 6:14 (NKJV) says, "Stand therefore, having girded your waist with truth."

In the Garden of Eden, the serpent convinced Eve that she would be like God if she ate the forbidden fruit. Adam and Eve chose to ignore the instructions of God and believe the serpent. From that time forward, our carnal nature has warred with following the *truth*. That's why God has given us the written Word. It's infallible and is just as applicable today as it was when written. Isaiah 55:8 says that the Lord's thoughts are not our thoughts and His ways are not our ways. That's why we cannot afford to lean on our own understanding (Proverbs 3:5). This may sound stern, but it is *truth*. It really doesn't matter what I think or what you think—what matters is what the Word of God says. I realize my own thoughts can be influenced by personal desire, pride, and immaturity, but the *truth* of God's Word will keep my posture balanced if I will heed its instructions.

Father, I accept Your Word as *truth*. Teach me to go to Your Word for the answers I need. Teach me to live by Your Word that I may receive all that You have promised. "Your word I have hidden in my heart, That I might not sin against You" (Psalm 119:11 NKJV).

Word for the Day

RIGHTEOUSNESS

When standing our ground against the enemy, the Scriptures tell us to take on the whole armor of God. The prior devotion talks about girding our waist with truth. Ephesians 6:14 also says that we put on the breastplate of *righteousness*, which happens when we confess our sins and become a new creature in Christ. We're marked as God's children; we wear His label. Our Father no longer sees our sin but the *righteousness* of His Son in us.

The devil also recognizes the *righteousness* of Christ, and he well knows that we belong to our Father! The breastplate protects crucial body parts—areas that can be fatally wounded, specifically our heart and soul. When the devil comes calling, our Father wants us to remember that we're wearing His *righteousness*. No one can snatch us out of His hand (John 10:29). The devil may get in your face, but he can't cross the bloodline of Jesus! Your heart and soul are safely secure because you wear the breastplate of *righteousness*!

Word for the Day

PEACE

Isn't it comforting to know our heavenly Father fights our battles? In Ephesians 6, the scriptures tell us how to stand our ground. Verse 15 (NLT) says, "For shoes, put on the peace that comes from the Good News so that you will be fully prepared."

This kind of *peace* far exceeds man's capability! The *peace* that God has available to you and me teaches us how to live in the miracle—not the moment! It takes us above our circumstances and allows us to live in faith and confidence—not in fear and failure. The *peace* of God surpasses all understanding (Philippians 4:7). This kind of *peace* is God-birthed—not understood by the world, not always understood by other believers.

So how do we get this *peace*? Isaiah says righteousness brings peace (32:17). The *peace* of God becomes yours as a child of God. How do we keep it? Isaiah says we will have perfect *peace* if we maintain our focus on God and His Word (26:3). That's a little harder because it requires us to become intentional with our thoughts.

The enemy wants us to focus on our problems, but if we will focus on the Peacemaker, we can successfully get through the dark seasons. Then we are able to take the *peace* we have experienced to a helpless and hopeless world. Then we are prepared to comfort others with the comfort that God gives us (2 Corinthians 1:4). I'm praying for your *peace* today!

FAITH

Ephesians 6 says if we want to be successful in standing our ground, above all, take up the shield of *faith* (verse 16). It takes *faith* to become born again. As we mature in our daily walk with the Lord, I believe we have the opportunity to grow our *faith*.

It may be easy to say, "God can." As we mature, our *faith* elevates to believing "God will." There is an even greater level of *faith* that can take us to trusting "God has" even when we don't see or feel it. *Faith* doesn't have to be complicated. We don't have to be spiritual giants to reap rewards of *faith*. We simply must have the *faith* of a little child—*faith* that is not contaminated with what others think, what is politically correct, or what is society-accepted. Simply take the Word of God at face value and believe. We must understand that childlike *faith* is based on the Word—not where we are, what we see, or how we feel.

So how do we grow our *faith*? We must get into the Word and get the Word into us. Romans 10:17 (NKJV) says, "So then faith comes by hearing, and hearing by the word of God." When our focus is on the Word, we are shielded from the fatal darts of the enemy. We are empowered to doubt our doubts, but if we allow our focus to shift, our present circumstances will invade with a vengeance. We must run to the Word for renewal. When our *faith* collides with the Holy Spirit, things change! It's no wonder the Scriptures tell us to take up the shield of *faith* above all!

Word for the Day

SALVATION

Ephesians 6:17 gives us a *heads-up* for standing our ground against the enemy—that is, we are instructed to put on *salvation* as our helmet.

Romans 8 asks these questions: "If God is for us, who can ever be against us?" (verse 31 NLT). "Can anything ever separate us from Christ's love?" (verse 35 NLT). In short, the answer is resounding: no one—nothing! The enemy will attempt to convince us differently. Our minds are his playground and the battlefield for his schemes. He would love nothing more than to fill our minds with his lies. While we cannot control every thought that pops into our heads, we can identify its source. If that thought doesn't bare the character of God, we know it comes from the enemy. Once we identify the source, then we must take appropriate action.

I prefer not to waste my time talking to the devil! I may find myself arguing all day long with him and getting nowhere. James 4:7 (NKJV) says, "Submit to God. Resist the devil and he will flee from you." What better way to submit than to offer praise and worship, declare the promises in His Word, and simply speak the name of Jesus! We may not feel like it, but that's how we successfully fight. Intentional worship puts the devil on the run!

Your protective headgear was given the day you received Jesus in your heart. It's yours forever now. It can't be taken away unless you choose to lay it down. Understand your mind is going to be a favorite battlefield, but the Lord has you safely wrapped in His helmet of *salvation.*

Word for the Day

WORD

The last piece of armor described in Ephesians 6 is the *Word*—which is the sword of the Spirit. Hebrews 4:12 (NLT) says, "The Word of God is alive and powerful. It is sharper than the sharpest two-edged sword, cutting between soul and spirit, between joint and marrow. It exposes our innermost thoughts and desires."

After Jesus fasted forty days and nights, the devil attempted to appeal to His hunger, physical weakness, and His royalty. In each case, Jesus responded to him with the *Word*, I believe, as a model for us. My words will never intimidate the enemy, but the *Word* of God will!

The *Word* connects and works with every other piece of armor described in Ephesians 6. The *Word* contains the truth. The *Word* tells us if we confess with our mouth and believe in our heart, we receive salvation and take on the righteousness of God. The *Word* guards our heart and minds so that we can live in peace. The *Word* grows our faith so that the impossible becomes possible.

Get into the *Word* and let the *Word* get into you! Then stand your ground and watch the Lord fight your battles!

CHILDREN

*C*hildren are precious gifts. At the time we receive them, parental care feels like a lifetime. Before we know it, they're grown and gone, and how we wish for a return of those early years. Well, perhaps not a repeat of those years, but we cherish those child-rearing days and often reflect on what we could have done better.

In 1 Samuel 1, we meet a woman who deeply wanted a child and prayed earnestly that the Lord would open her womb. She told the Lord that if He would bless her with a son, she would give him back—he would belong to the Lord for his entire lifetime. The Lord granted her desire, and Hannah honored her commitment. She stood before the priest and said, "I asked the LORD to give me this boy, and he has granted my request. Now I am giving him to the LORD, and he will belong to the LORD his whole life" (verses 27 and 28 NLT). No doubt this scripture pricks the soul of every Christian parent. This is our heart and prayer for our *children.*

Father, today I pray for every child. As parents, we've all made mistakes. Only You are perfect. We give our *children* to You. Place them in Your loving care—whether they be one year old or fifty. It's never too late because You are a Father who knows every intimate detail—where our *children* are and where they need to be. We ask You to take charge of their lives. We rebuke any generational curse over our *children* in the name of Jesus! May the enemy's plan to destroy and separate them from You be quickly severed. Father, speak wellness, wholeness, and godliness in our *children.* May they be Yours for the rest of their lives.

LISTEN

Listening seems to be a lost art. From the time we are born, we are introduced to the language of speech. The first words that come from a baby's mouth bring elation to the proud parents. We spend years learning how to speak grammatically correct. Some go on to perfect their language skills and become great orators.

I'm prone to think there is a greater gift in *listening*. Jesus said, "I say whatever the Father tells me to say" (John 12:50 NLT). If the Son of God spoke only what the Father gave Him, how much more do I need to acquire the art of *listening* to Him? Perhaps my words would be less regretted if I acquired a *listening* ear. There may be tools and methods that can teach us, but the greatest *listening* ear comes from seeking our heavenly Father.

Samuel was a young lad who assisted the priest in the tabernacle at Shiloh (1 Samuel 3). God audibly called his name multiple times. Each time Samuel would go to the priest, thinking he had called him. The priest reasoned the voice was coming from God and instructed Samuel to say, "Speak, LORD, your servant is listening" (verse 9 NLT). Each morning, in my *secret place*, I ask the Lord to speak. He may speak through His Word, through a song, through another individual, through my mind—and perhaps, one day, He may choose to speak audibly.

Father, I desire to speak Your words, because they are life and health to all those who hear them. Teach me how to *listen* at any given moment of the day so that Your words are communicated to a friend, a stranger, one who desperately needs to hear from You, one who is ready to give up on life. I consecrate myself to You that I may hear and speak Your words of life.

LEAST

Judges 6 describes how the Midianites reduced the children of Israel to starvation. Gideon asked why so many bad things had happened and where were the miracles if God was with them. The Lord told Gideon to become the miracle that the Israelites needed—go out and destroy the Midianites.

This was probably not the answer Gideon expected. Sometimes when we ask God to help someone in need, I believe He looks at us and says, "I will. Now you go help them. You are My hands and feet."

Gideon felt totally inadequate. He said, "But Lord...how can I rescue Israel? My clan is the weakest in the whole tribe of Manasseh, and I am the least in my entire family!" (verse 15 NLT).

When we can recognize our weaknesses, the Lord can step in and do God-sized things! He takes us out of our comfort zones so that we are compelled to rely solely on Him and not ourselves. God has given us gifts to use for His kingdom, but our talents will never match His anointing.

Heavenly Father, I desire to work in Your kingdom, but I realize my talents and efforts will never turn a head. I have little to offer, but You specialize in the *least*. Help me to be ready to say yes and be obedient, knowing You will handle the rest.

Word for the Day

SURRENDER

Our heavenly Father has promised to fight our battles, but for some reason (duh?) I am compelled to tell Him how to do it! And not to my surprise, the Lord doesn't need my direction. He often works on my behalf in a much different path than I envision.

In Judges 7, Gideon collected the army he needed—all thirty-two thousand of them—to defeat the Midianites. God reduced the army to three hundred so that the Israelites would know that the victory came solely through Him. The Scriptures say the Midianite army resembled a swarm of locusts and their camels were too numerous to count. Gideon and his army had no chance in their own strength! Gideon had to *surrender* the fate of the Israelites to the Warrior God.

Father, forgive me when I try to take matters into my own hands. I am not capable of fighting our enemy, but You are! I *surrender* my battles to You—Your ways, Your timing. Your thoughts are not my thoughts and Your ways are not my ways, so I fully *surrender* my circumstances to You, trusting You know best (Isaiah 55:8).

MERCY

The Old Testament records approximately sixty examples of people doing evil in the sight of the Lord. They often met swift punishment. The Israelites lost their freedom and peace for years at a time until God's *mercy* returned.

Now that we live in the dispensation of grace, the enemy deceptively portrays our freedom as an entitlement to do as we please. What he doesn't tell us is that our entitlements, our choices, can steal the freedom and peace that is available to us through Jesus Christ. But we serve a *merciful* God! When we confess our sins, the *mercy* of God returns. The world may not forgive—the enemy may dangle your past in front of you—but the *mercy* of God says, "I don't see what they see—what you see. I see the righteousness of my beloved Son in you. You are My child, and I will never let go."

> "As far as the east is from the west, So far has He removed our transgressions from us" (Psalm 103:12 NKJV).

Word for the Day

BLIND

My dad told me years ago that love can be *blinding*. I believe there is truth to his warning, as it allows us to see what we choose to see—or not see.

Judges 16 shares the popular love story of Samson and Delilah. The Scriptures describe how Delilah betrays her lover for wealth. The Philistines plotted with Delilah to learn the source of Samson's supernatural strength. Three times Delilah asked Samson what made him so strong and three times he misled her. You would think after the first time, with men ready to seize him, Samson would have seen Delilah's true color! Apparently, his love *blinded* him, because he continued his relationship with her and eventually shared the source of his power. Delilah betrayed his secret, and Samson lost his God-given strength.

This is a "duh?" moment for me as I read their story. How could Samson be so *blind*? Sadly, the enemy *blinds* the world. The Word is spoken, but they do not hear it. The love of God can be seen from Genesis to Revelation, but they do not see it.

Father, I thank You for opening my eyes to see such wondrous things from Your Word (Psalm 119:18). It is a lamp to my feet and a light to my path (Psalm 119:105). Sear Your Word in my heart that my senses do not dull. May Your light in me bring sight of a loving Savior to a *blinded* world.

Word for the Day

LORD

My generation and those before us grew up playing cowboys and Indians. To this day, most of us still watch the old western movies over and over and over (well, you get it).

Chapters 5 and 6 of Joshua describe how the *Lord* gave Joshua and the Israelites the town of Jericho. The *Lord* instructed Joshua and his men to march around the town gates in silence for six days. Seven priests were to walk ahead of the ark and blow their horns. As I was reading this passage, my mind flipped to the westerns, remembering how the Indians would start the drumbeat prior to an attack. The beating of the drums always played on the minds of those who were anxiously waiting for the first flaming arrow. (Wonder if the Indians learned this strategy from Joshua.) I can imagine the horns had a similar effect on the residents at Jericho. On the seventh day, the Israelites marched seven times as the *Lord* instructed. When the priests gave one long blast, the people were told to shout as loud as they could. The walls tumbled, the people charged, and Jericho was history!

How did they do it? Joshua 5:13–15 gives us the answer: The Commander of the *Lord's* army joined Joshua and his men as they were approaching Jericho. The Commander appeared as a man—He spoke as a man and He carried a sword like a man. But this was the *Lord* Almighty! He told Joshua to take off his shoes, as he was standing on holy ground! The marching, the blast of the horns, the shouts of the people, did not bring down the wall. The Captain of the *Lord's* host did!

Make no mistake: the *Lord* does the fighting for us. "Who is this King of glory? The LORD strong and mighty, The LORD mighty in battle. Who is this King of glory? The LORD of hosts, He is the King of glory" (Psalm 24:8, 10 NKJV).

WILL

Numbers 22 through 24 teach us the crucial difference between the perfect *will* of God and His permissive *will*. Why is it so important? God's perfect *will* opens the windows of heaven to abundant life—the best plan for our lives. His perfect *will* ultimately saves us heartache reaped from selfish desire. The Lord may allow us to proceed in the direction we are compelled to follow, but His permissive *will* comes at a cost. The "unknowns" can bring consequences that may last for a lifetime.

A Moabite king felt threatened by the Israelites and wanted Balaam to curse Israel. God told Balaam not to curse His people. Persistently, the Moabite king asked again, this time offering silver and gold. God had already told Balaam no, but Balaam requested the messengers hang around overnight to see if God would say anything else (as though the Lord might change His mind). The Lord allowed Balaam to go, but there were consequences. Angry that Balaam secretly desired the gold and silver, the Lord sent an angel to block his way. Had it not been for Balaam's donkey, the Lord's angel would have killed him.

Balaam should have learned an incredible lesson that day. He was allowed to continue the journey, but he had new respect for the perfect *will* of God—at least for the moment. Our uncontrolled desires can drive us totally out of God's perfect *will*—right past His permissive *will*—and take us down a destructive path. Eventually, that's what happened to Balaam.

Father, I desire to get so much of Your Word into me that it changes my desires to align with Your perfect *will*. I desire the abundant life that comes through You. May Your Word renew my desires daily.

> "And do not be conformed to this world, but be transformed by the renewing of your mind, that you may prove what is that good and acceptable and perfect will of God" (Romans 12:2 NKJV).

Word for the Day

DETOUR

D o you get annoyed when you approach a *detour*? I do, especially when I'm in unfamiliar territory. I'm not good at following directions. Once I'm off the main path, signage to get me back seems to disappear! According to Exodus 13, the children of Israel incurred a *detour* shortly after their departure from Egypt. God knew they were not ready for battle, so He led them down an alternate path. The route God used wasn't the shortest one or the quickest.

Sometimes we question the path our Father assigns us. But just like the Israelites, God knows every intricate detail about us. He will never set us up for failure! He already knows every challenge that lays before us. How comforting to know our heavenly Father never loses sight of us. His plan is always best.

Should we choose to *detour* from the path that God prepares, we must understand our rebellious choices will always lead to heart-ache. But regardless of how far we stray, our heavenly Father is waiting with outstretched arms to nudge us back on track.

> "Lead me, O LORD, in Your righteous-ness… Make Your way straight before my face" (Psalm 5:8 NKJV).

SLAVERY

The children of Israel lived in Egypt for 430 years. The Lord freed them from their oppression and rescued them from *slavery*. We've seen movies portraying the exodus, but I think only those who were there could fully grasp the glory of that day.

The celebration ended abruptly when the Egyptians came after them. In Exodus 14, the Israelites panicked and cried out to Moses, saying, "What have you done to us? Why did you make us leave Egypt? Didn't we tell you this would happen" (verses 11–12 NLT). It's easy for me to think how weak and ungrateful the Israelites were, but there are times when I react the same way to life's battles. Often our battles follow victory. Sometimes there's not enough time to celebrate the victory before the enemy comes back punching! Battles will come and go, but we don't have to fear them.

> "So you have not received a spirit that makes you fearful slaves. Instead, you received God's Spirit when he adopted you as his own children" (Romans 8:15 NLT).

Our victories should not be dampened by worry in anticipation of the next battle. Our Warrior God prepares us to stand our ground, and He fights our enemy. At the first sign, we can suit up for battle—get on the full armor of God (Ephesians 6:14–17). Focus on truth, know we're marked as His child, take on His peace, rev up our faith, and live—moment by moment—in the power and freedom of His Word!

We've been rescued from *slavery*, and our heavenly Father doesn't want us to go back there!

Word for the Day

SPARE

Long past their childbearing years, God gave Abraham and Sarah a son. Abraham was a hundred years old when Isaac was born (Genesis 21:5). Talk about a child being the apple of his father's eye! In Genesis 22, God instructed Abraham to offer his son as a burnt sacrifice to Him—Abraham's one and only beloved son. There are no words to capture the fierce emotions Abraham must have felt. Whether he believed God would *spare* his son or not, Abraham chose to obey the Lord. At the last moment, the angel of the Lord stopped Abraham.

God knew the great sacrifice Abraham was willing to make. Yes, God knew because He would sacrifice His one and only beloved Son, Jesus Christ. Our Father did not *spare* His Son, though He had the power to halt the process and deliver Him from the cross. Our Father did not *spare* His Son, knowing that people would reject Him, take His name in vain, and make a mockery of His Son's death. Our Father did not *spare* His Son because He wanted to give you and me a chance to know Him. He wanted to become our heavenly Father so we could live with Him eternally. He did not *spare* His Son (John 3:16).

Word for the Day

ALTAR

In Genesis 22, Abraham was instructed to sacrifice his greatest treasure—Isaac, his one and only son. The child was a miracle, a promise, everything Abraham wanted. In obedience Abraham laid his son on the *altar*, and then God intervened.

How this pricked my heart today! As parents, we should begin laying our children on the *altar* at an early age—praying for their health and growth, praying they will come to accept Jesus as Savior. We pray for their school years, protection, friends, future, and career. We pray for their life partner. We pray for the rest of our lives, because they are our greatest treasure.

As parents, we make mistakes. We may wish we could have done more, but the best thing we can do is lay our children on the *altar*—give them to God daily. When disappointments come, lay them on the *altar*. When we don't know where they are, lay them on the *altar*. When situations are out of our hands, put them in the mighty hands of our caring Father. Lay them on the *altar*, give them to God, and trust Him to intervene.

> "The love of the LORD remains forever with those who fear him. His salvation extends to the children's children" (Psalm 103:17 NLT).

Word for the Day

SUCCESS

What does *success* mean to you? To some, it may mean having a beautiful home and a nice car. To another, it may mean the executive job with the spacious office or being one's own boss. Certainly, there is a cost to *success*.

Genesis chapters 37 through 50 share the amazing story of a young man who faced one defeat after another to receive one *success* after another. The young man was Joseph. He was mistreated by his brothers, sold into slavery, and put into prison. One might assume Joseph's *success* came when he was put in charge of Egypt; but early on, the Scriptures say the Lord was with Joseph, and Joseph *succeeded* in everything he did. He even experienced *success* in troublesome times.

What can we learn from Joseph's story? We can conclude that our *success* comes from the Lord being with us. He establishes the work of our hands (Psalm 90:17). We can also conclude that *success* may coincide with hardship. While Joseph served as a slave to Potiphar, the Lord was with him, and his *success* got him promoted to oversee his master's property. While in prison, the Lord made Joseph a favorite with the warden. Forced to live in a foreign country, Joseph was pulled out of prison to interpret the king's dreams. Being able to do what no one else could, he was then placed in high position— being second only to the king. Joseph was a *successful* man because the Lord was with him.

The next time you're struggling with the pressures of everyday living, take a moment to thank your heavenly Father for being with you in every circumstance. Allow the peace, presence, and favor of God to rest on your soul, body, and mind.

> "You have allowed me to suffer in much hardship, but you will restore me to life again… You will restore me to even greater honor and comfort me once again" (Psalm 71:20–21 NLT).

Word for the Day

TRUST

O ne of our most beloved children's stories comes from Genesis: the story of Noah and the ark. Children's books have been written, movies have been made, toys have been manufactured, but in reality, the content of this account is for mature minds.

The Lord instructed Noah to build a boat that would house his family, two of every kind of animal on the face of the earth, and seven of every clean animal and bird. In addition, he had to store food for his family and the animals. I can only sum up this assignment with one word: impossible! How did Noah ever accumulate the supplies he would need? How could he build something so large? How could he organize the animals? The answer? This was God!

For Noah, there is only one word that sums up his actions—*trust*. He obeyed the voice of the Lord and followed His instructions to the letter! Some believe Noah may have entered the ark before the rain started, while others believe he entered when the flooding began. In any case, I wonder what Noah thought when God shut the door. Did he have doubts? The Bible doesn't record his thoughts or conversations, but Noah did what God told him to do. I believe he *trusted* God for the rest.

In comparison, our assignments pale, but sometimes they can feel impossible. Father, help me to take a leap of faith and *trust* Your Word for every part of my life. Your Word is living and powerful and will accomplish Your will. When doubt exalts itself, may You bring my every thought into captivity to the obedience of Christ (2 Corinthians 10:5).

Word for the Day

PRIORITIES

Do you ever wonder where your time goes? Some days, my time feels like a four-hour day instead of a twenty-four-hour day. Okay, I confess I'm a bit slow in the mornings, and I do like living in my PJ's! The years have taught me that best time-management practices won't work miracles when your plate is overloaded. Think of it as stacking a plate with pancakes. You can keep piling your plate, but at some point, those pancakes will topple!

We live in a pressure-filled world where career, family, relationships, and the desire to have more compete for our time. I find myself having to reset my *priorities* often. In Philippians 3:7–8, Paul says that things he once considered valuable became worthless compared to the infinite value of knowing Jesus. I will do well to follow his mind-set. Putting God first in my life will give me God-inspired wisdom to arrange all the rest.

Father, teach me how to put You first. Reveal the worthless things that consume my time and help me lay them aside. Following Your Word and Your wisdom will transform my day, my choices, my life. "Search me, O God, and know my heart… And lead me in the way everlasting" (Psalm 139:23–24 NKJV).

Word for the Day

FRUIT

My mother had an incredibly green thumb. Her yard was filled with gorgeous flowers. I have wonderful memories of strolling the gardens with her. Sadly, I didn't inherit her green thumb; even my artificial plants look withered! How gratifying it must be to harvest the *fruit* of one's garden—be it flowers or produce.

John the Baptist said we should bear *fruits* worthy of repentance (Matthew 3:8). The *fruit* he speaks of comes from knowing Christ and allowing Him to grow His character in us. Salvation begins with a prayer of repentance but doesn't end there. Salvation is about taking on new life—turning from our old lifestyle and taking on the character of God. While salvation is instantaneous, the growth of our *fruit* is a process. When I read the words of John the Baptist, I am compelled to examine my *fruit*. Is it worthy of what God has done for me? Is my Father delighted in the work of His hands? Does my *fruit* please Him?

Father, I cannot make myself righteous. Resolutions and self-help programs pale to Your design—who I can be in You. Your Word is the life-changer. I desire to dig into Your Word so You can speak change, healing, and growth into me. May the *fruit* of Your Spirit grow to maturity in me and flow bountifully to others: love, joy, peace, longsuffering, kindness, goodness, faithfulness, and self-control (Galatians 5:22–23).

RAINBOW

There are very few sights that compare with the magnificence of the *rainbow*. It's worthy of taking a second glance! Every time I see a *rainbow*, I think of God's mercy. He destroyed the earth by flood because of man's wickedness. Afterward, God made a covenant with Noah and with every living creature that the entire earth would never be destroyed again by flood waters.

While the same wickedness of Noah's time exists today, God's covenant stands. The *rainbow* reminds our Father of His everlasting covenant, and it reminds us of His everlasting mercy. We may disappoint each other, fail to live up to our promises, but there is a God in heaven who is faithful! Aren't you glad you know Him?

> "Your faithfulness endures to all generations; You established the earth, and it abides" (Psalm 119:90 NKJV).

Word for the Day

SECRET

Things done in *secret* often carry a stigma of wrongdoing. However, in Matthew 6, Jesus instructs us to do some things in *secret*. He says the good we do for others should be done in *secret*. Our personal prayer time should be done in the *secret* place. Our fasting need only be seen by God. When our works are done *secretly*, the Lord is glorified and we are blessed.

When our works are done primarily to throw us into the spotlight, God is not glorified and the attention we receive becomes our only reward. Looking spiritual should not be our objective. Jesus says to "lay up for yourselves treasures in heaven" (Matthew 6:20 NKJV). This comes by giving God the glory so that we receive everlasting rewards. I've often heard the word *character* defined as what we do when no one is looking. Our public image does not impress God, nor does it have a lasting impression on our neighbor.

In Luke 21, Jesus witnessed a poor widow woman giving two mites into the treasury. Others gave much more. Her offering didn't turn the heads of those around her, but her giving touched the heart of Jesus. He knew she had given more than all the rest because she had given all she had. Colossians 3:23 (NKJV) says, "Whatever you do, do it heartily, as to the Lord and not to men."

"Your Father who sees in secret will Himself
reward you openly" (Mathew 6:4 NKJV).

Word for the Day

HARD

In Genesis 18, the Lord visited Abraham and told him that Sarah, his wife, would bear him a son. Sarah was listening at a distance and laughed at the prospect of having a child at the age of ninety. The Lord asked Abraham why Sarah reacted with disbelief, and asked the question, "Is anything too hard for the LORD?" (verse 14 NKJV).

Hebrews 13:8 (NKJV) says, "Jesus Christ is the same yesterday, today, and forever." As we age, our human strength may fail us, but we serve the Almighty God who is infinite and all-powerful! He performs miracles today just as He performed in biblical times. Luke 1:37 (NKJV) says, "For with God nothing will be impossible." I believe our Father is asking us the same question today: "Is anything too hard for the LORD?"

As parents, there is absolutely nothing we would withhold from our children if it is within our means to provide. We delight in giving our children good things. Our heavenly Father delights even more to bless us. We may be ridiculed when asking for the impossible, but I believe God is honored by our bold prayers. The first step is to ask. The second is to believe without doubting. The third step is to obey and expect the manifestation of His Word. First John 3:22 (NKJV) says, "Whatever we ask we receive from Him, because we keep His commandments and do those things that are pleasing in His sight."

No, nothing is too *hard* for the Lord—absolutely nothing!

FORGIVE

We all know the Bible is God's anointed Word that will last throughout the ages of time. It's living and powerful and connects to every part of our lives, not just the spiritual part. The Bible teaches us to *forgive*. The commandment is not optional. Unforgiveness is not justified by the severity of wrongdoing. *Forgiveness* is a requirement for sustaining our spiritual, emotional, and physical health.

Medical studies show *forgiveness* lowers the risk of heart attack and improves sleep. It reduces pain, blood pressure, anxiety, depression, and stress. When we fail to *forgive* as the Word commands, we suffer! We step out from the umbrella of God's blessing.

Matthew 6:15 (NKJV) says, "If you do not forgive men their trespasses, neither will your Father forgive your trespasses." This is plain and simple: there are no attached exemptions to His commandment. I say this with all love intended, because I've personally witnessed what unforgiveness can do. Perhaps you have too. Our Father didn't *forgive* us because we deserve it. People may not necessarily deserve *forgiveness*, but our Father requires it, and we owe ourselves total wellness and wholeness available through Jesus Christ.

> "So if you are presenting a sacrifice at the altar…and you suddenly remember that someone has something against you, leave your sacrifice there at the altar. Go and be reconciled to that person. Then come and offer your sacrifice to God" (Matthew 5:23–24 NLT).

Word for the Day

RUSH

We live in the age of the microwave, the instant pot, fast food, carry-out groceries, express checkout lanes, instant photography, jet travel, and the list goes on. I admit I enjoy things that make life easier. We may reminisce about the old times in a dreamy sort of way, but if you're like me, we value our time in a fast-paced world and enjoy anything that helps us keep up.

If only God's timing were like ours, right? I imagine He thinks the same about us, if only our timing could be like His. In Genesis chapters 15 through 18, God makes a covenant with Abraham and promises him descendants as numerous as the stars. Unable to bear children, Sarah and Abraham decide to have a child through her servant, Hagar. Ishmael is born, and life becomes rocky at Abraham's place!

Sarah and Abraham were in a *rush* to make God's plan happen; consequently, they created conflict that continues to this day. We pray for things and want them instantly. God understands this, but He will always work for our good. He sees the days, weeks, and years ahead that we can't see. His works always promote the greater purpose for life—not the quick fix. What He teaches us in the process is to be cherished and treasured, lived and shared for the rest of our lives.

Father, you know my timing is not like Yours, but I will yield to Your plan because I trust You. I cannot afford to trust my will over Yours. Forgive me when I *rush* Your plan. I desire to stand still, wait on You, and rest in Your perfect care.

"Be still, and know that I am God" (Psalm 46:10 NKJV).

WORRY

Jesus asked the question in Matthew 6:27 (NLT), "Can all your worries add a single moment to your life?" Powerful question, isn't it? I think we can answer it unanimously—no! Medical studies even show that excess *worry* and stress are unhealthy, so why do we do it?

I think it's a natural response to everyday living, but we need to be aware that the enemy preys on our weaknesses and vulnerabilities, using them to feed unhealthy thoughts. Our minds are the favorite battlefield of the devil. He loves to play the "what-if" game. If he can get us focused on the what-if's, a frenzy of *worry*, fear, doubt, and anxiety can block the spiritual flow of peace and rest our Father wants us to have.

Jesus tells us in Matthew 6:25–33 not to *worry* about everyday basic needs. The next time we look at a bird or the wildflowers, we should remember that our Father takes care of them, and as Jesus says, "Aren't you far more valuable to him than they are?" (Matthew 6:26 NLT). In verse 33, Jesus says we should seek the Kingdom of God above all else. When we do that, He will give us everything we need.

Worry may come without invitation, but we don't have to entertain it. We can send it away with intentional worship and praise. The struggle may last for a while, but it can't stay when we are persistent in worshipping the Prince of Peace.

> "Don't worry about anything; instead, pray
> about everything. Tell God what you need, and
> thank him for all he has done. Then you will

experience God's peace, which exceeds anything we can understand. His peace will guard your hearts and minds as you live in Christ Jesus" (Philippians 4:6–7 NLT).

HEED

I've heard all my life that Jesus is coming. Based on the Scriptures, we are living in the end times, but it's easy for us to get complacent in looking for our Lord's return. I admit I didn't wake up this morning wondering if Jesus was coming today. If we thought we were going to be raptured this week, I wonder what we would do differently.

In Genesis 9, God decided to destroy the cities of Sodom and Gomorrah for their wickedness. Angels were sent to rescue Lot and his family. They instructed Lot to leave Sodom quickly. Lot rushed to tell his future sons-in-law that they needed to leave, but the young men didn't *heed* his warning. The angels waited for Lot and his family to get safely outside the city. One of the angels told them to keep running and not look back. Lot's wife did not *heed* the angel's instruction, and she glanced back to view the blazing inferno. According to the Scriptures, she turned into a pillar of salt.

Their story serves as a reminder for us to *heed* the Word of God. His Word is faithful and sure. Every letter, promise, and prophecy will be fulfilled.

> "Therefore you also be ready, for the Son
> of Man is coming at an hour you do not expect"
> (Matthew 24:44 NKJV).

Word for the Day

SPECK

D oes a *speck* of dust annoy you? How embarrassing is it to spot a dust ball in your house while company is there? Even worse, you spot it after they leave and wonder if they saw it. Okay, I admit it bothers me, but yes, I've learned how to ignore it. I don't know if that's a good thing. Just saying.

I'm also notorious for spotting someone else's *speck.* I'm talking about faults here. Just ask my sister! If there are any other *speck*-spotters out there, Jesus left a message for us in Matthew 7:1–5. Jesus speaks with authority, wisdom, and sincerity, so I will just let Him do the talking.

> "Why worry about a speck in your friend's eye when you have a log in your own? How can you think of saying to your friend, 'Let me help you get rid of that speck in your eye,' when you can't see past the log in your own eye? Hypocrite! First get rid of the log in your own eye; then you will see well enough to deal with the speck in your friend's eye" (Matthew 7:3–5 NLT).

It just may be that once we get the log out of our own eyes, the *speck* will not even phase us. Got it, Lord! Can anyone join me and say, "Ouch!"

TRADE

As a child, did you ever *trade* valuables with a brother or sister or friend? There's just something about what the other person has—it's intriguing and appealing. Perhaps that's why flea markets and yard sales are so popular.

Genesis 25 records the story of twin brothers who made a serious *trade*. One day, Esau came home hungry and wanted some of the stew that his twin brother, Jacob, was cooking. Jacob took advantage of his brother's hunger and offered to *trade* his stew for Esau's rights as the firstborn son. This *trade* was far beyond childish games boys and girls play. In those days, the birthright of a firstborn included inheritance, leadership, choice of family lands, and more. Who would *trade* their future for a bowl of stew?

Sadly, Adam and Eve *traded* their home in paradise for a piece of fruit. We find it difficult to comprehend, yet the enemy is walking right among us doing the same thing. He persuades some to *trade* their God-given joy for temporal happiness, their inheritance in Christ for a moment of pleasure, their home and family for a lustful affair. He convinces some to *trade* their confidence and trust in God for his lies of humanism and relativism.

Father, teach me to hide Your Word in my heart that I might not sin against you (Psalm 119:11). I don't want to miss heaven for the world! It's not worth the *trade*.

ASK

It's a simple word. We use it all the time. We say, "If you need something, just *ask*." I love the word because its letters remind me of Matthew 7:7–8 (NKJV), "Ask, and it will be given to you; seek, and you will find; knock, and it will be opened to you. For everyone who asks receives, and he who seeks finds, and to him who knocks it will be opened."

A-S-K: *ask*, seek, knock. This could be a cheerleading jingle! Jesus reminds us to keep *asking* for things we need and desire. Seek the deep things of God. Knock at His door for opportunity—His door of blessing. John 16:24 (NKJV) says, "Ask, and you will receive, that your joy may be full."

Our Father delights in giving us good things. Do you live beneath the abundance available in Christ? Our Father wants us to *ask*, understanding our request has to line up with His will and His Word, for He knows best. Our faith must be consistent; that is, we choose to believe even when we don't see or feel it. Then we wait, trusting our Father's timing instead of our own.

> "If you then, being evil, know how to give good gifts to your children, how much more will your Father who is in heaven give good things to those who ask Him!" (Matthew 7:11 NKJV).

HONOR

The book of Genesis records the covenant God made with Abraham, promising him descendants as numerous as the stars. In Genesis 26:5, God told Isaac that He would fulfil His covenant and bless him because his father obeyed the Lord. When I read this passage, my heart swells. I so desire for my children and their children to be blessed because I please my Father and He *honors* my righteous living.

This is the greatest gift I can give my children. The material things I leave pale to the promise of God's blessing over them. Our Father gives us all freewill to choose Him. Like Abraham's descendants, we sometimes stray to follow our own paths. Here's the good news: It's not too late to receive the mercy of God and *honor* Him with righteous living. In so doing, our Father *honors* our commitment by spreading His blessing over our children.

> "The righteous man walks in his integrity;
> His children are blessed after him" (Proverbs 20:7
> NKJV).

Word for the Day

RULE

Did you know the golden *rule* was spoken from the lips of Jesus? Matthew 7:12 (NLT) says, "Do to others whatever you would like them to do to you. This is the essence of all that is taught in the law and the prophets." Versions of the golden *rule* have been adopted by every major world religion. The *rule* is popular among religious and secular cultures everywhere because it speaks to the heart of mankind. The Bible may not have been first to record it, but certainly the spirit of the *rule* originated with our Creator!

The golden *rule*, if practiced by all, would restore peace, generosity, goodness, and love to the world. The golden *rule* would end poverty, division, and lawless chaos. Living the golden *rule* would be living heaven on earth!

Since the golden *rule* was spoken from the lips of Jesus, it is not merely a thought to bring on a warm, fuzzy feeling or a motto we post on a classroom chalkboard; it is a commandment, a *rule* to be practiced among believers. The golden *rule* is so simple yet so powerful.

Thank you, Jesus, for speaking truth and life! Sear the *rule* in my heart today—help me live it. The *rule* is not my nature; it requires Your character.

> "Create in me a clean heart, O God, And renew a steadfast spirit within me" (Psalm 51:10 NKJV).

Word for the Day

FREEDOM

There's an old cliché that says blood is thicker than water. Some will agree with that statement while others will challenge it. I also hear folks say those who are closest to you can hurt you the most. Family is wonderful. Family squabbles? Well, they can wreck relationship and even divide households for a lifetime.

Genesis 25 records the birth of twin brothers Esau and Jacob. They struggled with each other from the womb of their mother. Jacob cheated Esau out of his birthright and blessing as the eldest son. The blessings Isaac passed to his sons are recorded in Genesis 27. Isaac's blessing to Jacob included richness, abundance, and lordship. Isaac's blessing to Esau was the opposite. "You will live away from the richness of the earth and away from the dew of the heaven above. You will live by your sword, and you will serve your brother" (Genesis 27:39–40 NLT). However, Isaac did give Esau a glimmer of hope in verse 40 (NLT), saying, "But when you decide to break free, you will shake his yoke from your neck."

Isaac gave Esau a truth that is available to us: We can choose to live in anger, hurt, and bitterness, reaping the destruction it has on us spiritually, physically and emotionally; or we can choose to release the hurts of our past, forgive, and find *freedom*. The choice we make affects us more than our adversary. Our choice makes us a victim or a victor. Our Father wants us to choose forgiveness and receive *freedom*! As John 8:32 (NLT) says, "Know the truth, and the truth will set you free."

FAITH

In Matthew 8, a Roman officer asks Jesus to heal his servant. Jesus tells the officer that He will go home with him and heal the man. Being an officer, this man understood rank and authority. He also perceived the authority Jesus held over sickness and disease. "The officer said, 'Lord, I am not worthy to have you come into my home. Just say the word from where you are, and my servant will be healed'" (Matthew 8:8 NLT).

Jesus was amazed at the officer's *faith*! I wonder what the Father thinks about my *faith*. Does my trust grab His attention with delight? In spite of our weak moments, our loving, caring, patient Father continues to encourage us to trust Him. His Word is full of healing testimonies, miracles, and instructions to grow our *faith*. Is He worthy of our trust? The answer is absolutely, unequivocally, *yes*! I want to have the kind of *faith* that says, "Here's what the Word says about this situation. I accept this promise, this truth, with no reservation—no hesitation."

> "But without faith it is impossible to please Him, for he who comes to God must believe that He is, and that He is a rewarder of those who diligently seek Him" (Hebrews 11:6 NKJV).

GOOD

There's only one baby in a family. I happen to be the baby in mine. While my siblings would disagree, we all know who the favorite is! Genesis records the rival story of Joseph and his brothers. Being the younger sibling and the favorite of his father, Joseph was treated harshly by his brothers. They sold him to a caravan of Midianite traders and concocted a story of how he was killed by a wild animal. They never dreamed they would ever see him again.

In hard times, Jacob sent his sons to Egypt to buy food. There they met the man in charge, only to discover the man was their brother Joseph. It was a fearful reunion for them, but Joseph cared for them, their families, and his father, moving them to Egypt where they would have plenty and live comfortably. Once Jacob died, the siblings became fearful again that Joseph would punish them for their wrongdoing. The brothers begged for forgiveness and threw themselves down before him as slaves. Joseph reassured them he had no ill feeling by saying, "You intended to harm me, but God intended it all for good" (Genesis 50:20 NLT).

When we live under the blessing of God, bad things cannot defeat us. That's not to say bad things can't happen. But just as He did for Joseph, God will turn our ashes into beauty and mourning into joy (Isaiah 61:3). As Romans 8:28 says, "God causes everything to work together for the good of those who love God and are called according to his purpose for them" (NLT). When hard times come, know your Father will work things out for your *good*.

Word for the Day

FOUNDATION

I've always believed a job worth doing is worth doing right. Do you ever watch the high-drama disaster movies where buildings or structures are not built to standard? Someone gets greedy and decides to alter the plans to cut cost or time. In the end, the cost for substandard work is intensely multiplied. The disaster that follows costs countless dollars, time, and even lives.

Jesus says in Matthew 7:26–27 (NLT), "Anyone who hears my teaching and doesn't obey it is foolish, like a person who builds a house on sand. When the rains and floods come and the winds beat against that house, it will collapse with a mighty crash."

The Word of God is the *foundation* of our salvation and our faith. We are not saved by emotion, nor can we live by our own convictions. The Word identifies sin, teaches us how to live successfully, grows our faith, and it is our spiritual weapon. The Word is more than a book to read before we go to bed. Its contents are living and powerful. Reading from Genesis to Revelation will not change us unless we choose to obey the words we read. The Word contains the *foundation* for everyday living. Either we believe the Word, or we don't; either we obey it fully, or we don't fully obey.

Father, You provide the *foundation* for spiritual, physical, and emotional health. I desire Your Word to guide every part of my day. Teach me to walk according to Your Word so that the difficult times do not shake me.

"Blessed is the man who fears the LORD, who delights greatly in His commandments. Surely he will never be shaken" (Psalm 112:1, 6 NKJV).

Word for the Day

CHOSEN

When Joseph and all his generation passed, his descendants were still living in Egypt. In fact, they had prospered so much that the king felt threatened by them. This king came into power after Joseph died and knew nothing of the role Joseph played in sustaining Egypt during the famine years. The king's fear of Joseph's descendants resulted in him making them slaves, forcing them to build and do all the work in the fields. His paranoia escalated to the point of ordering Hebrew newborn boys to be killed by the midwives. However, the midwives feared God and didn't carry out the orders. In turn, the Scriptures say God was good to the midwives, and the Israelites continued to thrive.

They were God's *chosen* people. That's why they flourished even in the midst of hardship. They lived under the blessing of Abraham. Galatians 3 says that those who know Jesus Christ as Savior also live under the blessing of Abraham. We're marked as God's *chosen*! We're redeemed and live as an heir through Jesus Christ. Being *chosen* doesn't mean we won't meet opposition or escape suffering, but it does mean that our Father is on our side, watching every move made against us. He will not allow more than we can handle. As His *chosen*, we cannot be defeated or separated from the love of God. Being on the *chosen* side means we win!

"Blessed is the nation whose God is the LORD, the people He has chosen as His own inheritance" (Psalm 33:12 NKJV).

CRY

A baby's *cry* is their first language. The *cry* may mean they're hungry, wet, tired, want to be held, and sometimes we can't figure out what it means! They quickly learn to associate their *cry* with the attention they desire. As they continue to grow, children may even resort to a fake *cry* to get what they want. (I didn't do that, but my siblings did.)

The Israelites lived under the burden of slavery in Egypt. Exodus 2:23 (NLT) says, "They cried out for help, and their cry rose up to God." How comforting it is to know our *cries* rise to our Father. Sometimes we call out in a gentle whisper, other times in a resounding *cry*. There's not a prayer prayed, a groan made, or a tear shed that does not rise up to God. He is moved by our *cry*! While we may be operating by the alarm clock, our Father may be on calendar time, but He is forever compassionate and faithful. Psalm 34:15 (NKJV) says, "The eyes of the LORD are on the righteous, And His ears are open to their cry."

Don't give up on what you need from the Lord! Know your *cry* turns the face of your loving Father to you.

> "Evening and morning and at noon I will
> pray, and cry aloud, And He shall hear my voice"
> (Psalm 55:17 NKJV).

DEPENDENCE

I've often heard people say one can't be helped until they seek help. The first step in getting help is to acknowledge the need for help.

Matthew 9 (NLT) tells how Jesus and his disciples were invited to dinner by Matthew, a tax collector. The Pharisees observed in disgust, wondering why Jesus would associate with a sinner like Matthew. Jesus responded, "Healthy people don't need a doctor—sick people do… I have come to call not those who think they are righteous, but those who know they are sinners."

Our *independence* lies in our total *dependence* on God. We cannot receive salvation until we realize our sin. We can never be good enough or do enough good things to earn a place in heaven. We can never be wise enough to successfully map our own lives. We can never be strong enough to be our own master. The air we breathe belongs to God. The beats of our hearts are numbered by the Creator. The only thing you and I control is our destiny: heaven or hell—only because our heavenly Father gives us the choice.

When we place our *dependence* solely in Him, we are no longer bound by human limitations or the bondage of evil, but we sit in heavenly places (Ephesians 2:6). Freedom doors open! "Trust in the LORD with all your heart, And lean not on your own understanding" (Proverbs 3:5 NKJV). Only our heavenly Father is worthy of our trust. *Depend* on Him for everything!

Word for the Day

CONSUMED

Did you know an entire house can burn to the ground in minutes? It's no wonder that Moses stared in amazement at a blazing bush engulfed in flames and not being *consumed*. This was not a natural occurrence; this was the actual presence of God! The event is recorded in Exodus 3.

Daniel 3 records the event of three men who were thrown into a blazing furnace. The furnace was so hot that the flames killed the soldiers who threw them into the fire. The king looked on with amazement to witness the three men walking around in the fire unharmed. With them was a fourth figure—again, the company of God!

If the enemy were allowed, we would all be *consumed*! But there is a God who fiercely loves us, allowing His own Son to be *consumed* on a cross to pay our sin debt. Jesus Christ suffered and died for us. He rose on the third day, conquering death, hell, and the grave. The same power that resurrected Him lives in His followers! The same power shields us from the destruction that the enemy desires to inflict on us.

Second Corinthians 4:8–9 (NKJV) says it best: "We are hard-pressed on every side, yet not crushed; we are perplexed, but not in despair; persecuted, but not forsaken; struck down, but not destroyed."

Father, thank You for Your fierce, amazing love. I will not be *consumed* by trouble because You are merciful. Your compassion does not fail but rains fresh on me every single morning (Lamentations 3:22–23).

Word for the Day

EXTRAORDINARY

The Bible is filled with many examples of how the Lord used ordinary circumstances, objects, and people to perform *extraordinary* things. The book of Exodus describes how God chose a shepherd to lead His people out of Egypt. He used Moses's staff to perform supernatural events: turning it into a snake to demonstrate God's power. He used the same staff to initiate the plagues God imposed on Pharaoh and the Egyptians. Moses used the staff to part the Red Sea and produce water from a rock.

We don't have to be credentialed or hold impressive titles and position to be used by God. We must simply be willing—regardless of how big or small the assignment is. The end result is to glorify our Father. I'm personally glad I don't own a shepherd's crook. I really prefer the Lord not ask me to lay it down and watch it turn into a snake, then tell me to pick it up! There's always a cost to the call of God; but with every assignment, big or small, there is God! He makes the *extraordinary* happen!

> "May the God of peace who brought up our Lord Jesus from the dead…make you complete in every good work to do His will" (Hebrews 13:20–21 NKJV).

TOUCH

One Christmas season, my son and I took an overnight bus trip to New York. We were dropped off early morning and had the entire day to take in the beautiful sights and sounds of the big city. The streets were filled with more people than I could imagine. By end of day, my patience was growing thin with umbrellas poking my head, struggling through herds of bodies moving in the opposite direction, being pushed and prodded out of the way, and coming to a halt to stand in endless lines. One might describe me as a person who likes my space and doesn't like others in it!

Luke 8 describes a crowd of people who eagerly awaited the arrival of Jesus. The crowd was apparently large, and the people pushed each other to get near Him. Jesus felt healing power go out of His body, and He immediately stopped, asking who *touched* Him. "Everyone denied it, and Peter said, 'Master, this whole crowd is pressing up against you'" (Luke 8:45 NLT). However, Jesus knew this was more than an accidental bump. He recognized the *touch* of faith.

Our Father is *touched* by our faith—it doesn't go unnoticed! With countless people all over the globe calling out to Him daily, our Father instantly recognizes the *touch* of faith! It is our faith that saves us, heals us, moves mountains, births miracles. Hebrews 11:6 (NLT) says, "It is impossible to please God without faith. Anyone who wants to come to him must believe that God exists and that he rewards those who sincerely seek him."

"According to your faith let it be to you"
(Mathew 9:29 NKJV).

Word for the Day

VALUED

What makes you feel *valued*? People seek *value* in different places. Some measure their *value* by the size of their bank account. Others measure their *value* by family name, credentials, position, title, or popularity. The list can go on and on. There is nothing wrong with achieving things, but they are temporary. Circumstances and relationships change. Trophies rust. A winning streak eventually ends.

Lasting *value* comes from accepting Jesus Christ as Savior. We take on His righteousness and become adopted sons and daughters. We can't win it or work for it; our Father simply gifts His *value* to us. John 3:16 (NKJV) says, "For God so loved the world that He gave His only begotten Son, that whoever believes in Him should not perish but have everlasting life."

According to Matthew 10, not even one sparrow falls to the ground without our Father knowing it, and we are more *valuable* to Him than a flock of sparrows. Relationships and circumstances can destroy us to the core when our *value* is founded upon anything other than God. Our *value* comes from understanding we are made in God's image. Our *value* comes from knowing who we are in Christ. Our *value* comes from grasping the intense love our Father has for us. Our *value* comes from trusting that absolutely nothing can separate us from His love (Romans 8:31–39). We are forever His! If that doesn't make us feel *valued*, what will?

DISCOURAGED

Is there anyone who has never been hurt, disappointed, *discouraged*? I doubt it! Life has a way of disappointing us all. Life was certainly harsh on the Hebrew children who were being forced to serve the Egyptians. Their groans and cries captured the attention of God, and He sent Moses to lead them out of their oppression.

Exodus 5 describes how Moses and Aaron went to Pharaoh on their behalf. Their first attempt quickly multiplied into additional attempts—each one carrying increasingly drastic consequences to the Egyptian people. Not only did the Egyptians suffer consequences, the Hebrew children did as well. They were spared from the plagues God placed on the Egyptians, but they were forced to work harder. When Moses tried to reiterate God's promise to the Hebrew children, Exodus 6:9 (NLT) says, "They refused to listen anymore. They had become too discouraged by the brutality of their slavery."

Had I been Moses, I might have said, "Well, all righty then! Just stay in Egypt." That's the difference between God's patience and mine! God kept sending Moses and Aaron back to Pharaoh and sending harsher consequences. Our Father doesn't give up on us, even when we become too *discouraged* to reach out to Him. He's right there, ready to pour His peace and comfort in us, empowering us to bring our thoughts captive to the obedience of Christ (2 Corinthians 10:5).

Friend, you may be too *discouraged* to see it, but know God is there all the time working on your behalf.

"In the multitude of my anxieties within me, Your comforts delight my soul" (Psalm 94:19 NKJV).

Word for the Day

KNOW

Ever feel like you're always the last person to find out something? Sometimes our choices would be different if we had only *known*. Jesus created the very world we live in and chose to live among us, but the world did not *know* Him. His chosen people did not recognize Him as the promised Messiah. Even the disciples who lived with Jesus did not *know* Him. They ran away when He was arrested and put on trial.

Matthew 8 describes how Jesus met and healed two demon-possessed men. The demons knew Jesus immediately and "began screaming at him, 'Why are you interfering with us, Son of God? Have you come here to torture us before God's appointed time?'" (Matthew 8:29 NLT). I marvel how demons can immediately *know* and bow to the authority of Jesus, yet God's most beloved creation does not *know* Him.

Our Father wants us to *know* Him intimately—as one who lives in us, nurtures us, provides for us, and defends us. He desires to open our eyes to the treasures He has for us. He's always there eagerly waiting to spend time with us. There's more to relationship than saying, "God is great, God is good" and "Now I lay me down to sleep." The more we *know* Him, the more we are changed into His image. The more we *know* Him, the richer our lives become. His Spirit and His Word will marry with our faith and diligence in seeking Him as He reveals Himself to us.

"Eye has not seen, Nor ear heard, nor have
entered into the heart of man The things which

God has prepared for those who love Him... No one knows the things of God except the Spirit of God. Now we have received...the Spirit who is from God, that we might know the things that have been freely given to us by God" (1 Corinthians 2:9–12 NKJV).

HAPPEN

There are some people who just make good things *happen*! My pastors are like that. If it's remotely within their means, they step up and do it! I love that, and I want to be this kind of person. There are things, however, that are beyond our abilities. Thank God in heaven who has no limits!

Matthew 9 describes two blind men who followed Jesus to the place He was staying and asked for mercy. Jesus asked them if they believed He could make them see. "'Yes, Lord,' they told him, 'we do.' Then He touched their eyes and said, 'Because of your faith, it will happen'" (Matthew 9:28–29 NLT).

I have a list of things that need to *happen* in my life. My Father will come through—speak the same words He said to the blind men—if I am consistent in my faith. Do you need something to *happen* in your life? Jesus said in Mark 11:23–24 (NLT), "I tell you the truth, you can say to this mountain, 'May you be lifted up and thrown into the sea,' and it will happen. But you must really believe it will happen and have no doubt in your heart. I tell you, you can pray for anything, and if you believe that you've received it, it will be yours."

Believe God and watch it *happen*!

Word for the Day

HERE

In Exodus 17, the children of Israel found themselves in a place where there was no water, and they were thirsty. Feeling parched, frustrated, tired, and perhaps scared, they asked Moses, "Is the LORD here with us or not?" (Exodus 17:7 NLT).

Have you ever been in a place like that? I confess I've been there. The psalmist wrote, "O God… Why must I wander around in grief, oppressed by my enemies? They scoff, 'Where is this God of yours?'" (Psalm 42:9–10 NLT). The psalmist continues in verse 11, "Why am I discouraged? Why is my heart so sad? I will put my hope in God! I will praise him again—my Savior and my God!"

When we ask if the Lord is *here* with or us not, the resounding answer is yes! He is not offended by our cries of frustration. He knows and understands our deepest hurts. May I encourage you to follow the psalmist's example and begin to bring intentional praise to our Savior and God. The words of a beautiful song come to mind: "Praise the Lord! He can work through those who praise Him. Praise the Lord, for our God inhabits praise. Praise the Lord, for the chains that seem to bind you serve only to remind you they drop powerless behind you when you praise Him."

Word for the Day

HAVE

No doubt this Christmas, there were children who asked Santa for the Jedi light saber or the princess magical wand. These toys have a way of stirring the imagination. I remember my sister and I taking turns standing in a chair and using a pencil to magically sing on stage with microphone.

Moses had a shepherd's hook that performed such feats as transforming into a snake, casting plagues, dividing the Red Sea, and producing water from a rock. There was no imagination, magic, or power within the staff; it was a simple trade tool Moses *had*, and God used it to carry out His missions. God used what Moses *had* to help him make a difference in his time.

What do you *have*? Maybe it's the "gift of gab" or the ability to befriend a stranger. Maybe it's skillful hands that can help a neighbor in need. Maybe it's the car you own to take a friend to a doctor's visit, or that simple dish you can share with a shut-in. God will use whatever we *have*. It's His power and anointing that changes lives—not who we are, what we do, or how much we possess.

> "Present your bodies a living sacrifice, holy, acceptable to God, which is your reasonable service. Having then gifts differing according to the grace that is given to us, let us use them" (Romans 12:1, 6 NKJV).

COMMANDMENTS

A couple of months after the Israelites left Egypt, the Lord gave them a set of rules we commonly call the "Ten Commandments." The first *commandment* is probably the one I struggle with the most: "You must not have any other god but me" (Exodus 20:3 NLT).

That sounds fair enough, right? We wouldn't think of labeling anyone or anything "God." The truth is, however, anyone or anything we prioritize above God becomes an idol. Our Father wants us to have good things. Psalm 84:11 (NKJV) says, "No good thing will He withhold From those who walk uprightly." But if God is not lord of everything, He's really not lord at all. When our desire to accumulate wealth exceeds our desire to become rich in His character, wealth becomes a god. When we chase after pleasure more than we chase after our Creator, then pleasure rules. When our affection for human relationship is stronger than our relationship with the Father, then that person takes God's place.

The first *commandment* seems simple but can be complicated by our own human nature. Perhaps that's why the Lord made it the first of the Ten Commandments. If we can faithfully practice this one, the other *commandments* might come naturally. Jesus sums it all saying, "'You must love the LORD your God with all your heart, all your soul, and all your mind.' This is the first and greatest commandment. A second is equally important: 'Love your neighbor as yourself'" (Matthew 22:37–39 NLT).

Word for the Day

CHOICE

The Lord is not one to mince words. What He says, He means and what He means, He says. We may not always understand His Word, but it never changes—it's truth and enduring through the ages.

In the beginning, God gave Adam and Eve rules to follow. He warned them of consequences if they disobeyed. God has given us His Word to follow. He outlines the blessing connected to living by His Word and the consequences of disobedience.

Deuteronomy 30:19 (NLT) says, "Today I have given you the choice between life and death, between blessings and curses. Now I call on heaven and earth to witness the choice you make. Oh, that you would choose life."

Exodus 20:5–6 (NLT) says, "I lay the sins of the parents upon their children; the entire family is affected… But I lavish unfailing love for a thousand generations on those who love me and obey my commands."

Think about it. To be lavished by God's unfailing love for a thousand generations! What's your *choice*?

YOKE

By definition, a *yoke* is a type of harness that is fastened over the necks of two animals and attached to a cart. The *yoke* provides control to the driver of the cart. Jesus said in Matthew 11:28–30 (NLT), "Come to me, all of you who are weary and carry heavy burdens, and I will give you rest. Take my yoke upon you. Let me teach you, because I am humble and gentle at heart, and you will find rest for your souls. For my yoke is easy to bear, and the burden I give you is light."

Taking on the *yoke* of Jesus implies giving up our self-control for His peace. We all want peace, but we struggle with laying down our *yoke* to take on His. The truth is our *yoke* is hard. Life just gets to be more than we can handle. The reality of wearing our *yoke* of self-control means we try to solely bear the pressures of life's demands and heartaches. We exhaust our energies, time, and resources trying to create balance and order out of chaos. Often, we become trapped under the load.

Jesus wants us to let go and let Him do for us what we cannot do for ourselves. Our Father offers "beauty for ashes, the oil of joy for mourning, the garment of praise for the spirit of heaviness" (Isaiah 61:3 NKJV). Wearing His *yoke* is much lighter than our own. Are you ready to lay down your *yoke* for His?

Word for the Day

REAL

Desire for quality products at a cost savings has generated knock-offs, simulations, and artificial products in the marketplace. Years later, the movement to return to the "*real* deal" is on. While the artificial products offer savings in time, dollars, and calories, some believe these products don't quite measure up to the original and can even be harmful.

In Matthew 13, Jesus shares a parable of the wheat and tares, likening the kingdom of heaven to a farmer who sowed good seed. Later that night, the enemy planted seeds of weeds among the wheat. One source says the weed is a plant that comes from the darnel seed. In its early stages of growth, the plant looks like the wheat, but as it continues to grow, the plant takes on a separate identity. By this time, the weed is intertwined with the wheat and cannot be separated without destroying some of the wheat.

Our enemy offers counterfeit values to replace the *real* deal. His imitation of love, tolerance, power, and servanthood appeals to our desire to do good, feel good, and look good, but the enemy's imitation eventually takes on his identity and reaps the destruction he planned all along. That's why it's important to know the Word of God.

The Word ensures that we don't stray from the *real* deal. God gave us the written Word so we wouldn't be deceived by imitations. If you want the *real* deal, get planted in the Word! It brings life, healing, health, and richness.

"Your word I have hidden in my heart, That I might not sin against You" (Psalm 119:11 NKJV).

133

Word for the Day

BEST

Disciplinary action felt like a ceremonial process in my child-hood years. My mother handled the day-to-day corrections, but it was my father's family meetings I always dreaded. When least expected, he would call us together for one of his "talks." One by one, he would address our wrongdoings accumulated over a period of time. My sister and I would tear up as soon as we were summoned to the meeting. Our father would preface phase two of his meeting (the more intense hands-on-part) by saying, "Now this is going to hurt me more than you. I do this because I love you." I didn't under-stand that as a child, but maturity and parenting has opened my eyes to my father's love. I can look back now and know that everything he did for me was for our *best*.

In Exodus 23, God told the Israelites He would go before them and set the stage for them to drive out the inhabitants of the land He was giving them. God said, "I will not drive them out in a single year, because the land would become desolate and the wild animals would multiply and threaten you. I will drive them out a little at a time until your population has increased enough to take possession of the land" (Exodus 23:29–30 NLT).

Sometimes I want it all and I want it now. Our Father knows what's *best*, and His plan never sets us up for failure.

Father, You know waiting is hard for me, but I know Your tim-ing, Your plan, Your way is *best*. I yield to You because I trust You. "For who is God, except the LORD? And who is a rock, except our God? It is God who arms me with strength, And makes my way per-fect" (Psalm 18:31–32 NKJV).

Word for the Day

TRACK

These days it's difficult to stay on *track* without a personal planner or techy device. Of course, we ladies know the most reliable source is a mother who never needs batteries or updates!

In Numbers 15, the Lord instructs the Israelites to make tassels for the hems of their clothing. The tassels were worn to remind them to follow all the commands God had given them. Being attached to their clothing, the tassels were always with them as a constant reminder.

Under the grace dispensation, we aren't required to wear tassels to keep us on *track*. Our Father has sent the Holy Spirit to live inside us and be our personal teacher, reminding us of His Word. While the Word identifies sin, it does not itemize every possible sin, but the Holy Spirit will send us a warning signal when we get off *track*. The warning may be subtle, but the Holy Spirit is protective. He will always keep us on the right *track* if we listen.

Father, thank you for sending Your Holy Spirit. You will always show me the right way, and when I get off on the wrong *track*, Your Holy Spirit gently nudges me toward You. "I have tried hard to find you—don't let me wander from your commands" (Psalm 119:10 NLT). Holy Spirit, condition my heart, soul, ears, and mind to recognize Your voice—Your unction, Your teaching, and Your warnings. You are teacher and protector of my soul!

Word for the Day

SPEAK

Did you know our words say more than the syllables we utter? Our words say who we are; words describe our hearts. Our words reveal the inner person. Jesus said in Matthew 15:11 (NLT), "It's not what goes into your mouth that defiles you; you are defiled by the words that comes out of your mouth."

When we *speak* our fears and doubts, we allow the enemy to gain advantage of our weaknesses. When we *speak* out of uncontrolled anger, bitterness, and envy, we inflict damaging words that can never be taken back. These words form images of our character that do not glorify God. So what should we *speak*? *Speak* the Word!

When you need the peace of God, *speak* Philippians 4:6–7. I will be anxious for nothing, but in everything by prayer and supplication with thanksgiving, I will make my requests known to You. And Your peace will guard my heart and mind.

If you need healing, *speak* Isaiah 53:5. By His stripes I am healed!

If you need to overcome your fears and doubts, *speak* 2 Timothy 1:7. God doesn't make me fearful. He has given me power, love, and a sound mind!

If you need freedom, *speak* John 8:32, 36. I know God's Word is true, and His truth makes me free. I am free indeed!

If you have a material need, *speak* Philippians 4:19. My God will supply all my needs according to His riches.

If your family needs the mercy of God, *speak* Hebrews 4:16. I come boldly to Your throne to obtain mercy and grace.

The more we *speak* the words of God, the more the words transform our thinking. *Speak* the Word till you believe it, then watch GOD *speak* miracles in your life!

GIFTING

Does something come naturally for you that others find difficult? Do people tell you that you're good at certain things? These are *giftings* from God. He endows a measure of talents to each individual to fulfill His purpose and bring Him glory. We all have talents because God has purpose for each of us.

In Exodus 31:3 (NLT), God chose Bezalel to take charge of building the tabernacle and all the furnishings. The Lord said, "I have filled him with the Spirit of God, giving him great wisdom, ability, and expertise in all kinds of crafts." The Lord personally appointed Oholiab to be his assistant, and He gave special skills to other workers to complete the tabernacle.

First Corinthians 12 says we make up the body of Christ and He has a place for each of us. With our place comes purpose, and with every purpose comes the *gifting* to complete it. Your *gifting* may not look like mine. We do well to ignore the temptation to compare; rather, be accountable to use what God has given us.

"Whatever you do, do all to the glory of God" (1 Corinthians 10:31 NKJV).

Word for the Day

DOUBT

The tiniest flaw can degrade the quality of a diamond. A tenth of a second can make the difference in winning or losing a race. A small stain can ruin the appearance of an outfit. That's what *doubt* does to our faith.

In Matthew 14, Jesus met the disciples on the lake. They were in a boat, but Jesus, well, He was simply walking on the water! Peter asked Jesus if he could come to Him and walk on the water too. Jesus told Him to come ahead. Being a play-it-safe kind of gal, I would have waited for all the other disciples to do it first. Being a let-me-do-it kind of guy, Peter went overboard and actually started walking on water; that is, until *doubt* gripped him. *Doubt* caused Peter to set his focus on the wind and waves. At the moment he took his eyes off Jesus, Peter began to sink. Jesus said, "Why did you doubt me?" (Matthew 14:31 NLT).

We may not be able to control thoughts that enter our minds, but we are accountable for what we do with them. First, we must identify the source of that thought. If it does not come from God, then we must intentionally counteract it with the Word. When *doubt* pays you a visit, run to the Word to resist it! Don't entertain it. Don't speak it. Fill your mind with the goodness of God (Philippians 4:8) and *doubt* will have to go (James 4:7)!

Word for the Day

RADIANCE

The marketplace is filled with products promising beauty and youthfulness. I must admit I can use all the help I can get, but nothing remotely compares to the *radiance* of God.

In Exodus 24, Moses spent forty days and nights with the Lord on Mt. Sinai. When he returned to camp, the children of Israel were afraid of him because his face was so *radiant*. This kind of *radiance* only comes from spending time with the Lord.

There's no specific number of hours to be logged. It's not based on the number of times we read through the Bible. The *radiance* comes from building relationship with the Father. As we talk to Him and read His Word, He reveals Himself to us and our need for Him. Day by day, month by month, year by year, He continues to work on us, purging the carnal things and filling us with godly things. As we grow in obedience, the glow of His character shines through us.

Father, I desire our time to change me from the inside out! May others see less of me and more of You.

> "And the Lord—who is the Spirit—makes us more and more like him as we are changed into his glorious image" (2 Corinthians 3:18 NLT).

WORTH

What does your value lie in? I can definitely say it's not in my bank account! We all place different levels of value on our possessions. The philosophy behind flea markets, garage and yard sales is "One person's trash is another's treasure."

In Matthew 16:26 (NLT), Jesus asks a very important question: "Is anything worth more than your soul?" It's a question we all must answer for ourselves. Our Father owns it all, and He desires to lavish His abundance on us. First and foremost, however, He wants relationship with us, and nothing else can compete. Matthew 6:33 (NKJV) says, "Seek first the kingdom of God and His righteousness, and all these things [our material needs] shall be added to you."

Understanding our *worth* in Christ teaches us how to live the good life. Gratitude becomes our mind-set. Contentment becomes our path. Sharing becomes our action plan. Blessing becomes our reward. In every temptation, in every battle, in every decision we make, we do well to ask ourselves if anything is *worth* more than our soul. As Jesus says, "What do you benefit if you gain the whole world but lose your own soul?" (Mathew 16:26 NLT).

MISS

Have you ever tried to watch a clock to see the minute or hour digit change? If you're like me, I get distracted and *miss* it. The children of Israel *missed* the Messiah because they were not looking for a baby in a manger or a carpenter's son from Nazareth. The religious leaders of the day taught the people that Elijah would return before the Messiah came. Jesus said John the Baptist came (having the power of Elijah), but no one recognized him. Thomas almost *missed* out on the miraculous resurrection of Jesus because he believed only in what he saw.

If the religious leaders of that day and the disciples of Christ struggled to see the glory of God, how likely am I to *miss* it? Is it possible that we become desensitized to the greatness of God? Do we *miss* the voice of God for the noise of the world? Do we *miss* miracles because our faith is stuck in present circumstances? What if we were to *miss* heaven because we're too busy with life here on earth?

Father, I don't want to *miss* You! I don't want to *miss* out on what You have for me. "Turn my eyes from worthless things, and give me life through your word" (Psalm 119:37 NLT). I don't want to *miss* one minute with You, one blessing, one miracle!

Word for the Day

CONFIDENCE

Life is full of changes, requiring us to change with it. Change often takes us out of our comfort zones. Joshua was chosen by God to assume leadership of the Israelites when Moses died. Joshua knew he had big shoes to fill. The Lord told him He would be with him and encouraged him to be strong and courageous.

As they crossed the Jordan, the Lord miraculously dried up the river for Joshua just as He dried up the Red Sea for Moses (chapters 3 and 4). Joshua 4:14 (NLT) says, "That day the LORD made Joshua a great leader in the eyes of all the Israelites, and for the rest of his life they revered him as much as they had revered Moses."

We may be unaware of the changes tomorrow brings. Whether it's Kingdom work, career, or personal obligations, the Lord already knows the changes that may be required of us. He wants us to know He will be with us every step of the way. We are to be strong and courageous because our Father is leading us. He is rich in strength, power, knowledge, and wisdom. We never have to face anything on our own. God is more than enough!

"For the LORD will be your confidence" (Proverbs 3:26 NKJV).

Word for the Day

CHILDREN

In Matthew 18, the disciples ask Jesus who is greatest in His kingdom. Some would probably think John the Baptist was greatest. Certainly, those who were martyred for the faith would be at the top of the list. But Jesus called a little *child* to Him and responded, "Anyone who becomes as humble as this little child is the greatest in the Kingdom of Heaven" (Matthew 18:4 NLT).

I'm reminded of a testimony shared with me by a precious prayer partner. A lady who had been diagnosed with cancer called her pastor and requested that she be prayed over in the next church service. She said she only wanted people of faith to surround her in prayer; she didn't want any doubters in the group. The pastor told her the Lord had already been speaking to him about her need and who should pray for her. The next service came, and the pastor called the lady to the front. Next, he summoned the prayer warriors of faith. The deacons nor the prayer team were included. The pastor didn't ask anyone who had faith to come forward. Instead, he called the *children* to surround this lady, lay hands on her, and pray. The lady received her healing, and the woman is cancer-free!

We need the faith of a little *child*—faith that is not contaminated with what others think or what is society-accepted; *child*like faith that believes if Jesus said it, He will do it! "Jesus said, 'Let the children come to me. Don't stop them! For the Kingdom of Heaven belongs to those who are like these children'" (Matthew 19:14 NLT).

Father, I want *child*like faith!

Word for the Day

HIDE

I imagine the Lord shakes His head when we try to *hide* our offenses from Him. We may *hide* things from our family, friends, and coworkers, but we are in denial if we think we have *hidden* them from our Creator.

In Joshua 7, an Israelite named Achan took items that were to be set apart for the Lord and kept them for himself, *hiding* them beneath his tent. Consequences followed. What should have been an easy raid turned to defeat for the Israelites. Joshua and the elders went before the Lord and asked why defeat had come to the children of Israel. "But the LORD said to Joshua, 'Get up! Why are you lying on your face like this? Israel has sinned and broken my covenant!' Hidden among you, O Israel, are things set apart for the LORD. You will never defeat your enemies until you remove these things from among you" (Joshua 7:10, 11, 13 NLT).

Blessing and disobedience just don't mix! Father, I desperately need Your favor. Reveal anything within me that is ungodly so that I may confess and repent. You know my deepest thoughts and desires. Teach me to *hide* Your Word, not my sinful ways. "Search me, O God, and know my heart; test me and know my anxious thoughts. Point out anything in me that offends you, and lead me along the path of everlasting life" (Psalm 139:23–24 NLT).

LOVE

There are so many things we get to enjoy in life, but they don't last forever. There's a season where we enjoy innocence, beauty, strength, and accomplishment. The Scriptures, however, describe attributes available to us for our entire lives: "Three things will last forever—faith, hope, and love—and the greatest of these is love" (1 Corinthians 13:13 NLT).

Love is an endless circle of receiving and giving—following the model of Christ. When asked what the greatest commandments were, Jesus said to *love* God with everything you have; and secondly, *love* your neighbor as yourself. Jesus spent time with a Samaritan woman—someone with whom the Jews wouldn't associate. He had compassion on the weak, the poor, and the rejected. Jesus teaches us that *loving* our enemies sets us apart from the world. If everyone obeyed this one commandment, life might feel like heaven on earth!

Sharing God's *love* requires selflessness, tolerance, our time, and our means. Our actions must mirror our words. One is worthless without the other. We must ask the Lord who we can *love* on today. When we *love* others, we'll find the *love* coming right back at us! What we give comes back to us "pressed down, shaken together, and running over" (Luke 6:38 NKJV).

TOUCH

Jesus shares the parable of the lost sheep in Matthew 18. "If a man has a hundred sheep and one of them wanders away, what will he do? Won't he leave the ninety-nine others on the hills and go out to search for the one that is lost? And if he finds it, I tell you the truth, he will rejoice over it more than over the ninety-nine that didn't wander away! In the same way, it is not my heavenly Father's will that even one of these little ones should perish" (Matthew 18:12–14 NLT).

The heart of Jesus is *touched* by the lost. He gave His life for them just as He gave His life for us. Our Father loves them and is *touched* by our prayers for them. First John 5:14–15 says, "We are confident that he hears us whenever we ask for anything that pleases him. And since we know he hears us when we make our requests, we also know that he will give us what we ask for" (NLT). Prayers for the lost *touch* the heart of God!

We can be confident that our Father extends mercy and grace, sending His Word to speak to our loved ones, as we continue to pray for them. God allows each individual the privilege of choice; nevertheless, He can be most persuasive! If you are praying for a lost one, don't stop! You are *touching* the heart of God and aligning your prayer with His will. We can be confident He is working to bring them home.

INCLUDE

God brought terror to the inhabitants living on the land He promised to the Israelites. Battle by battle, the Israelites were conquering the "ites" (Amorites, Canaanites, Perizzites, Hivites, and Jebusites). In Joshua 9 (NLT), the Gibeonites wanted to make a peace treaty with the children of Israel, so they created a scheme to deceive the Israelites into thinking they were from a distant country. Their scheme was convincing to the natural eye. The Israelites listened to the Gibeonites, but verse 14 says, "They did not consult the LORD." Believing their story, the Israelites made a peace treaty with the Gibeonites. When we fail to *include* God, we may be making adverse decisions that will affect the rest of our lives.

Father, I desperately need You to partner with me every day in every part of my life. You see what I cannot see. You know what I do not know.

> Show me Your ways, O LORD; Teach me Your paths. (Psalm 25:4 NKJV)

> Teach me Your way, O LORD, And lead me in a smooth path. (Psalm 27:11 NKJV)

> So teach us to number our days, That we may gain a heart of wisdom. (Psalm 90:12 NKJV)

I desire to *include* You in everything I do and in every place I go. One step out of Your will can change everything!

Word for the Day

AGREE

Jesus says in Matthew 18:19–20 (NLT), "If two of you agree here on earth concerning anything you ask, my Father in heaven will do it for you. For where two or three gather together as my followers, I am there among them."

There are times when it's just me and the Lord. I'm so grateful that I can get into my secret place anytime and meet with my Father, but I'm also grateful for the community of believers who stand together, unite in belief, and pray for each other. I am strengthened by worshipping with my church family. There's just nothing else like it!

I also enjoy the nearness of God when another believer and I begin to encourage each other in the Word. Our Savior leans in and joins the conversation! Seriously, that's what the Word says! The goodness just doesn't stop there. Jesus says that when we *agree* on what we ask for, our Father will do it for us. Watch out, prayer partners, here I come!

SERVE

Our lives play a continuous cycle of "follow the leader." From a tot, we learn through our parents, and they continue to be role models for our entire lives. Our teachers (God bless them) spend many hours feeding educational and behavioral concepts into our minds, and the process continues into college. We transition into adulthood and assume leadership roles; thus, the cycle continues.

Sometimes our understanding of authority and leadership is skewed. I'm grateful that the Word defines and models true leadership. Matthew 20:26–28 (NLT) says, "Whoever wants to be a leader among you must be your servant, and whoever wants to be first among you must become your slave. For even the Son of Man came not to be served but to serve others and to give his life as a ransom for many." Jesus's model is to *serve*, and that ultimately defines leadership.

Father, teach me to demonstrate leadership by *serving*. Position and title may come packaged with authority, but *service* defines leadership. We may have more *chiefs* than we do *Indians* these days, but how we need *leaders*!

Word for the Day

POSSESSION

I read a passage of scripture today that ignites a freeing resolve in a troubled part of my spirit. Joshua asked seven tribes of Israel who had not yet been allotted their land this question in chapter 18, verse 3 (NLT), "How long are you going to wait before taking possession of the remaining land the LORD, the God of your ancestors, has given to you?"

These words jumped off the page as though my Father were speaking them directly to me! Every spiritual, physical, and material need we have is already provided through the cross. To receive, we must take *possession* by faith!

It's time to start claiming the promises of God over our homes, our children, our bodies, and the giants we are facing. No matter how bad things look, no matter how big our situations are, no matter the prognosis, we stand by faith and take *possession* of God's redemptive wholeness. Today, I resolve to take *possession* of Calvary's benefits and start thanking my Redeemer for what is yet to be manifested! Will you join me?

Word for the Day

BLEND

Fashion sets the trend for what we wear, how we style our hair—even the colors we use. I guess I'm one of those who prefer *blending* with the crowd instead of venturing out to become a trendsetter. When it comes to our spiritual identity, however, our Father sets us apart from the world.

First Peter 2:9 says that we are a chosen generation and His own special people. We have been called out of darkness, and the character of God changes us from the inside out. When we begin to *blend* with the culture of the world, we start losing the resemblance of Christ. The worldly trend does not mirror the Christian name.

In 1 Samuel 8, the Israelites decided they wanted to *blend* in with their surrounding nations. They wanted a king, rejecting the Great King—GOD Almighty—just to be like everyone else. Samuel tried to warn them of the consequences, but the people refused to listen.

Father, teach me how to be a trendsetter when it comes to modeling Your character. I don't want to hide the light, the Good News, under a basket. May I honorably wear the Christian name in word and deed, wherever I am, whoever I'm around, that the world may follow and be drawn out of darkness into Your marvelous light (see 1 Peter 2:9, Matthew 5:14–16).

Word for the Day

REMIND

Numbers 23:19 (NLT) has attached to my spirit: "God is not a man, so he does not lie. He is not human, so he does not change his mind. Has he ever spoken and failed to act? Has he ever promised and not carried it through?"

God's Word stands when everything else is falling around us.

His Word lasts when our patience diminishes.

His Word holds when we are ready to give up and let go.

His Word rings true when our minds are bombarded with Satan's lies.

His Word speaks truth when our minds are clouded with the ideas of others.

His Word strengthens when we feel our weakest.

His Word brings a holy hush over our spirits when voices inside us scream panic.

His Word anoints our head with oil, comforting us when we are hurting and bruised.

His Word changes circumstances when our faith marries with His will.

His Word *reminds* me today to be still and abide in my Father.

Word for the Day

FOG

Photographers often try to capture the romance that *fog* brings to a waterfall or a mountain peak. The stage often dispels a manmade *fog* to create a specific ambience for its audience. At a distance, I admit *fog* appears dreamy and beautiful, but for me, it's not pleasant to be in the middle of it. *Fog* limits my vision and makes my skin feel clammy. It's annoying to us who contend with natural curl!

Just like *fog*, the enticement of what the enemy offers may look appealing. It's only when we're in the middle of it that we recognize we've lost sight as the weight of sin settles upon us. By that time, we're in the thick of it and there seems to be no way out but God!

Recently I read an article by Kenneth Copeland about living in the *fog*. At first glance of the title, I assumed he was talking about circumstances overwhelming our minds, but he was actually talking about living in the "favor of God—FOG."

Jesus Christ made it possible for us to trade the *fog* of sin for the favor of God (FOG). Psalm 5:12 says the Lord blesses the righteous and surrounds us with favor. Psalm 30:5 (NKJV) says, "His anger is but for a moment, His favor is for life." Proverbs 8:35 says when we tap into the wisdom of God, we obtain favor from the Lord.

The next time I see nature's *fog*, I will remind myself of the favor I have through Jesus Christ!

NOW

When Jesus was in the synagogue in His hometown, He unrolled the scroll of Isaiah and read the prophet's powerful words recorded in Isaiah 61:1–2 and Luke 4:18–19 (NLT): "The Spirit of the LORD is upon me, for he has anointed me to bring Good News to the poor. He has sent me to proclaim that captives will be released, that the blind will see, that the oppressed will be set free, and that the time of the LORD's favor has come." Jesus went on to say, "The Scripture…has been fulfilled" (Luke 4:21 NLT).

Jesus is the Good News! Through Him we become adopted sons and daughters of the Most High, who brings abundant living *now* and promises the greatest inheritance to come. He proclaims our freedom from sin, bondage, and oppression. He opens our eyes so that His light surrounds us even in the darkest times. The time of the Lord's favor is *now*!

Father, thank You for Your favor that blankets Your children—for the freedom, victory, and abundance we have through Jesus Christ. "Now is the accepted time; behold, now is the day of salvation" (2 Corinthians 6:2 NKJV). I can begin this day knowing that the favor of the Almighty One is upon me!

Is there anything or anyone who can defeat Your plan for me? The answer is a resounding no! "Does it mean he no longer loves us if we have trouble or calamity, or are persecuted, or hungry, or destitute, or in danger, or threatened with death? No, despite all these things, overwhelming victory is ours through Christ" (Romans 8:35–37 NLT).

Word for the Day

TIMING

As a musician, I'm well aware of how important *timing* is. Starting a second early forces me to play an unintentional (and unwelcomed) solo. Starting a second late can throw off the other musicians. *Timing* is just as important as the notes that are played.

God's *timing* is perfect, although it doesn't always feel that way. My pastor says God sometimes works by the calendar, while we sit and wait by the alarm clock! In 1 Samuel 13, King Saul was facing a mighty army of Philistines. Before commencing battle, King Saul was instructed to wait for the prophet Samuel to join him and intercede for the children of Israel. The wait felt long, and his anxious soldiers began to abandon him. King Saul felt compelled to take this situation into his own hands. He decided to wait no longer and sacrificed the burnt offerings himself. When Samuel arrived, he rebuked King Saul for disobeying the Lord's command.

The destiny of Saul changed that day. He would eventually be replaced by another king who would follow God's heart. Getting ahead of God's *timing* never works.

Father, teach me to reverence Your Word, Your way, and Your *timing*. Getting ahead of Your plan, taking situations into my own hands, shows lack of trust and will never accomplish what You would have. No one knows Your work from beginning to end, but we do know that You make everything beautiful in its *time* (Ecclesiastes 3).

Word for the Day

RECEIVE

First Samuel 14 records the event of King Saul making a foolish oath that injured his army and nearly cost the life of his own son. Saul's army had engaged in battle with the Philistines, and they were exhausted. Saul imposed an oath over his army saying, "Let a curse fall on anyone who eats before evening—before I have full revenge on my enemies" (1 Samuel 14:24 NLT). His soldiers honored the oath, though they desperately needed food to revive them. Everyone abstained from nourishment except Jonathan, Saul's son. He was unaware of the oath his father had made. Being informed of the oath, Jonathan said, "My father has made trouble for us all!" (1 Samuel 14:29 NLT).

The unnecessary vow Saul made resulted in three detrimental consequences. First, the hunger of the soldiers led them to devour the plunder of their enemies without following God's instructions. Second, Jonathan would have lost his life had his fellow soldiers not stopped King Saul. And third, total victory was not accomplished that day. Some of the Philistine soldiers escaped and returned home.

Sometimes there is a fine line between our words being helpful or harmful. How we need the wisdom of God to speak life—not curse! Proverbs 20:25 says, "Don't trap yourself by making a rash promise to God and only later counting the cost" (NLT). Ecclesiastes 5:5 says, "It is better to say nothing than to make a promise and not keep it" (NLT). We don't have to bargain with God; rather, we do well to simply *receive* what He freely gives. His love, His peace, His protection and provision are not deserved, nor can ever be earned. It is His gift (Romans 6:23).

HOPE

Health is a wonderful blessing we sometimes take for granted. We often fail to nurture it until our health is threatened. The label "disease" often blankets us with dread and fear. Luke 4 (NLT) describes how people brought their sick family members to Jesus. Verse 40 says, "No matter what their diseases were, the touch of his hand healed every one." Don't you just love that? No matter what their diseases were, Jesus made everyone whole! Sickness must bow to the authority of Christ.

We may live in a fallen world, but Calvary redeems us from the curse! I love the way F.F. Bosworth said it in his book, *Christ the Healer*, "Sin and sickness have passed from me to Calvary—salvation and health have passed from Calvary to me."

There's not a disease that can't be healed by the blood of Jesus. There's not a sickness that can stand against the Word of God. According to Isaiah 53:5 (NKJV), we have a Savior who took a beating for our spiritual, physical, and emotional health. "By His stripes we are healed." Psalm 91:5–6 (NLT) says, "Do not be afraid of the terrors of the night, nor the arrow that flies in the day. Do not dread the disease that stalks in darkness, nor the disaster that strikes at midday."

We have a *hope*. I believe our Father wants us to walk in it!

GLORIFY

"One day Samuel said to Saul, 'It was the LORD who told me to anoint you as king of his people, Israel'" (1 Samuel 15:1 NLT). While God desired to be the people's king, He consented to the people's desire and bestowed this great honor upon Saul. He made him a great man who did great things, but Saul was impulsive to act without following the specific instructions God gave. Saul's leadership was clouded by repetitious acts of disobedience. Verses 10 and 11 say, "Then the LORD said to Samuel, 'I am sorry that I ever made Saul king, for he has not been loyal to me and has refused to obey my command.'"

Why do you think Saul continued to repeat the same mistakes? I believe it's because he did not revere the Lord. Saul did not grasp who God was and the honor of God's anointing over him; rather, he gleaned *glory* in what he (Saul) could do. I believe Saul had zeal to complete the missions God gave him, but he thrived on the thrill of self-accomplishment.

Everything we do should *glorify* God. Our worship is not confined to singing songs, paying tithes, and giving offerings in church. Our everyday living reveals worship and defines who we are in Christ.

Father, help me to realize every word that comes from my mouth, every action I take, every move I make, is to be done with You in mind. The task is not important—it's doing the task to *glorify* You.

> "So whether you eat or drink, or whatever you do, do it all for the glory of God" (1 Corinthians 10:31 NLT).

Word for the Day

INTERCEDE

I had a fifth-grade teacher who could only be called "teacher" by credentials—certainly not by gifting. On foggy mornings to this day, I have flashbacks of that awful school year. I got off the bus one afternoon and burst into tears as my mother tried to console me. She knew I was struggling with this teacher and encouraged me to hang in there as things would get better. But after hearing my story that day, my mother transformed into battle mode as only mothers can. She went to *intercede* on my behalf. She shot straight to the top!

As I was reading 1 Samuel 15 (NLT) today, I was reminded of how my mother *interceded* on my behalf. Samuel did the same thing for Saul. The Lord chose Saul to be king over Israel, but Saul kept disobeying God's instructions. The Lord told Samuel He was sorry He had ever made Saul king. Verse 11 says, "Samuel was so deeply moved when he heard this that he cried out to the LORD all night."

That portion of verse really pricks my heart today. When we hit our knees to *intercede* for our loved ones, we touch the heart of God. We go straight to the top! We can't afford to stop *interceding* for them! Our prayer may be the one that draws them back from making devastating decisions. No matter how desperate, how irreversible circumstances may seem, the mercy and grace of God can change everything.

While the Lord did not change His mind about Saul remaining king, the Lord is most longsuffering, gracious, and compassionate when it comes to souls. Lamentations 3:22 (NKJV) says, "Through the LORD's mercies we are not consumed, Because His compassions fail not." We must keep *interceding*. The destiny of our loved ones depends on it!

Word for the Day

CONVERSATION

Being an introvert, I don't always have a lot to say, but there are certain people who bring out the "talk" in me. You can bet it's always someone who loves God, and our *conversations* can last for hours!

Luke 6:12 (NLT) says, "One day soon afterward Jesus went up on a mountain to pray, and he prayed to God all night." That's a long time! At daybreak, Jesus summoned His followers and chose twelve of them to be His apostles. I've pondered about the *conversation* between Jesus and the Father. What would they have talked about all night? I believe Jesus spent some of this time seeking God's wisdom for appointing twelve apostles. I believe their *conversation* included a time of mutual honor and love. I don't think Jesus was spending hours complaining, although He certainly could have! The imagery that comes to mind is a *conversation* between father and son, cherishing the time they had together at that moment, catching up with what's happening on earth and what's happening in heaven. They may have laughed together, spoke of their love for each other, and finally got down to business.

The Scriptures do not share the content of their *conversation*, but I think it was a time they both looked forward to—the way parents feel when their children are grown and come home for a visit or connect by phone. Our Father cherishes our *conversation* time. It's where we get to know Him. We can sit at His feet as He teaches us. We can sit in His lap as He comforts us. We can kneel before Him with worship and praise. We can have the face of our Father looking intently and compassionately on us as we share our heart with Him.

My mind cannot fathom how the God of the universe delights to have *conversation* with someone like me. How amazing it is to know He's never too busy or uninterested to partner in *conversation*.

> "The eyes of the LORD watch over those who do right, and his ears are open to their prayers" (1 Peter 3:12 NLT).

HEART

First Samuel 16 (NLT) describes how David is anointed king of Israel. The Lord instructs Samuel to go to Bethlehem to find the one He has selected to replace King Saul. God's selection was to be one of Jesse's sons. Verses 6 and 7 say, "Samuel took one look at Eliab and thought, 'Surely this is the LORD's anointed!' But the LORD said to Samuel, 'Don't judge by his appearance or height, for I have rejected him. The LORD doesn't see things the way you see them. People judge by outward appearance, but the LORD looks at the heart.'"

Aren't you glad God sees the *heart*? Our facade can transform us into what we want others to see, but God goes straight to the *heart*. Our Father knows our most secret desires, our deepest hurts, our greatest insecurities, our intense passions, and every motive that drives our actions. He knows the real you and me while we may still be trying to own our identity.

That's why He is constantly working to fashion us in His likeness from the inside out. We cannot depend on our own understanding; rather, trust that He sees the *heart* and is working for our good (Proverbs 3:5). Perhaps things are happening in your life, like mine, for which you have no answers.

May we resolve to trust and yield to God's divine work, praying, "Search me, O God, and know my heart; test me and know my anxious thoughts. Point out anything in me that offends you, and lead me along the path of everlasting life" (Psalm 139:23–24 NLT).

BATTLE

My husband and I enjoy watching old war movies—from the western classics to world war stories. In every *battle*, there is a victory. First Samuel 17 describes a *battle* between two people—David and Goliath. It's a story most of us learned as kids in Sunday school. From human perspective, the victory should have easily gone to the giant, Goliath. How could a small boy conquer a champion fighter towering over nine feet tall? Goliath's armor weighed more than the boy, David! The answer is in verse 47: this was the Lord's *battle*!

The Old Testament records numerous *battles* where the Israelites were outnumbered yet victorious. The Lord of heaven's armies fought for them as He does for you and me! *Battles* will come, but our Father doesn't want us to live in fear or dread. Take comfort in knowing He has provided the protective gear we need to stand. God's truth, peace, faith, salvation, and His Word will enable us to stand our ground as He fights our battles (Ephesians 6).

Romans 8:37 (NLT) says, "Overwhelming victory is ours through Christ, who loved us."

We stand—we win—because our *battles* belong to the Lord!

Word for the Day

REWARD

We live in a generation who expects *reward*. Our pets get treats. Teachers use a *reward* system to motivate learning and good behavior. Credit cards offer cash *rewards*. Retail offers *reward* for auto-ships, memberships, and reaching purchase plateaus. I am always ready to check out available instant *reward* programs. You shoppers out there with me?

When it comes to Kingdom work, however, *reward* is not always instantaneous, or at least complete, at the present time. I believe there is an immediate *reward* when we glorify God in our daily work. There is consolation in doing the right thing even when others don't acknowledge it, but there is a greater *reward* coming for living God's plan.

If we are waiting for acknowledgment, a thank-you, or a pat on the back, we may get it, but that becomes our *reward*. How much greater it is to give—to serve without expectation. Jesus says in Luke 6:35 (NLT), "Then your reward from heaven will be very great, and you will truly be acting as children of the Most High, for he is kind to those who are unthankful and wicked."

Living our daily lives is Kingdom work if we live it to represent our heavenly Father. Jesus goes on to say in Luke 6:38 (NLT), "Give and you will receive. Your gift will return to you in full—pressed down, shaken together to make room for more, running over, and poured into your lap."

Enjoy the *reward* that righteous service brings and know the greater *reward* comes!

ME

In 2 Samuel 7:20 (NLT), David prayed these words to the Lord, "What more can I say to you? You know what your servant is really like, Sovereign LORD." These words are the epitome of my heart today. God knows *me*! He knows every shortcoming and every desire. He knows what I'm going to think or say before I do it! If there is any pretense on my part, it doesn't fool God, for He discerns the heart.

I may try to justify myself, but God's Word corrects *me*. I may struggle to understand things that happen, but my Father reminds *me* that He is always working for my good. I may feel inadequate, but His Word assures *me* that I can do all things through Him. Simply said, I can just be *me* with my Father! I can pour my heart out to Him about anything—about everything.

David goes on to say in 2 Samuel 7:29 (NLT), "When you grant a blessing to your servant, O Sovereign LORD, it is an eternal blessing!"

God doesn't wake up in a bad mood. He doesn't know *me* one day and not the next. He doesn't get tired of my tears. He knows my tendencies, and His Holy Spirit gently redirects my focus. His love toward *me* will never change. That, my friend, is an eternal blessing worth all my praise and worship! (Psalm 139).

FENCE

Do you know anyone who sits on the *fence*? I'm talking about someone who prefers to be neutral when others openly support their conviction or belief. From a spiritual perspective, there is no such thing! The devil would like people to think they can take a position of neutrality, not make a commitment to serve anyone. Seriously, how many people publicly acknowledge they serve satan? On second thought, there are more than I would care to count!

Jesus says in Luke 11:23 (NLT), "Anyone who isn't with me opposes me, and anyone who isn't working with me is actually working against me."

Speaking of salvation, we must not buy into satan's lie that we can sit on the *fence* and serve no one. Speaking of Kingdom work, we cannot afford to sit on the *fence* when it comes to standing up for truth. Truth may bring offense. First Peter 2:7 (NKJV) says, "To those who are disobedient, 'The stone which the builders rejected Has become the chief cornerstone, and A stone of stumbling And a rock of offense'." Knowing offense may come, however, does not give us an open platform to blast sinners.

Lord, teach us how to be hard on sin and tender with sinners. Teach us how to speak the truth with boldness and speak truth with love. As the truth of Your Word is twisted by our culture, empower us to get off the *fence* and speak with the anointing of Your Holy Spirit.

COST

In 2 Samuel 24 (NLT), David was instructed to build an altar on a threshing floor that belonged to a Jebusite man. David told the man he would buy the threshing floor so that he could build an altar and present a burnt offering to God for his sin. The Jebusite offered to give the threshing floor and wood to the king, but David said, "No, I insist on buying it, for I will not present burnt offerings to the LORD my God that have cost me nothing."

Jesus paid a great price for our sins. While repentance is freely given to all who believe, worthy repentance comes with *cost*. We cannot purchase or earn it, but repentance requires sincerity and intention to walk away from the sins of our past. I'm so glad our Lord's forgiveness is available as often as we need it, but our Father also knows if our repentance is merely words or if it conveys the heart. Simply said, worthy repentance changes our life and our lifestyle!

We can't continue to live our sinful ways and think the now-I-lay-me-down-to-sleep bedtime prayer fixes everything. Jesus says in Luke 14:27–28 (NLT), "If you do not carry your own cross and follow me, you cannot be my disciple. But don't begin until you count the cost."

Second Corinthians 5:17 says (NLT), "Anyone who belongs to Christ has become a new person. The old life is gone; a new life has begun!"

Being a follower of Christ means we start walking the high road, forsaking the low road. Our inheritance through Jesus Christ will absolutely be worth the *cost*!

Word for the Day

DESIRES

If you were granted one wish, would you find it difficult to identify your most important, passionate *desire*? In 1 Kings 3:5 (NLT), the Lord comes to Solomon in a dream and says, "What do you want? Ask, and I will give it to you!"

Solomon has just assumed the throne of His father, David. He realizes his inadequacy and says, "I am like a little child who doesn't know his way around. Give me an understanding heart so that I can govern Your people well and know the difference between right and wrong. For who by himself is able to govern this great people of yours?" (1 Kings 3:7, 9 NLT). God was so pleased that He made Solomon the wisest of all men; furthermore, He granted him above and beyond what he asked, giving him riches and fame.

God owns it all! I believe He *desires* to lavish blessings on us, but our *desires* must align with His will. Our Father *desires* that we seek an intimate relationship with Him. Jesus says in Matthew 6:33 (NLT), "Seek the Kingdom of God above all else, and live righteously, and he will give you everything you need."

The more we seek God, the more we come to know Him. The more we come to know God, the more our *desires* align to His plan for us. Psalm 37:23 (NLT) says, "The LORD directs the steps of the godly. He delights in every detail of their lives."

Let us first seek the Blesser, and the blessings will come! "Take delight in the LORD, and he will give you your heart's desires" (Psalm 37:4 NLT).

IMPORTANT

In Matthew 19, there was a young man who asked Jesus what he needed to do to have eternal life. Jesus told him to keep the commandments. When the young man asked what else he should do, Jesus instructed him to give his earthly possessions away and follow Him. Jesus required this of the young man only because He knew the man's riches were more *important* to him than becoming His follower.

Our Father doesn't take second place to anyone! His commandments are *important* for us to keep. They keep us from straying outside God's boundaries, but His desire for us to know Him intimately is more *important*.

Jesus told the Pharisees in Luke 11:42 that they should tithe but should not neglect the more *important* things. There are *important* scriptural principles to practice, but they don't save us. Salvation cleans us from the inside and then changes the outside as we develop our relationship with Him.

We won't become better Christians by trying harder or giving more; rather, it's relationship we build in Christ that transforms us into His image. "You must love the LORD your God with all your heart, all your soul, and all your mind" (Matthew 22:37 NLT).

This is most *important* to God. When we do this, His commandments will become easier for us to follow.

GREAT

Children are often taught a prayer of grace to recite at mealtime that begins with "God is *great*, God is good! Let us thank Him for our food." I was taught about the *greatness* of God at a young age. Those early years have long gone, and I'm still not sure I grasp the *greatness* of my heavenly Father.

In Luke 12:6–7 (NLT) Jesus says, "What is the price of five sparrows—two copper coins? Yet God does not forget a single one of them. And the very hairs on your head are all numbered. So don't be afraid; you are more valuable to God than a whole flock of sparrows." It's easy to miss the power of this verse because our minds simply cannot comprehend God knowing every single sparrow—not just the ones in my yard or yours. Jesus goes on to say that the hairs on our head are numbered. Can you imagine a God so *great* that He counts the hairs on every human head?

Psalm 147:4 (NLT) says, "He counts the stars and calls them all by name."

Isaiah 40:12 (NLT) says, "Who else has held the oceans in his hand? Who has measured off the heavens with his fingers?"

I don't know if I will ever totally grasp the *greatness* of God because it is beyond my limited understanding. How I desire to recognize the *greatness* of God in everything around me and the *greatness* of His love for me.

Father, You are *great*, and You are good! Your *greatness* in all its glory may be more than this mortal body can absorb, but please reveal as much as You will in me!

Word for the Day

PROVIDER

The Scriptures records numerous events where God graciously *provides* for man. Though mankind has continuously failed to honor God throughout history, He has made *provision* for us again and again.

In 1 Kings 17 (NLT), the Lord instructs Elijah to camp by a brook. The Lord says, "Drink from the brook and eat what the ravens bring you, for I have commanded them to bring you food" (1 Kings 17:4 NLT). Verse 6 says, "The ravens brought him bread and meat each morning and evening."

God saw the need of this one man and instructed the ravens to feed him! Elijah served God, and God takes care of His own. The God of Elijah is our God, and He still takes care of His children! Through His Son, Jesus Christ, our Father has made *provision* for soul, body, and mind.

There's not a person that can't be forgiven, not a sickness that can't be healed, no bondage—mental or physical—that can't be severed through the blood of Jesus! Our heavenly Father sacrificed His Son to meet every need we will ever have. While hanging on the cross, I believe every human face flashed before our Savior—your face and mine! Second Chronicles 16:9 (NLT) says, "The eyes of the LORD search the whole earth in order to strengthen those whose hearts are fully committed to him."

Know the *provider* has already met your needs and is watching over you!

Word for the Day

TELL

Nothing pleases the Father more than His children having a heart for the lost. This is the heart of the Father. In John 6:39–40 (NLT), Jesus says, "And this is the will of God, that I should not lose even one of all those he has given me, but that I should raise them up at the last day. For it is my Father's will that all who see his Son and believe in him should have eternal life. I will raise them up at the last day."

Think about it: God does not want His Son to lose even one soul! How comforting it is to know when we pray for the lost, we are in total harmony with God's will. When we reach out to sinners, love them, witness to them, we are sharing the heart of God.

We don't have to be credentialed or speak from a platform. God simply wants us to *tell* our story with whomever He places in our path. His love and the Holy Spirit will do the rest! Let's go *tell*!

> "But how can they call on him to save them unless they believe in him? And how can they believe in him if they have never heard about him? And how can they hear about him unless someone tells them?" (Romans 10:14 NLT).

WEPT

Memorization doesn't come as easy as it once did, but even I can recite the shortest verse in the Bible: "Jesus wept." This is recorded in John 11:35. Jesus met with His friends, Martha and Mary, as they mourned their brother's passing. When Jesus saw Mary crying, "A deep anger welled up within him, and he was deeply troubled. 'Where have you put him?' he asked them. They told him, 'Lord, come and see.' Then Jesus wept. The people who were standing nearby said, 'See how much he loved him!'" (John 11:33–36 NLT).

There are two other instances where Jesus *wept*. Luke 19 records Jesus *weeping* over Jerusalem. Just as God had given Adam and Eve a perfect garden, He gave His chosen people the city of Jerusalem—a place where He would dwell. And just as Adam and Eve lost everything through their disobedience, Jesus *wept* for Jerusalem when He saw the city of God losing its divine heritage to pagan practice.

In Luke 22, Jesus prays earnestly in the garden about the sin He was to bear for the entire world. The human part of Him may have dreaded the physical pain He would endure, but I believe it was the heaviness and the stench of sin that made Him *weep* as He prayed to the Father. Jesus experienced every emotion we have, and He understands our tears. They tell the story of His heart and ours. The tears of Jesus reveal His love for us. First John 4:19 (NKJV) says, "We love Him because He first loved us."

Each time you look in the mirror, profess the love of God over your life and do your day in confidence that the love of the Most High—His most unimaginable, intense, powerful love—is abiding within you!

Word for the Day

PREPARE

I'm not one of those people who are constantly in trouble, but I am one of those people who have a guilty face! Through the years, I have practiced controlling my words, but I haven't learned how to silence my face!

In John 13, being with His disciples at the Last Supper before being arrested, Jesus said one of them was going to betray Him. Had I been sitting around the table, I'm sure my face would have said plenty, like, "No, who could ever do that?" or "Is it me?"

Just as Jesus knew who was going to betray Him, the Holy Spirit has insight to spiritual realm battles. He tugs at our heart, warning us to stay close to God's umbrella of protection and blessing. It often begins with a gentle nudge and can lead to a sterner warning when we fail to respond.

Holy Spirit, how grateful I am that You *prepare* me for the day. You've already been there. You have already *prepared* me for success. You may have impressed me to pray for things approaching, because You know I will need Your strength. I will need Your provision. You impress others to pray for me. Our prayers, with Your leading, touch the throne of grace. You intercede, and the battle may get halted before it ever surfaces. If the battle is to be played out in my presence, I know You've already been there and have *prepared* me for it.

> "LORD, it is nothing for You to help, whether with many or with those who have no power; help us, O LORD our God, for we rest on You" (2 Chronicles 14:11 NKJV).

175

Word for the Day

JOY

Who doesn't want *joy*? To me, that's like asking who doesn't want chocolate. I'm confident we would all answer, "Yes, we want *joy*!" One of the hardest scriptures that I have struggled to get into my spirit is James 1:2–4 (NLT): "When troubles of any kind come your way, consider it an opportunity for great joy. For you know that when your faith is tested, your endurance has a chance to grow. So let it grow, for when your endurance is fully developed, you will be perfect and complete, needing nothing."

This week, these words have come alive in my spirit! Personally, I have been desiring great faith. I have struggles (and you probably do too), but for the first time in my life, my eyes have been opened to see my struggle as a door to grow great faith. That's why I must count this season as *joy*. This season of testing is opening a door for me to grow my faith to a new level. Great faith brings great results!

The growing process can be painful, but the faith it brings will be worth it, for when my faith becomes great, every need I will ever have will be met by my Father.

> "For his anger lasts only a moment, but his favor lasts a lifetime! Weeping may last through the night, but joy comes with the morning" (Psalm 30:5 NLT).

SEED

Sometimes when we start a diet or a new health fitness program, we get "pumped" and want to share it with everyone—whether they want to hear it or not. (Just ask my sister!) I've begun a spiritual health fitness program, and I'm so pumped! Friend, this means I have to share, and will you be gracious enough to listen?

I've been walking a faith journey, and now I'm ready to move to the next level. Recently, a dear friend loaned me a book on faith (thank you, Terry). This book is simply entitled *Faith* by Faye Penland. The book has reenergized my desire to grow great faith. According to Romans 12:3, God has planted the *seed* of faith in each of us. We've all been given a measure of faith to receive salvation, but great faith has to be grown, matured, and developed in us. In reference to having faith as a grain of mustard *seed*, I quote from Ms. Penland, "Most people think Jesus was saying, 'A little dab will do you.' Jesus was not saying, 'Little faith does great things.' That concept just doesn't work and I think we all have the scars to prove it. It takes mature, developed faith to do great things."

The mustard *seed* is tiny, but it has the potential to develop into a strong tree. *Seed* faith is a gift, but great faith—mature faith—is a process that we intentionally work to develop. It takes more than wanting and wishing. We dig, dig, and dig more into the Word, allowing the Holy Spirit to become our teacher, opening our eyes and ears so that the Word becomes alive in us. The love of God will join the Word and the Holy Spirit to renew, revive, and reveal. When we act on what has been revealed to us, our faith has nowhere to go but up!

"According to your faith let it be to you"
(Matthew 9:29 NKJV).

Word for the Day

MOUNTAINS

I'm a *mountain* girl! I always loved our family trips to the *mountains*. As a child, I would always ask my dad if we could climb a blue one. I could never understand why *mountains* looked blue in the distance but transformed into a hilly forest at close range.

Mountain peaks are beautiful, but the climb can be challenging! Spiritually speaking, God has given us the authority to move them. It sounds spiritual to say, "God *can* move *mountains*!" But in reality, are we simply making a safe proclamation—one that demands little in return? The word *can* is a verb that denotes possibility, but it also suggests uncertainty. Can we really expect this kind of faith to move *mountains*?

Seed faith (undeveloped faith) is vulnerable to circumstance. When circumstances deteriorate, seed faith may become shaken. Circumstances set limits where mature faith removes them! Have you ever noticed how restricted you feel when walking in the dark? You may take baby steps and move with outstretched hands to feel your way. You may stumble, run into a wall, or get off course. But when we walk in the light, we do not have to resort to "feeling" our way; we can see. Our steps are plain in sight, and we can move freely. That's what the Word of God does for our faith. Psalm 119:105 (NLT) says, "Your word is a lamp to guide my feet and a light for my path."

We don't have to settle for "feeling" the way through our faith journey when we can walk in the light of God's Word. We can know what we know because the Word says so!

Word for the Day

BELIEVE

"There's more than what meets the eye." Have you heard that cliché? We live, breathe, see, and touch things in the natural world, while not always being aware of the spiritual world around us. We don't see all that goes on in the spiritual world, but we can live in the comfort of knowing our Father does and He has already made provision for us.

To receive God's promises, we must first *believe* that we receive. If the enemy cannot keep us from *believing*, then he feeds us his next best lie that says, "*Believe* it when you see it!" This is contrary to Scriptures! We are to act on God's Word when we don't yet see the results. We base our *belief* on what God's Word says He will do in spite of what we see or feel. Romans 8:24–25 (NKJV) says, "Hope that is seen is not hope; for why does one still hope for what he sees? But if we hope for what we do not see, we eagerly wait for it with perseverance."

We accept God's offer right now. Our *belief* is based solely on the promises provided in the Word. We think it, we speak it, we live it, and we wait for it! This activates the power of God that works in us. When we see the results we have prayed for, then we are no longer exercising faith; we are reaping the rewards of our faith.

Steadfast faith and obedience to the Word will always demand the evil forces of nature to yield to the spiritual will of God. The period of time it takes for the natural forces to bow to the authority of Christ is the period of time you and I are walking by faith. That

WORD FOR THE DAY

period of time can be as short as an instant or as long as a season. What matters is that we keep walking by faith. Jesus said, "I tell you, you can pray for anything, and if you believe that you've received it, it will be yours" (Mark 11:24 NLT).

COMMUNION

I have participated in the Lord's Supper since early childhood, but it's only been in recent years that I have been enlightened to its significance. I was taught at an early age that *communion* was sacred, serious, and should be practiced on a regular basis, but the extent of my participation was mostly obligatory—something we just did in church.

I now realize how significant *communion* is! Without the shedding of Jesus's blood, there would be no remission of sin, no redemption, no salvation. It's also important to recognize Jesus's body was broken for us so that we can be redeemed from the curse of sin. The curse includes separation from God. It also includes sickness and disease, worry and fear, poverty and suffering.

The body and the blood of Jesus cover every part of us—everything we will ever need. His sacrifice brings the promise of both eternal and abundant life. When we partake in *communion*, we should be ready to receive everything Jesus's sacrifice provides: healing for soul, mind, and body.

Communion should be more than a mere exercise of remembrance; rather, a means of appropriating our faith, accepting everything available through Jesus's sacrifice. I'm grateful to be part of a church body that provides the Lord's Supper. We can also establish this practice at home in our personal devotion time.

> "Jesus on the same night in which He was
> betrayed took bread...broke it and said, 'Take,
> eat; this is My body which is broken for you; do

this in remembrance of Me.' In the same manner He also took the cup after supper, saying, 'This cup is the new covenant in My blood. This do, as often as you drink it, in remembrance of Me'" (1 Corinthians 11:23–25 NKJV).

WHICH

I've talked about wanting childlike faith, and I've talked about needing matured, developed faith. So *which* is it? I believe the faith of a little child can be as effective as the faith of a spiritual giant. Spiritually speaking, childlike faith is unadulterated belief in God. Childlike faith accepts what God says because God says it! I think matured faith mirrors childlike faith in that it continues to believe what God says because God says it, and that's enough.

The common denominator is believing—accepting what God has to say because He is God! Perhaps matured faith takes it a step further by requiring us to consistently act on what God says, refusing to entertain doubt. James 1:6–8 (NKJV) says, "Ask in faith, with no doubting, for he who doubts is like a wave of the sea driven and tossed by the wind. For let not that man suppose that he will receive anything from the Lord; he is a double-minded man, unstable in all his ways."

I'm not a credentialed scholar in the Word. I have a lot more questions than I have answers, but any way I look at it, I come to the same conclusion: I need great faith! It can't be just wished down. It must be grown into my spirit by getting into the Word and getting the Word into me. "So then faith comes by hearing, and hearing by the word of God" (Romans 10:17 NKJV).

Word for the Day

FIRST

We live in a me-*first* society. I admit I struggle with that mentality sometimes, but there's always blessing when we put God *first* and others next. In 1 Kings 17, Elijah meets a poor widow woman who is down to her last meal. He asks her to make a little bread for himself *first* and then use what's left to fix herself and her son a meal. Elijah tells her the Lord will continue to provide for her if she will take care of his need *first*.

That takes faith! Verses 15 and 16 (NLT) say, "So she did as Elijah said, and she and Elijah and her family continued to eat for many days. There was always enough flour and olive oil left in the containers, just as the LORD had promised through Elijah."

Matthew 6:33 (NKJV) says, "Seek first the kingdom of God and His righteousness, and all these things [your needs] shall be added to you."

Putting God *first* in our lives is all about making our relationship with Him priority. When we are striving to put God *first*, we don't have to keep score on how charitable we are, nor how empty our cupboards are. The Lord will open opportunities for us to give, and He will abundantly bless what we have for giving. *First* and foremost, He desires relationship with us. All the money and time we can give will never substitute relationship with our Father. When we grow intimate with the Blesser, the blessings follow.

Father, we live in a world that demands our time, resources, and energies. Nothing or no one can ever be as important as You are! I desire to put you *first* in my life. For me, it's a daily choice. Forgive me when I miss the mark. You should be *first* always!

NAME

My maiden *name* is often mispronounced. When I took my husband's *name*, I no longer anticipated having this problem since "Barker" is such a common *name*. To my amazement, it's often mispronounced as "Baker" or "Parker" or "Barkley!" Oh well! My *name* doesn't turn a head, but there's something powerful about the *name* of Jesus!

The devils tremble at His *name*! (James 2:19).

The moon and stars hang in precise order at His *name*'s command (Psalm 8:3–4).

His *name* is above all others, and every knee in heaven and earth will bow to it (Philippians 2:9–10).

As Christians, we are born again and adopted into His Kingdom. We carry the *name* of Jesus Christ! Jesus told His disciples in John 16:23 and 24 (NLT), "You will ask the Father directly, and he will grant your request because you use my name. You haven't done this before. Ask, using my name, and you will receive, and you will have abundant joy."

Just think about it: We have the *name* of Jesus! And in His *name*, we can do all things. When only two or three of us come together in His *name*, He will be in our midst (Matthew 18:20). We should all find ourselves standing a bit taller today, knowing Jesus has given us His *name* and His authority to live abundantly as children of the Almighty!

Word for the Day

FAITHFUL

First and Second Kings record the history of the kings of Israel and Judah from the reign of Solomon to their Babylonian captivity. God desired to be Israel's king and for good reason. History shows man isn't capable of successfully ruling himself or the world. God blessed them and was with them when they were *faithful* to His commandments, and they met His judgment when they were not.

In 2 Kings 18:5–7 (NLT), the Scriptures say, "Hezekiah trusted in the LORD, the God of Israel. There was no one like him among all the kings of Judah, either before or after his time. He remained faithful to the LORD in everything, and he carefully obeyed all the commands the LORD had given Moses. So the LORD was with him, and Hezekiah was successful in everything he did."

According to the Scriptures, there were several kings who followed some of the commandments, but not all. They never lived under the full blessing of God. Our Father is *faithful* to every single promise in His Word, but the hard truth is this: either we are *faithful* to obey His Word or we're not. He is Lord of all or not Lord at all. Is it possible that we want to settle for a portion of blessing with a portion of obedience?

Father, I desire to be all in! I know all of heaven is behind Your words, and I want my everyday living to mirror my words. Thank You for your mercy when I'm less than *faithful*, for Your diligence when I am less than deserving. "Search me, O God, and know my heart; Try me, and know my anxieties; And see if there is any wicked way in me, And lead me in the way everlasting" (Psalm 139:23–24 NKJV).

Word for the Day

LOVE

Isn't *love* a powerful emotion? Books are written about it, movies attempt to capture it, and dreams are driven by it. Human *love* is wonderful, but it cannot compare to the *love* of our Father. As Jesus was praying to the Father, He spoke of God's *love* for us, saying, "The world will know that you sent me and that you love them as much as you love me" (John 17:23 NLT).

Don't let this bypass you! God *loves* you as much as He *loves* His Son, Jesus! For those of us who have children, we know how intense a parent's *love* is for a child. We will do for our children what we will do for no one else. It's hard to fathom, but the *love* of God is exponentially deeper—so much greater that it is off the charts!

God's *love* is as unique as God Himself. I believe God *loves* His Son, Jesus, more than we can humanly *love* our own children, and He *loves* you and me that much too! "For God so loved the world that He gave His only begotten Son, that whoever believes in Him should not perish but have everlasting life" (John 3:16 NKJV).

Oh, how I desire to grasp how fierce my Father's *love* is for me!

SPIRIT

Wrapping up His mission on earth, Jesus told His disciples that He would return to His Father and the Father would send the Holy *Spirit*. The *Spirit* would not live among the disciples in the flesh as Jesus did, but the *Spirit* would live in them.

Acts 2 describes the incredible arrival of the Holy *Spirit*. The scriptures say Jews from every nation, living in Jerusalem at that time, heard a great noise as the *Spirit* descended. The people came out to see what was happening. Amazed at what they heard, the Jews said, "These people are all from Galilee, and yet we hear them speaking in our own native languages…about the wonderful things God has done!" (Acts 2:7–11 NLT).

I just love that! While the *Spirit* is here to comfort, teach, and guide us, He is also here to take the gospel to the world and empower us to help Him do it. The followers of Jesus were not even aware they were testifying of our great God. The Holy *Spirit* continues the Kingdom work of Jesus. Just as Jesus only spoke what He heard from the Father, the Holy *Spirit* reveals to us what He receives from the Son and the Father.

I pray I pass on what the *Spirit* speaks into my heart. He will always agree with the written Word. I pray my everyday living welcomes and yields to the working of the Holy *Spirit* as He embodies my temple. My testimony within itself is powerless, but I pray the Holy *Spirit* directs my path, my words, and my ways, making a difference in my family, a neighbor, a stranger, a community.

> "Therefore glorify God in your body and in your spirit, which are God's" (1 Corinthians 6:20 NKJV).

MADE

The book of Esther records the beautiful story of how a young Jewish woman became queen to King Xerxes. Esther wasn't born through a royal line. Prior to becoming queen, she didn't have wealth, name, or status. Her parents died, and she was raised by her uncle. During her reign as queen, a plot was born to assassinate the Jews. Esther became the instrument God used to save His people. Mordecai, Esther's uncle, says it best concerning her role: "Who knows if perhaps you were made queen for just such a time as this?" (Esther 4:14 NLT).

Have you ever thought about what you were *made* for? God has designed a plan for each of our lives, and He designed it with specific purpose. How sad it would be should we live out our days and miss the plan the Creator *made* for us!

God's plan included wealth and title for Esther, but those things were given to her to use for His purpose. God provides abundance to us. His abundance, however, is not only for our comfort and enjoyment but often serves a greater purpose.

Father, I pray I don't miss who You've *made* me to be. The dates of my birth and death are insignificant. It's that span between that counts. I pray You look at me with delight as You did when you *made* the heavens and earth, seeing all is good.

> "You saw me before I was born. Every day of my life was recorded in your book. Every moment was laid out before a single day had passed" (Psalm 139:16 NLT).

LESS

John the Baptist was a spiritual giant. Jesus spoke of his greatness, and John the Baptist spoke of Jesus being far greater than him. John's followers became concerned that a bigger crowd was going to Jesus to be baptized. John quickly addressed his followers by saying, "You yourselves know how plainly I told you, 'I am not the Messiah. I am only here to prepare the way for him.' I am filled with joy at his success. He must become greater and greater, and I must become less and less" (John 3:28–30 NLT).

As I read these words, my heart swells with desire to become *less* so my Father can become more. I realize it's my Father's nature that really matters. My own human character is flawed with toxic seeds of selfishness, stubbornness, and pride. The more room I make for God, the *less* room I have for things that steal my joy, confidence, and peace. As we become *less* and *less*, our Father becomes greater and greater. His nature spills into our attitude, conversation, and every-day living. When we become *less* and God becomes more, the world takes notice. That, my friend, is how the world is changed—one soul at a time.

> "I long for Your salvation, O LORD, And
> Your law is my delight" (Psalm 119:174 NKJV).

Word for the Day

JOB

The Bible describes a man who had many servants and was the richest man in the entire area. The last words in the book say, "He died, an old man who had lived a long, full life" (Job 42:17 NLT). This man sounds like the kind of person we want to be, right? Sometimes we can look at others and think how easy life comes to them. The description of this man's life between the beginning of the book and the end, however, is quite unsettling. The man I am talking about is *Job*. His name instantly brings images of grief and pain as the greater portion of his book deals with devastation that consumed him.

Job feared and followed God, so much that satan begged God to let him take away material possessions and his family, thinking *Job* would blame God and walk away from Him. Instead, *Job* worshipped God! Chapter 1, verse 22 (NLT) says, "In all of this, Job did not sin by blaming God."

Satan again challenged *Job's* faith by taking away his health. Having lost everything, *Job* spills his heart out to God wishing his life were over. Trying to be "spiritual," his friends told *Job* he needed to repent, for such devastation could only come from sin in his life. (Father, help me to speak words of wisdom to those who are struggling. Give me wisdom to sense when there are no words and simply love in silence.)

Fast-forwarding to the end of the book, the Lord sets *Job* straight as well as his friends. Chapter 42, verse 10 (NLT) says, "The LORD restored his fortunes. In fact, the LORD gave him twice as much as before!"

When God Almighty is our Lord, who is there to fear? (Psalm 27:1). The enemy may snatch precious things from us, but he can never snatch us from our Father who brings hope, help, and healing.

Word for the Day

MEDITATE

What do you spend most of your time thinking about? Wouldn't it be wonderful if only God's Word came to mind, nothing contrary? Psalm 1 speaks of those who constantly *meditate* on God, saying, "They are like trees planted along the riverbank, bearing fruit each season. Their leaves never wither, and they prosper in all they do" (Psalm 1:3 NLT).

The enemy continuously hurls thoughts in our mind, but we don't have to own them. Our own human nature will bring selfish thoughts to mind, but we don't have to entertain them. Friends can say and do things that clog our minds with frustration and hurt, but we don't have to act on them. Circumstances can bring thoughts of fear and doubt, but we don't have to succumb to them. We can take authority over contrary thoughts by *meditating* on God's Word!

His Word sends the enemy running, feeds us a humble spirit, heals the hurts, and brings the miracles to spiritual sight. *Meditating* on God and His Word is an intentional thing—it's work, but it will clean out the trash and allow the promises of God to sink in!

> "Whatever things are true, whatever things are noble, whatever things are just, whatever things are pure, whatever things are lovely, whatever things are of good report, if there is any virtue and if there is anything praiseworthy—meditate on these things" (Philippians 4:8 NKJV).

Word for the Day

IGNITE

Chapter 7 of Acts records the horrific stoning of Stephen for his faith. Just before the crowd began to stone him, the Lord opened Stephen's eyes to see "Jesus standing in the place of honor at God's right hand." What a glorious revelation that would be! Acts 8:1 (NLT) describes a "wave of persecution" hitting the church and believers being scattered.

As I read this, I can visualize a piece of dough on my kitchen bar, covered in flour. As I pound my fist into the bread, the powdery flour spews, forming a cloud of flour dust settling over the bar. The flour doesn't disappear; it just spreads to a larger circumference. Verse 4 of chapter 8 (NLT) says, "But the believers who were scattered preached the Good News about Jesus wherever they went."

The persecution against the church could not stop the gospel; it *ignited* it! God has a mission for each of us, and the enemy works to desecrate it. We may feel blown off course, isolated from our goals and expectations, and even find ourselves in new territory that feels foreign. The devil means it for harm, but these places set us up to rely solely on the promises of God. Our faith is sparked, and our testimony is *ignited*! Whatever the enemy throws at us, our Father can make it work for us!

> "And we know that all things work together for good to those who love God, to those who are the called according to His purpose" (Romans 8:28 NKJV).

Word for the Day

FAVOR

We may not all know what it's like to be a parent, but we all know what it's like to be a child. We may know what it feels like to await the "wrath" of a parent when we have done wrong. As a parent, we may feel anger and disappointment when our children make bad choices, and we often feel broken as we carry out appropriate discipline. Our children may not understand how it can hurt us as much as it hurts them; nevertheless, we suffer with our children.

Psalm 30:5 (NLT) says, "His [God's] anger lasts only a moment, but his favor lasts a lifetime!"

Father, thank You for correcting me when I get off track. Thank You for teaching me, opening my eyes to Your Word. You desire to put me in a place where You can pour Your best into me. Your correction can be subtle and swift; it can be a nudge or what feels like a nightmare. But You will never turn Your back on me, never leave me comfortless. I am my Father's child. I have His name and His *favor* for the rest of my life!

DETAILS

Do you like a "bird's eye view" or do you need the *details*? For me, the answer depends on the subject or the task. My attention span prefers the big picture. (This doesn't say much for my listening skills, does it?) When I'm in charge, however, I'm all about *details*. Psalm 37:23 (NLT) says, "The LORD directs the steps of the godly. He delights in every detail of their lives."

Don't you just love that? Our Father cares about every *detail* of our lives! He cares about what makes us happy and what makes us sad. He has planned every step of our journey. He is fully aware the moment we step out of His plan. The Scripture says He delights in every *detail* as though each one of us has His sole attention.

Not one tear escapes His presence. Whatever is important to you is important to Him. He delights when we share the good times with Him and the bad, our moments of gratitude and our moments of grief. He delights when we ask Him to partner with us daily— when we seek His wisdom and guidance in every decision and in every action. We can take anything to Him. We can take everything. He is never too busy to bother with the *details*!

Word for the Day

LIFETIME

Getting out of school for the summer as a little girl seemed to last forever. These days, summer vacations seem to end before they barely get started! Christmas now feels like it comes around every six months instead of twelve.

At an early age, we often wish away our birthdays. We can hardly wait till we turn thirteen, then sixteen, eighteen, and twenty-one. When our children are born, we see a *lifetime* of parenting ahead of us. Before most of us are ready, our babies are grown and gone. Is it the times or is it an age thing? I think it's a little of both.

Psalm 39:4–5 (NLT) says, "LORD, remind me how brief my time on earth will be. Remind me that my days are numbered... My entire lifetime is just a moment to you."

It's really not about how many days we have here but what we do with the days we have. I confess I've wasted too many! The good Lord gives me this day, and it's up to me what I do with it.

Father, may the rest of my days honor You. Forgive me for yesterday's failures. By Your strength and guidance, I want to make this day count for You as though tomorrow never comes.

Word for the Day

TESTIMONY

There are so many gifted speakers who feed us words of wisdom, inspiration, and encouragement. My pastor is one of them. He knows how to preach an hour's sermon in twenty-five minutes! My friend, Melissa, is a wonderful teacher who amazes me with her ability to teach a Sunday school class. What she shares would take me a month of Sundays to prepare. Like me, you may not be an exceptional orator, but each one of us can be a walking *testimony*.

Words are important, but our daily living may speak louder than our words. To have a *testimony*, we will have tests. Self-accomplished wealth, power, and success do not glorify God. But when battles are won, miracles are manifested, and the unexplainable happens, God gets all the glory. You may be in a *testimony*-building season. Don't get discouraged, for the tests must come to produce the *testimony*. And it is our *testimonies* that will preach sermons to a helpless and hopeless world.

> "Many will see what he has done and be amazed. They will put their trust in the LORD" (Psalm 40:3 NLT).

Word for the Day

PRAISE

The sixteenth chapter of Acts describes how Paul and Silas were miraculously delivered from jail. They had been placed in prison for preaching the gospel. Verse 24 (NLT) says, "The jailer put them into the inner dungeon and clamped their feet in the stocks." If anyone had the right to sing the blues, Paul and Silas did! Beaten and chained, they sang hymns—they had church! The scriptures also say the other prisoners listened as Paul and Silas prayed and sang.

Freedom came, not by a seal team or a raid by fellow believers. The Almighty sent an earthquake to shake the prison to its foundation. "All the doors immediately flew open, and the chains of every prisoner fell off!" (Acts 16:26 NLT). And just as amazing, the prisoners made no attempt to escape. No one can deny this was a God-thing! The jailer fell before Paul and Silas and asked what he needed to do to be saved.

Hopefully you and I will never find ourselves in prison like these men were, but we may find ourselves prisoners of circumstances. The good news is that we don't have to stay there! Paul and Silas have modeled the battle plan: *praise* and worship. Our problems won't seem near as big when we focus on the nearness of a bigger God.

> "Why am I discouraged? Why is my heart so sad? I will put my hope in God! I will praise him again—my Savior and my God!" (Psalm 42:5–6 NLT).

OPPORTUNITY

We are so blessed to live in a country where we have freedom to worship. Our pledge of allegiance acknowledges that we are "one nation under God." Our currency is inscribed with "In God We Trust." While there is a growing movement against godly values in our country, we are still blessed with religious freedoms that many countries don't have.

Paul says, "I don't know what awaits me, except that the Holy Spirit tells me in city after city that jail and suffering lie ahead. But my life is worth nothing to me unless I use it for finishing the work assigned me by the Lord Jesus" (Acts 20:22–24 NLT).

Paul and other early church pioneers paid dearly for the *opportunity* to spread the gospel. I recently read an article from *The Torch* (Christians United for Israel Magazine) saying this is the most dangerous time in history to be a Christian. One Christian is martyred somewhere in the world every six minutes. This is only one of many shocking statistics about ongoing persecution today. How we need to pray for believers across the globe, for missionaries who are facing violence and even death to share the Good News!

What excuse can I possibly have to hoard the gospel when I live in an environment that gives me the freedom to speak for Jesus? I must take advantage of every *opportunity*. The door is wide open. The time is now!

> "Live wisely among those who are not believers, and make the most of every opportunity" (Colossians 4:5 NLT).

Word for the Day

DEFAULT

We often function by *default*—from our contact lists to timer settings to computer options. Menus and macros are built for us to eliminate mundane choices, to rid ourselves from unnecessary, repetitive steps that can slow our production to a crawl. It's often advantageous to go with the *default* option, but not always.

Have you ever considered mankind's *default* destiny? Contrary to what some believe, our *default* destiny is not heaven. We don't go to heaven because our parents are good people or because we attend church every Sunday. Our good works won't do it either. Romans 5:12 (NLT) says, "When Adam sinned, sin entered the world. Adam's sin brought death, so death spread to everyone, for everyone sinned."

We are all born sinners, and each individual must make the choice to change our *default* destiny. We can accept Jesus Christ as Lord and Savior, allowing the blood He spilled on the cross to pay our sin debt, or we can spend eternity paying our own sin debt. First John 1:9 (NLT) says, "If we confess our sins to him, he is faithful and just to forgive us our sins and to cleanse us from all wickedness."

Don't assume heaven is yours by *default*!

NEED

The word *need* is often misused, as it sometimes represents our *wants*. Our heavenly Father has promised to supply our *needs*. I cannot expect to get everything I want, but I can trust God for any *need*.

One of my favorite scripture verses is recorded in Psalm 84:11 (NLT). "For the LORD God is our sun and our shield. He gives us grace and glory. The LORD will withhold no good thing from those who do what is right."

I so enjoy the warmth of the sun—the feeling of energy it gives me. Then there are other times when a little shade is just what I *need*. There are times in my life when the Lord gives me grace to endure, to wait, to be still. There are other times when His favor surrounds me and glory blessings overflow!

We don't give in to our children's every want, but as parents, we will do what it takes to give them what they *need*. Jesus says in Matthew 7:11 (NKJV), "If you then, being evil, know how to give good gifts to your children, how much more will your Father who is in heaven give good things to those who ask Him!"

God's big enough and rich enough to handle every *need* everywhere to everyone every day of our lives! Aren't you glad you know Him?

> "And my God shall supply all your need according to His riches in glory by Christ Jesus" (Philippians 4:19 NKJV).

Word for the Day

REMOVED

My husband says I can remember everything he's done wrong, or failed to do, since we've been married. Of course, that's not true! I can only remember most things! *Chuckle.* The truth is we may extend mercy to people, but we don't always forget. Aren't you glad our heavenly Father is not this way? He doesn't just forgive us, but He *removes* the evidence!

Our Father doesn't see our sin; He sees His loving Son, Jesus Christ, in us. When we ask Jesus to be our Lord and Savior, He *removes* our self-righteousness and replaces it with His pure righteousness. He doesn't bring up our past when we fail, because our past is forgiven—*removed*, erased, gone!

People may still be interested in our garbage and the enemy will help us search for it, but the Word is our final answer. "He does not deal harshly with us, as we deserve. For his unfailing love toward those who fear him is as great as the height of the heavens above the earth. He has removed our sins as far from us as the east is from the west" (Psalm 103:10–12 NLT).

We're stank-free!

QUESTIONS

Do you hear people ask *questions* like, "Why does God let bad things happen? If God is so powerful, why doesn't He stop the unspeakable crimes against innocent people?" Sometimes a *question* isn't being asked to seek an answer, rather to justify an action. My pastor says the appropriate *question* is, "Why are people so evil? Why do people do the horrible things they do?" Romans 1:18–32 gives us God's answer.

When people decide to worship things other than God and choose to trade the truth of God for a lie, He abandons them to their shameful desires. Verse 28 (NLT) says, "Since they thought it foolish to acknowledge God, he abandoned them to their foolish thinking and let them do things that should never be done." Not only do such people commit horrible sins, but verse 32 (NLT) says they "encourage others to do them, too."

Does this not describe the culture of the world? The enemy would like for us to think we're in the minority, even alone in our principles of faith, but God Almighty has raised an army of followers who stand on the truth of His Word. May we forever be branded as followers of Jesus Christ, immersed in His Spirit, and boldly empowered to proclaim the gospel—being ready to correctly explain and defend the words of truth (2 Timothy 2:15).

AM

Who *am* I? That's a loaded question, isn't it? Identity is important, and we all have the need to "make our mark." We go through phases that change our roles and challenge our identity. As children, we imitate our parents playing house. A few years roll by, and we watch our own children imitating us. We become labeled by our careers. Then comes retirement, and we look forward to a pace we can set for ourselves. During our latter years, we may find ourselves in caregiving roles or learning how to live without our soul mate. All these things shape who we are, but Psalm 104:35 (NLT) says it best for me: "Let all that I am praise the LORD!"

We often tend to value who we are by what we own or what we've accomplished, but my greatest value comes from who I *am* in Christ.

I *am* forgiven! (Ephesians 1:7).

I *am* redeemed! (Colossians 1:14).

I *am* more than a conqueror! (Romans 8:37).

I *am* healed! (Jeremiah 17:14).

I *am* a joint-heir with Jesus Christ! (Romans 8:17).

I *am* free! (John 8:36).

Father, I pray that everything I *am* glorifies You and brings honor to Your name.

Word for the Day

RELATIONSHIP

Just how much will you do for a friend? I am blessed with friends who have been there for me, and I desire to be that kind of friend in return. Romans 5:8 (NLT) says, "But God showed his great love for us by sending Christ to die for us while we were still sinners."

He loved us long before we ever knew or loved Him. That kind of love is greater than I can grasp. God sent His Son to the cross to pay for our sins—knowing some would reject Him, knowing some would curse Him, knowing some would walk away from Him, knowing none could ever repay Him.

Amazingly, God did this so He can have a *relationship* with each of us. I'll never understand what He sees in me, but I am forever honored to be in *relationship* with my Lord! Romans 5:11 (NLT) says, "So now we can rejoice in our wonderful new relationship with God because our Lord Jesus Christ has made us friends of God."

This friendship is more than I will ever deserve, but I cherish it with all my heart!

Word for the Day

WATCH

Growing up in a home with brothers and sisters, I never had my own bedroom until my high school years. Sharing a bedroom, one sister felt it was her duty to warn me of suspicious activity during the night hours. The only problem was she concocted suspicious activity most every night, and she would have to wake me to say she saw something at our window. I had quite a few sleepless nights under her *watch*! (Still love her though.)

Psalm 121 tells us we have a God in heaven who keeps *watch* over His children. Let that sink in for a moment. "The LORD himself watches over you!" (Psalm 121:5 NLT). He doesn't miss anything on His *watch*! "The LORD keeps you from all harm and watches over your life. The LORD keeps watch over you as you come and go, both now and forever" (Psalm 121:7–8 NLT).

When you wake up, take a deep breath. Know God is *watching* over you today. The Lord has your back!

When your head hits the pillow tonight, rest easy knowing Your Creator continues His *watch* in the night hours.

This is His promise.

DESTINY

Two men changed the *destiny* of mankind. The first man, Adam, changed the *destiny* for every human born thereafter. Romans 5:12 (NLT) says, "When Adam sinned, sin entered the world. Adam's sin brought death, so death spread to everyone, for everyone sinned." The second man who changed our *destiny* is Jesus Christ, the incarnate Son of God, who left his throne of glory, for a season, to live as a man among us. He preached the Good News and ultimately gave His very life to fulfill it.

I love the way Paul compares the two in Romans 5:16–17 (NLT): "Adam's sin led to condemnation, but God's free gift leads to our being made right with God, even though we are guilty of many sins. For the sin of this one man, Adam, caused death to rule over many. But even greater is God's wonderful grace and his gift of righteousness, for all who receive it will live in triumph over sin and death through this one man, Jesus Christ."

Our lives were indeed changed by the sin of Adam, but aren't you glad we don't have to live out its *destiny*? Jesus Christ brings a new *destiny* for the asking. An old chorus I grew up with comes to mind. I bet you know it! "Thank You, Lord, for saving my soul. Thank You, Lord, for making me whole. Thank You, Lord, for giving to me Thy great salvation so rich and free."

Father, may You be blessed as those who read this post today join me in singing this song to You.

Word for the Day

BENEFITS

I read Psalm 112 yesterday and felt so comforted by the Lord's promises. Today, I am drawn back to this chapter again, feeling overwhelmingly grateful for the *benefits* that God gives His children. We can never be good enough or do enough to deserve His *benefits*. The Scripture says His *benefits* are freely given when we know Jesus as Savior and delight in following God's Word. Take a moment to discover the delightful *benefits* the Scripture describes in Psalm 112.

We are filled with joy.

Our children will be successful.

We will be blessed and wealthy.

Good will come to us through our generosity.

We won't have to fear bad news because we trust God to care for us.

We will have influence and leave an honorable legacy.

Who could want more than this?

> "Blessed be the Lord, who daily loads us with [these] benefits" (Psalm 68:19 NKJV).

SIDE

In Psalm 124:1 (NLT), David asks, "What if the Lord had not been on our side?" Can we pause for a moment, and imagine what our lives would be like without the Lord? So many awful things come to mind that I cannot share. I would not want to trade one day with Jesus, troubles and all, for the best day this world can offer.

The enemy wants us to see pleasure in things that satisfy our natural desires, but he doesn't show us the consequences, the heartache, the ugliness that sin layers on our soul, mind, and body. People may enjoy pleasures for a season but are unaware of its traps. The devil doesn't show us the ugliness until we are snared with what seems to be no way out. He doesn't tell you there's a God in heaven who loves you and has sent His Son to rescue you from the hellish pit in which you find yourself. He doesn't show you the benefits you have when God is on your *side*.

Jesus says the Father "makes His sun rise on the evil and on the good, and sends rain on the just and on the unjust" (Matthew 5:45 NKJV).

Life has its troubles, but if we know Jesus as our Savior, we can do our day in confidence, knowing the Lord God is on our *side*!

> "If God is for us, who can ever be against us?" (Romans 8:31 NLT).

Word for the Day

BROKEN

Sin's power is *broken* through the death and resurrection of Jesus Christ! Best news ever! Where is the glory in our relationship with God if we continue to be enslaved to sin? Jesus died to *break* the power of sin so we can experience new life in Him. This experience liberates our complete being—soul, body, and mind!

The same resurrection power that raised Jesus from the grave lives in every believer and severs the chains of our past. What does all this mean? We aren't slaves to sin anymore. Romans 6:22 (NLT) says, "But now you are free from the power of sin and have become slaves of God." Does this mean sin never tempts us? Of course not! The devil continues to bobble sin before us and then make us feel guilty for being tempted. We live in a world of sin, and we're bound to run into it every day. Romans 6:16 (NLT) says, "Don't you realize that you become the slave of whatever you choose to obey?"

God always has and always will allow us to choose. Sometimes our choices distance us from our Father, but He stands ready to forgive and restore (1 John 1:9). His Word teaches us how to "become slaves to righteous living" (Romans 6:18 NLT).

Father, I make mistakes and often wander from Your presence, but the Holy Spirit leads me back to You. I'm so grateful sin's power is *broken*, fully confident that "I can do all things through Christ who strengthens me" (Philippians 4:13 NKJV).

Word for the Day

KNOW

Have you ever spent so much time around someone that you can predict what they are going to say? You can imitate their expressions and behaviors, because you observe them routinely. Those who *know* me best, however, still don't *know* everything. This knowledge is reserved for my Creator.

Psalm 139 so beautifully describes how He *knew* me before I was born. "Every day of my life was recorded" and "every moment was laid out before a single day had passed" (verse 16 NLT).

Our heavenly Father *knows* everything about us. He *knows* every word—spoken or thought. He even understands what our tears say. We might as well be open, honest, and real with Him, because He already *knows*.

There's no need for pretense, no point in hiding anything, as His presence brings light to darkness. Most incredibly, He loves us fiercely, fully *knowing* every mistake and failure we will ever make. As David says in verse 6 (NLT), "Such knowledge is too wonderful for me, too great for me to understand!"

CONDEMNATION

My precious poodle, Benji, would always meet me at the door when I arrived home, except when he had done something bad. Then he would sit quietly and try not to look at me. Guilt shows!

When we confess our sins and accept Jesus as Lord and Savior, we don't have to wear a guilty face or carry the burden of *condemnation*. Our sins are gone! The enemy may try to resurrect our past, but the great news is our sins are erased!

There may be people who are not as gracious to forgive and may attempt to recall our past. Paul was guilty of murdering Christians, and the Christian community was reluctant to accept him. But thank God for Paul, as he is responsible for contributing significant writings to the New Testament! Paul tells us in Romans 8:1 (NLT), "There is no condemnation for those who belong to Christ Jesus." He goes on to say in verse 33 (NLT), "Who dares accuse us whom God has chosen for his own? No one—for God himself has given us right standing with himself."

So what should we learn from Paul's writing? Don't be hanging out dirty laundry—yours or anyone else's! If God forgives, who are we to *condemn*? And if the devil tries to haunt you with your own past, set him straight with Romans 8!

Word for the Day

HEART

Solomon says in Proverbs 4:23 (NLT), "Guard your heart above all else, for it determines the course of your life." Our ticker plays a vital role in our overall health, and we should certainly do all we can to keep it functioning well. However, Solomon was referring to the core of our being where we hold our deepest emotions and beliefs. Jesus says in Matthew 6:21 (NKJV), "For where your treasure is, there your heart will be also."

This kind of *heart* bears our character and convictions. In Matthew 22:37, Jesus says the first and great commandment is to love God with all our *heart*, soul, and mind. The physical organ impacts our quality of life and length of days on earth. The *heart* Solomon speaks of drives the conduct of our everyday living and our ultimate destiny.

We all know how to stay *heart* healthy when it comes to the physical body—eat a proper diet, exercise, and get adequate rest. We will do well to follow the same basics for our spiritual *heart*:

Feed our *heart*, soul, and mind a proper dose of the Word daily (Psalm 119:11).

Exercise the commandments given in the Word (Deuteronomy 28:1–2).

Rest in the hope of the Word, being confident His Word does not fail (1 Peter 1:13).

May God bless your *heart*!

Word for the Day

RESCUE

I've always enjoyed watching disaster movies, especially when the good characters get *rescued*! Throw in a little romance, and it's perfect!

Proverbs 11:6 (NLT) says, "The godliness of good people rescues them; the ambition of treacherous people traps them."

Believers are not exempt from trouble, but our cries move the heart of God. Psalm 34:17 (NKJV) says, "The righteous cry out, and the LORD hears, and delivers them out of all their troubles."

Perhaps you're in a hard place and you're wondering where the *rescue* is. I'm reminded of a time when my son was preschool age, and we were visiting Granny and Papa. Edging toward the creek bank, Papa warned my son, Tyler, not to get any closer, or he might fall in the creek. Being curious, Tyler decided to get just a l-i-t-t-l-e closer. You can probably guess what happened next. My son slid into the edge of the water. Struggling to free himself from the murky mud, Tyler said, "Aren't you going to help me, Papa?" He was allowed to struggle for a moment, but my father never took his eyes off my son. My father told me all about it, assuring me he was in control the whole time.

There are times when we look at Abba Father and say, "Aren't you going to help me?" We may not realize it, but He's been there the whole time, never taking His eyes off our situation. There's always a purpose for the struggle. Sometimes we're enlightened to the whys, and sometimes we're not. Just know your "godliness" touches the heart of God and He comes to your *rescue*! Trust until you know!

LEADER

What image comes to mind when you think of a *leader*? I believe God has called us all to be *leaders*. A *leader* doesn't necessarily have to be in charge, but a *leader* must know what to follow and when to follow.

God has chosen each of us to *lead* others to Christ. We don't have to be credentialed, have the gift of gab, or a platform. We are simply called to tell our individual stories. Deuteronomy 28:13 (NKJV) says, "The LORD will make you the head and not the tail." The Holy Spirit is our backbone, and He empowers us with the character of *leadership*. I love what Proverbs 12:24 (NLT) says: "Work hard and become a leader; be lazy and become a slave."

Everything we say, everything we do, tells our story. What does your story say? Our Father gives us His wisdom, direction, truth, power, goodness, and favor to make our mark in this world.

Father, I pray my mark *leads* others to receive Your Son's name and all the inheritance that comes with it.

Word for the Day

LOVE

First Corinthians 13:13 says, "Three things will last forever—faith, hope, and love—and the greatest of these is love" (NLT). I am guilty of underestimating the power and beauty of *love*. If I were to describe a Christian hero, my first thoughts would probably focus on the dynamics of their prayer life, their faith, works, and their knowledge of the Word. Certainly, these characteristics are strong evidence of Christian living, but the Word says *love* is the greatest. Prioritized above gifts and works, 1 Corinthians 14:1 (NLT) says, "Let love be your highest goal!"

Want to take a pop quiz with me? Rate yourself against 1 Corinthians 13:4–7 (NLT):

> "Love is patient and kind.
>
> Love is not jealous or boastful or proud or rude.
>
> It does not demand its own way.
>
> It is not irritable, and it keeps no record of being wronged.
>
> It does not rejoice about injustice but rejoices whenever the truth wins out.
>
> Love never gives up, never loses faith, is always hopeful, and endures through every circumstance."

Wow, I am humbled! I think I will keep my score to myself!

WORK

Proverbs shares practical life lessons. Solomon speaks frequently about *working* hard, *working* faithfully, and *working* with integrity. God created human life in all its wholeness—soul, body, and mind. His Word teaches us how to live successfully in every way. Proverbs 13:4 (NLT) says, "Lazy people want much, but get little, but those who work hard will prosper."

This truth applies to our physical, spiritual, and mental well-being. Prosperity is not a handout but a promise from our Father, when we are faithful to His Word. Our *work* says who we are and brings glory to God. Our Kingdom *work* should be performed with the same vigor as our bread-n-butter labor. First Corinthians 15:58 (NLT) says, "Always work enthusiastically for the Lord, for you know that nothing you do for the Lord is ever useless." Jesus says in Mark 9:41 (NLT), "If anyone gives you even a cup of water…that person will surely be rewarded."

The only one who buys into our excuses for doing less than our best is the devil. He's the one who plants excuses in our minds to begin with. To say we have nothing to offer says little about our Creator. Never underestimate what God can do through you!

Word for the Day

PLANS

How often do your *plans* change? Please tell me your *plans* do change on occasion, and it's not just me! Change is not always comfortable, but I'm learning change is inevitable. God will equip me with the ability to switch directions when He deems it profitable.

Proverbs 16:1–2, 9 (NLT) says, "We can make our own plans, but the LORD gives the right answer. People may be pure in their own eyes, but the LORD examines their motives. We can make our plans, but the LORD determines our steps."

What I begin undergoes the scrutiny of my Creator and may look totally different when He's finished with it, but His will always brings success, fulfillment, and glory to Him.

Father, You know I tend to shy away from change, but I trust in your *plans* for me. You know best, and I never want to settle for less. I desire a teachable heart to follow Your path. I desire to hear Your voice when I wander in the wrong direction. I desire to hear Your voice when I'm celebrating and when I'm hurting. With every *plan* I make, You will determine my steps. If I surrender my actions to You, I know my *plans* will succeed (Proverbs 16:3).

Word for the Day

RELY

Have you ever found yourself in a place where you can't come up with one single answer, where every direction leads to nowhere? It's the hardest place to be, but it can also be a teachable season. Exhausting our options, running out of resources, watching every attempt fail, brings us to the realization that our situation is too big to fix. That's when we can look to our heavenly Father and learn how to *rely* on His faithful promises.

Paul describes his personal experiences in 2 Corinthians 1. He says, "We were crushed and overwhelmed beyond our ability to endure, and we thought we would never live through it. In fact, we expected to die. But as a result, we stopped relying on ourselves and learned to rely only on God" (2 Corinthians 1:8–9 NLT).

When there are no answers, no backup plans, no options, we find ourselves in the same place as Paul. As we learn how to *rely* solely on God, the windows of heaven open as His glory is manifested. The outcome is God-orchestrated—greater than anything we can imagine or think! (Ephesians 3:20).

The test can be difficult, but the testimony is invaluable!

INSTALLMENT

I remember buying my first stereo system. I didn't have credit, so my older brother purchased it with the agreement that I would repay him in *installments*. I loved that stereo system! I wore it out playing music by Christian artists like Andrea Crouch, the Imperials, and Lannie Wolfe. Records are obsolete these days, but I still have my stash! Oh, the memories—good memories—I have when I flip through my collection. Just for the record (pardon the pun) I faithfully made each *installment* payment and eventually paid my debt in full.

In 2 Corinthians 1:22 (NLT), Paul says, "He [speaking of God] has identified us as his own by placing the Holy Spirit in our hearts as the first *installment* that guarantees everything he has promised us."

Having the Holy Spirit in our lives is the greatest gift our Father could give us.

The Holy Spirit prays for us (Romans 8:26).

The Holy Spirit comforts us (Romans 15:13).

The Holy Spirit empowers us (Acts 1:8).

The Holy Spirit teaches us (John 14:26).

Just think: the Holy Spirit is the first *installment* of what God has for us! Too incredible to grasp!

Word for the Day

GIFTS

Who doesn't like a *gift*? There are certain times of the year when we expect to receive a *gift*—days like Christmas, birthday, and anniversary. I especially love when my husband surprises me with a *gift* outside these events. Recently, his *gift*-giving went awry when he decided to order me something online. Out of town and unaware of his doings, I was startled by a text message alerting me of a purchase in progress. Convinced my credit card had been stolen, I immediately called and cancelled my card. Then I decided to call my husband and give him the bad news. That's when I found out about his surprise! I botched it big time!

Often the best *gifts* can't be purchased. Proverbs 20:12 (NLT) says, "Ears to hear and eyes to see—both are gifts from the LORD." These are natural *gifts* we often take for granted, but I believe the verse refers to more than just the physical anatomy.

Father, I want to be close enough to You to hear Your voice above all others. I desire to hear and discern the struggles that others carry. I want to see the world the way You see it. I want to see through the eyes of faith. I hold Your *gifts* in gratitude and pray You are blessed delightfully in giving them to me.

Word for the Day

FRAGILE

I love to pump myself with scriptures like Philippians 4:13 (NKJV), "I can do all things through Christ who strengthens me" and Romans 8:37 (NKJV), "We are more than conquerors through Him who loved us." Then there's Psalm 18:29 (NKJV), "For by You I can run against a troop, By my God I can leap over a wall." These scriptures make me feel like a bionic woman! Okay, that may be taking it a bit far!

So why does Paul refer to us as *fragile* clay jars in 2 Corinthians 4? I don't think his words were intended to burst our bubble or demean our faith. I believe his words were God-inspired for people like you and me who face challenges that can appear insurmountable. Christians aren't exempt from adversity. We too are *fragile* in our bodies and in our environment. The difference is we have God, and He brings all the victory we will ever need!

God becomes strong in our weakness. Our tests become our testimonies. Paul says in verse 18 (NLT), "So we don't look at the troubles we can see now; rather, we fix our gaze on things that cannot be seen." Through Jesus Christ, we may encounter troubles on all sides, but we will not be crushed by it. Our challenges may bring questions and tears, but they do not have to drive us to despair.

Sometimes we feel the enemy knows right where we are, and we wonder if God does. We may even get knocked down, but we get back up in the name of the Lord! Yes, we are *fragile* beings, but the Creator handles us with utmost care. Everything we endure is for our benefit. As Paul says in verse 16 (NLT), "That is why we never give up."

WAITING

Do you ever talk your dreams? It's a good starting place, but it's just that—only a starting place. Has anyone ever asked you, "What are you *waiting* for?" Dreams never get to first base until we put them into action. Just like personal aspirations, our Kingdom work and even our worship will remain dormant if we are *waiting* for a better time. We may be thinking, "I'll do more when my children get a little older. I'll give more when I get out of debt. I will have so much more time when I retire."

King Hezekiah said in Isaiah 38:18–19 (NLT), "The dead cannot praise you; they cannot raise their voices in praise... Only the living can praise you... Each generation tells of your faithfulness to the next."

My personal mission statement is "Do what I can while I can and live to minimize regrets." The years are teaching me that every day is a good day to serve God with all my heart, soul, and mind. *Waiting* only steals today's blessing.

Word for the Day

STANDS

The seasons bring an onslaught of change to nature. The earth's colors change as the plants respond to nature's call. Some seasons wake up the creepy, crawly things while other seasons lull them to sleep.

Isaiah 40:8 (NLT) says, "The grass withers and the flowers fade, but the word of our God stands forever." We live in a world that's always changing, and that can be a good thing. Even better is knowing that one thing *stands* forever—GOD's Word! Psalm 119:89–90 (NKJV) says, "Forever, O LORD, Your word is settled in heaven. Your faithfulness continues throughout all generations."

Man's thinking continues to change from year to year. Many wonderful inventions have evolved from the creative minds our Father has gifted. Unfortunately, evil schemes and devices have also been born from our sin nature. Proverbs 14:12 (NKJV) says, "There is a way that seems right to a man, but its end is the way of death."

That's why the Word is so important. It was written for all generations. It *stands* the test of time and will always be current, relative, and "spot-on" for every one of us. It's for the old and the young, those who have and those who don't. It's for every race, color, and kindred—applicable to every generation, gender, and culture. Who else but God could inspire life-giving words that last forever?

Word for the Day

EQUAL

As a young child, did you ever think your father was bigger, better, and smarter than all other dads? He could do anything! One of our old family videos shows my brother walking next to my dad, trying to imitate his movements. The truth is our dad has limitations like all dads. Our heavenly Father, however, exceeds every expectation we can imagine (Ephesians 3:20).

So why should we exhaust ourselves trying to fix things, work things out that are beyond our means? Can we do what God can do? Can anyone do what God can do? The answer is a resounding no! The Lord has no *equal*. When life's struggles get bigger than you can carry, remember your heavenly Father has no *equal*. There's no one like Him, above Him, or remotely comparable to Him!

Isaiah 40 says it best:

> Who else has held the oceans in his hand? Who has measured off the heavens with his fingers? Who else knows the weight of the earth or has weighed the mountains and hills on a scale? (Isaiah 40:12 NLT)

> No one can measure the depths of his understanding. (Isaiah 40:28 NLT)

Step back and let the Father do what no one else can—what He desires to do for His children. "He gives power to the weak and strength to the powerless…those who trust in the LORD will find new strength. They will soar high on wings like eagles. They will run and not grow weary. They will walk and not faint" (Isaiah 40:29–31 NLT).

Word for the Day

HARVEST

Most of my working career dealt with supporting offices throughout North Carolina that serve the farming community. I never grew up on a farm and didn't have the experience most of my coworkers had, but I can assure you I have great respect and admiration for the agricultural community. A farming background is not required, however, to understand the basic principles of *harvesting*: we reap what we plant, and *harvest* more than we sow.

Paul says in Galatians 6:7–8 (NLT), "You will always harvest what you plant. Those who live only to satisfy their own sinful nature will harvest decay and death from that sinful nature. But those who live to please the Spirit will harvest everlasting life from the Spirit."

I believe we get to enjoy some of the *harvest* now, and we will receive the great *harvest* later. It's easy to get discouraged while waiting for the *harvest*, but in verse 9 (NLT), Paul encourages us, "So let's not get tired of doing what is good. At just the right time we will reap a harvest of blessing if we don't give up."

The *harvest* will always be more than we can measure. "Give and you will receive. Your gift will return to you in full—pressed down, shaken together to make room for more, running over, and poured into your lap. The amount you give will determine the amount you get back" (Luke 6:38 NLT).

BODY

What's your definition of teamwork? Interestingly, my husband and I have held different views over the years. I've always thought of teamwork as being willing to lay my work aside to help a coworker for the greater good. My husband defines teamwork as each person taking responsibility to complete their own assigned tasks. If everyone does their part, the mission gets accomplished.

As I read Ephesians 4, I see a lot of value in my husband's concept. Paul says Christ is the head of His *body*, the church. Verse 16 (NLT) says, "He makes the whole body fit together perfectly. As each part does its own special work, it helps the other parts grow, so that the whole body is healthy and growing and full of love."

Paul says spiritual gifts enable us to grow our relationship and knowledge of God. The gifts should not spotlight the individual; rather, glorify God. Every believer belongs and is placed in the *body* to complete a work. Each one of us has purpose and a place. We aren't designed to solo this Christian journey. We need each other to grow individually and together as the *body* of Christ. I want to do my little part, and I'm so grateful you are doing yours! Together we're family strong, growing in the Lord, and who we're meant to be—one *body* with Christ as the head.

BLAME

When things don't go right, who or what do you *blame*? We all do it, right? Interestingly, none of us like to be where the finger is pointing. None of us like to be the one who receives the *blame*. Adam *blamed* Eve, and Eve *blamed* the serpent. Since then, the *blame* game has been on!

Isaiah 53:6–7 (NLT) says, "All of us, like sheep, have strayed away. We have left God's paths to follow our own. Yet the LORD laid on him the sins of us all. He was oppressed and treated harshly, yet he never said a word."

Jesus intentionally accepted *blame* for our sins and bore the horrific penalty—certainly not because He deserved it. He could have called angels to deliver Him from the cross and show the world who He was. Why did He take the *blame*, knowing He could have stopped it at any moment? This was all part of God's plan. He was God, and He didn't have to prove Himself to anyone. He chose to carry out the Father's plan because He loves the Father. The Father chose the plan of redemption for us because He loves us as much as He loves His own Son.

Father, I want to become secure in Your love for me. My faults are many. Teach me to accept responsibility and bring them to You for forgiveness. A little less finger-pointing and a little more repentance builds Your character in me.

Word for the Day

COVENANT

> "'My covenant of blessing will never be broken,' says the Lord, who has mercy on you" (Isaiah 54:10 NLT).

This is a promise God made the children of Israel. Their disobedience reaped dividends of heartache, but the Lord always showed compassion. The *covenant* of blessing covers you and me through Jesus Christ. We aren't exempt from troubles, but we are helped through every one of them. Psalm 46:1 (NLT) says, "God is our refuge and strength, always ready to help in times of trouble."

When God said His *covenant* would not be broken, He also told the children of Israel He would restore their homes, teach their children, and keep the enemy at a distance. Isaiah 54:17 (NLT) says, "No weapon turned against you will succeed."

With best intentions, we may break promises, but God is faithful to His Word. Sometimes I feel disappointed that He doesn't work things out the way I want them, but I must trust He's always working for good. In Isaiah 55:11, the Lord says His Word accomplishes what He sends it to do. Aren't you glad you're under the *covenant* of blessing?

FORWARD

Looking back has its consequences. Years ago, I visited my parents' home church. As service concluded, I headed toward the car, picking up my pace as raindrops began to fall. I remember hearing someone call my name. I made the mistake of looking back while continuing to sprint *forward*. I ran into a roped fence and fell face-down. Lying on the wet ground, my feet dangled on the rope. It wasn't a pretty sight! Years later, I returned to the church for my mother's funeral. A friend, whom I had not seen for a very long time, approached me to reminisce that embarrassing tumble! Like I said, looking back has its consequences!

In Philippians 3:13–14 (NLT), Paul says, "I focus on this one thing: Forgetting the past and looking forward to what lies ahead, I press on to reach the end of the race and receive the heavenly prize for which God, through Christ Jesus, is calling us."

It's difficult to move *forward* when we're stuck in the past. Perhaps your past is calling you. Maybe your past is haunting you. Paul encourages us to set our focus *forward*. The truth is we can't change the past, but we have every opportunity to make today count. Yesterday has its glory and its failures. Today is a clean slate—a new day that the Lord has made, a day to rejoice and be glad in it (Psalm 118:24).

CROSSROADS

Did you know fifty percent of vehicle accidents nationwide involve intersections? This isn't a shocking statistic. Most of us realize the potential dangers and understand the importance of exercising caution. We may not like traffic lights, but try navigating through an intersection when one is down.

God chose Jeremiah to warn His covenant people of the sinful path they had taken. "This is what the Lord says: 'Stop at the crossroads and look around. Ask for the old, godly way, and walk in it. Travel its path, and you will find rest for your souls'" (Jeremiah 6:16 NLT).

When we approach *crossroads* in our spiritual journey, the Word of God serves as our navigational system and the Spirit functions as a traffic light. Proverbs 14:12 (NKJV) says, "There is a way that seems right to a man, but its end is the way of death." Personal opinions, emotions, and self-will can get us on the wrong path, but the Word will always keep us on track.

When we reach a *crossroad*, the Spirit knows how to help us choose the right direction. Sometimes He gives us the green light to continue our path. Other times, He cautions us to slow down and examine where we are. Sometimes He brings us to a halt to reassess our position. The halt may be frustrating, but it is necessary to realign us to God's direction and timing. The next time you come to an intersection, thank God that He is in control. Without His Word and His Spirit, our journey would be chaos!

SAFE

Being *safe* is a great feeling, isn't it? Whether you've just run to first base and the umpire calls you *safe* or you've just made it home from a long trip. Perhaps you just made it to your car on a dark, lonely street. Maybe you get that feeling when everyone is finally home and tucked away in bed.

While being *safe* is a great feeling, feeling *safe* doesn't necessarily make it so. Apparently, the people of Judah felt *safe* in the Lord's temple, but God instructed Jeremiah to correct them. In chapter 7, verses 9–10 (NLT), Jeremiah says to the people of Judah, "Do you really think you can steal, murder, commit adultery, lie, and burn incense to Baal and all those other new gods of yours, and then come here and stand before me in my Temple and chant, 'We are safe!'— only to go right back to all those evils again?"

These words sound harsh, but they warn us to not be tricked into believing a lie. Our godly heritage can't save us. Our good deeds can't save us. The church can't save us. It's only when our sins are washed by the blood of Jesus! Repentance is more than saying, "I'm sorry." Godly sorrow causes us to walk in a new direction, forsaking sinful practices of our past. We are taught what our new life should look like by the Word. When our sins are covered by the blood, and we are walking in the light of God's Word, then we are truly *safe*! As I said earlier, being *safe* is a great feeling, isn't it?

PRAY

One of my favorite scriptures is Philippians 4:6–7 (NLT): "Don't worry about anything; instead, pray about everything. Tell God what you need, and thank him for all he has done. Then you will experience God's peace, which exceeds anything we can understand. His peace will guard your hearts and minds as you live in Christ Jesus."

God cares about anything that's important to you. Just as we want our children to feel like they can talk to us about anything, so does our heavenly Father. Matthew 7:11 (NKJV) says, "If you then, being evil, know how to give good gifts to your children, how much more will your Father who is in heaven give good things to those who ask Him!"

Worry doesn't just disappear. We may try methods that temporarily sidetrack our concerns, but it's only the peace of God that can conquer worry. The Word gives us the battle plan against worry: take your concerns to the Father, along with praise and worship (Philippians 4:6–8). When a negative thought surfaces, immediately put your praise game on! Speak the opposite; speak blessing! Go ahead and do it out loud!

The battle plan sounds simple, but it's hard work that involves obedience, persistence, and repetition. I've made the choice to believe the Word regardless of what my senses say. We can bank on His Word, His love, and His power! If we are faithful to execute the battle plan, He will be faithful to drape us in His incomprehensible peace!

I confess I haven't mastered execution of the battle plan yet, but I keep working at it!

CLING

These days, it's really important to keep small children within reach. It only takes a moment for a parent to look away while kids wander off quickly. Such incidents are frightening and can result in heartbreaking nightmares. We hear horror stories about children being abducted in public places. For their protection, we teach our kids to *cling* to us.

In 1 Timothy 1:19 (NLT), Paul says, "Cling to your faith in Christ, and keep your conscience clear. For some people have deliberately violated their consciences; as a result, their faith has been shipwrecked."

The Spirit works through our conscience to alert us when we are wandering from the umbrella of God's protection. The enemy will attempt to destroy our faith with subtle lies that eventually grow into bigger ones. If we continue to ignore His warnings, our conscience will grow dormant.

Paul is telling Timothy (and us) that the living Word of God never changes—never has, never will. Faith rooted and grounded in the Word will protect, sustain, and carry us through our entire lives. We must make every effort to *cling* to that faith and not be influenced by opinion, popularity, or changing times. Faith rooted in the Word will endure the test of time. I want to examine my faith to ensure it's grounded in the Word, and I resolve to *cling* to it with all my heart, soul, and mind!

ROOTS

Unfortunately, I didn't inherit my mother's green thumb. Even my artificial plants can look poorly. Oh well, that just gives them a more natural look, right? But even someone like me understands the life of a plant is in its *root* system. It's not the pretty part, not the producing part. We all know a plant will not bear beautiful blossoms, fruit, or life, without a healthy *root* system. It's the part that is hidden deep within the ground that produces what we enjoy on the surface.

Jeremiah says in chapter 17:7–8 (NLT): "Blessed are those who trust in the LORD and have made the LORD their hope and confidence. They are like trees planted along a riverbank, with roots that reach deep into the water. Such trees are not bothered by the heat or worried by long months of drought. Their leaves stay green, and they never stop producing fruit."

Father, I desire to indulge in Your Word so that it transforms my thinking, my mind-set, and my behavior. The kind of confidence I need in my life comes solely from being *rooted* in Your Word. "Open my eyes to see the wonderful truths in your instructions. Turn my eyes from worthless things, and give me life through your word. With all my heart I want your blessings" (Psalm 119:18, 37, 58 NLT). May Your Word take *root* deep inside me to produce the desires of Your heart and blossom the benefits of gracious living within me.

PLAN

Jeremiah 29:11 (NLT) is a very popular verse we often share at graduations and weddings. "'For I know the plans I have for you,' says the Lord. 'They are plans for good and not for disaster, to give you a future and a hope.'" This verse reveals the heart of God.

If you read these verses in context with the chapter, however, you will discover the children of Judah are living in exile. They have turned their backs on God. In spite of all His warnings, they fail to repent, and they end up living in Babylonian captivity. If they had only heeded the words of God, their lives would be different.

Notice what God says to them in verses 5 and 6 (NLT) about living in captivity: "Build homes, and plan to stay. Plant gardens, and eat the food they produce. Marry and have children." In verse 10 (NLT), the Lord says, "You will be in Babylon for seventy years. But then I will come and do for you all the good things I have promised."

Some choices we make can affect us for a long time—perhaps the rest of our lives. God is always ready to forgive, but circumstances we create don't always disappear the moment we tell God we're sorry. I hope this doesn't come across negatively. I mean just the opposite! The baggage we create when we fail to heed God's Word can become a consequence, but it doesn't mean life is over. Our Father brings wholeness and wellness even in our brokenness.

Know you have a loving Father who will never walk away from you. He's ready to give you new dreams to replace the shattered ones. He always has a *plan* for you.

Word for the Day

REJECT

Have you ever played the counting game with your children? You give them a certain number of chances before you impose punishment? I don't think God played the counting game with the children of Israel, but He was longsuffering. Despite His warnings, they continued to rebel. In the book of Jeremiah, the Lord told His chosen people that they were about to lose everything.

In chapter 33, the Lord asked Jeremiah, "Have you noticed what people are saying? 'The LORD chose Judah and Israel and then abandoned them!' They are sneering and saying that Israel is not worthy to be counted as a nation. But this is what the LORD says: I would no more reject my people than I would change my laws that govern night and day, earth and sky" (Jeremiah 33:24–25 NLT).

God was angry with His children and was ready to pour out punishment they well deserved, yet He loved them fiercely! It's like He was saying, "I can talk about my kids, but you better not talk about my kids! I can punish my kids, but you had better not lay a hand on them!"

We may be corrected from time to time, and it's not pleasant, but know His correction is for our good. Remember His words in Jeremiah 33:25, "I would no more reject my people than I would change my laws that govern night and day, earth and sky." Don't you love that? God created and set the solar system in motion. The sun rises and sets every day. The moon appears like clockwork. The functions of our solar system are so faithful, so dependable, we don't even think about them. God is that faithful to us!

The chances of Him *rejecting* us is as good as the chances of the sun not rising and setting tomorrow!

Word for the Day

FIRST

There's just something special about the *first* time—the *first* time we get to drive a car, the *first* time we go on a date, the *first* kiss. When we become parents, we are thrilled at all the *first* things our babies do—like the *first* time our babies say "mama" or "dada." After the thousandth time, it's not quite as special, is it?

Hebrews 3 tells us to be careful that we don't become immune to sin and, consequently, become hardened against God. When we *first* get saved, we have an appetite for the things of God. Our hearts are tender, and we crave worship, fellowship, and the Word. It doesn't take long, however, for the intensity to wane when we distance ourselves from God's fellowship. Distance invites other cares and passions to consume the heart. Our Father may have to nudge us a bit to regain our attention.

There's an old song my sister and I sang years ago, entitled "We're Not Home Yet." The start of our Christian journey will always be special and is a part of our story, but the final chapter is much more important. How we finish means everything.

> "For if we are faithful to the end, trusting God just as firmly as when we first believed, we will share in all that belongs to Christ" (Hebrews 3:14 NLT).

FAVORITE

My sister and I have an ongoing game where we claim to be the *favorite*. The truth is we were equally loved by our parents. We siblings bear common characteristics and yet are unique in personality. Our differences may have required different parenting skills, but we were loved just the same.

James 1:18 (NLT) says, "He [speaking of our heavenly Father] chose to give birth to us by giving us his true word. And we, out of all creation, became his prized possession."

Think of the most spectacular views across the globe, the solar system, the heavens, every living creature. Everything the Lord made is breathtaking, but mankind is His *favorite* creation! He made us in His image. He sent His Son to become one of us. He laid the sins of all mankind on His Son. Loving us fiercely and giving us His best, He allows each one the personal choice of relationship with Him.

Heaven and earth will pass away, but we have the promise of an eternal home with our Father. "For we are God's masterpiece" (Ephesians 2:10 NLT). We are the Creator's *favorite*!

Word for the Day

ENOUGH

There are those who do just *enough* to get by, while others are always compelled to exceed expectations. Either goal can be unhealthy, as one goal suppresses an individual's potential and the other drives an individual to burnout. Just how much is *enough*?

When it comes to faith, I believe God has given each of us a measure. A measure of faith is *enough* to believe Christ died for our sins and be saved. From there we should strive to grow great faith to move mountains, but James 2:17 (NLT), says, "Faith by itself isn't enough."

Faith must be married with our actions. One does not work sufficiently without the other. If we only talk our faith, we fail to be the hands and feet of Jesus. Others go lacking, and our faith becomes empty words. If we do good deeds without faith, then we are working for ourselves. Our accomplishments are our reward, and sadly, the opportunity to share Christ is missed. It is when the two function together that God-sized blessings are poured into both the receiver and the giver.

Father, I pray that my faith becomes an action word. I want my actions to make my faith complete—paving the way for me to share the gospel story. As I grow my faith, may my works grow as well so that others can receive more than provisions that go as quickly as they come. May they receive the knowledge of the Giver and benefits that last forever (Hebrews 10:23–24).

Word for the Day

TONGUE

Have you ever met someone who has the perfect body, the perfect hair, but when they open their mouth, they ruin their image? It's amazing how such a small member of the body can set us up for success or failure. The *tongue* can make a good impression or a bad one. It can attract friendship or alienate it. The *tongue* can spread joy or venom. James 3:2 (NLT) says, "If we could control our tongues, we would be perfect and could also control ourselves in every other way."

We consider committing murder a horrific crime—a blatant sin against God and our fellow man. We detest a murderer, yet we can excuse gossip, criticism, complaining, and unkind words. Is it possible to murder someone's reputation, murder someone's spirit? Can we possibly murder our own? I don't have to look far for the answer. I need only look in the mirror and admit I'm guilty!

The truth is the *tongue* can bring blessing or curse. Proverbs 18:21 (NKJV) says, "Death and life are in the power of the tongue, and those who love it will eat its fruit."

Father, I want to speak life over myself, my family, my neighbor, my circumstances. When I can't find the words to speak blessing, let my words be few (Ecclesiastes 5:2).

It never hurts to give the *tongue* a rest. Silence may just be the best gift we can give to ourselves and others.

Word for the Day

ASK

JR and I placed a bird feeder in our yard, hoping to enjoy watching birds eat at their pleasure. After a couple of days, to our disappointment, we did not observe any takers. This makes me think of how our heavenly Father must feel when we struggle day after day, while His table of blessing is abundant and there for the taking. I wonder how disappointed He must feel when we don't come to the table.

James 4:2–3 (NLT) says, "You don't have what you want because you don't ask God for it. And even when you ask, you don't get it because your motives are all wrong—you want only what will give you pleasure."

God desires to give us His best, just as you and I desire to give our children the best we have. Sometimes we can't give our children everything they want because it's not best for them. When we can, however, there is nothing that gives us more pleasure.

God will give us everything we need if we put Him first (Matthew 6:33). That's a promise! Take every need you have to your Father and *ask* boldly. If your request aligns with God's Word, know it's yours (1 John 5:14–15)! If you're not sure, share your desire with Him and *ask* for His will. He will be delighted!

WARNING

It's interesting to observe how people react to *warning* signs. Consider a "Keep Away" sign, for example. Human curiosity lures us to venture past the sign. What do some of us do when we see a sign that reads, "Wet Paint?" You guessed it. We need to touch for validation. How do we react when we see a yellow traffic light? We speed up to beat the upcoming red light. Our human nature drives us to challenge the *warning* signs.

God's Word is full of *warnings*. These instructions are set in place to bring life to our souls and success to our Christian journey. When we ignore His *warnings* and step across boundaries, we may get by for a while, or at least think we are. The consequences may be so subtle that we don't recognize the danger. First John 5:21 (NLT) posts a *warning* sign saying, "Dear children, keep away from anything that might take God's place in your hearts."

The Scriptures define keep-out areas for us, and the Holy Spirit reveals the danger areas to us. The *warnings* are not designed to restrict; rather, they are provided to free us from sins that so easily entangle us (Hebrews 12:1). The next time you see a *warning* sign, thank the Holy Spirit for the protective boundaries He has in place for you.

Word for the Day

SLIPPED

In Revelation, Jesus instructed John to write letters to seven churches. One letter was addressed to the church at Ephesus. The Lord praised the church for their hard work and standing for truth, but He spoke of one complaint against them. Revelation 2:4–5 (NLT) says, "You don't love me or each other as you did at first! Look how far you have fallen! Turn back to me and do the works you did at first."

I wonder if I had a tool to measure my passion for Christ, would I measure at an all-time high, or would I discover my passion—my love for Him, my worship, my relationship—has *slipped* from where it once was?

How do we keep our passion burning? Romans 12:2 says our minds can be renewed. We renew by getting the Word into us. We find time to get alone with God. We stay in fellowship with other believers where faith and works unite. Success in walking a Christian journey means doing what we know to do to maintain relationship with Christ first and foremost.

Our actions often reveal our priorities. At the end of the day, what do your actions say about your priorities? What do your priorities say about your passion for Christ? I admit these are hard questions, but a little soul-searching brings honest answers. If I ask myself these questions often, I don't stray so far that my passion depletes. My desire to give my best helps me get back on track.

Word for the Day

UNKNOWN

In Revelation 2:10 (NLT), Jesus sent a message to the church in Smyrna, saying, "Don't be afraid of what you are about to suffer. The devil will throw some of you into prison to test you." The Lord may not always reveal what is going to happen as He did with the church in Smyrna, but He will prepare us for every approaching battle—every challenge. He prompts us to pray, and He prompts others to pray for us. He will speak to us through His Word.

Whether He chooses to reveal the specifics or not, the Lord will prepare us spiritually, physically, and mentally for tomorrow's event, for nothing is *unknown* to Him. He's way ahead of it! What happens to you and me never takes the Lord by surprise.

When we feel a subtle nudge from the Holy Spirit to pray, we need to take time to do it right then and there! Our future may depend on it—maybe someone else's! We need not worry about the *unknown*. God's already been there and knows just what to do!

> "How joyful are those who fear the LORD and delight in obeying his commands. They do not fear bad news; they confidently trust the LORD to care for them. They are confident and fearless and can face their foes triumphantly" (Psalm 112: 1, 7–8 NLT).

Word for the Day

TOLERATE

In Revelation 2, Jesus sent a message to the church in Pergamum, saying He was displeased with them *tolerating* false teaching. There are hundreds of thousands of truths in the Bible. We can spend a lifetime preaching, teaching, and living these truths. In fact, that is just what we must do to make it to heaven. I have my opinions and you have yours, but at the end of the day, what really matters is what the Word says.

Time naturally changes everything. Change can be good. If we choose to stay behind, we lose our ability to adapt, function, and thrive. Churches may look different today, sound different, and operate differently, but one thing must never change. We must never trade truth for popularity, gain, convenience, or acceptance. We must never trade truth for anything!

"Jesus Christ is the same yesterday, today, and forever" (Hebrews 13:8 NLT). His Word remains the same. "All Scripture is inspired by God and is useful to teach us what is true and to make us realize what is wrong in our lives. It corrects us when we are wrong and teaches us to do what is right" (2 Timothy 3:16 NLT).

It stands the test of time and is relevant to every nation, age, and generation. We can *tolerate* change in fashion and trends, but the Word of God must not be added to or taken away. In evolving cultures and practices, it is our one constant—keeping our heads clear and our paths destined for heaven!

Word for the Day

PLAY

Most kids grow up *playing* house. I grew up *playing* church. My father was a pastor, and we often lived next to the church house. There were five of us kids. I was quite young when my oldest sister and brother left home, resulting in three of us—the exact number we needed to *play* church. One of us would *play* the part of the preacher, while one would assume the role of the song leader. Then the third person would be the sinner. We always made sure the sinner got saved. That's the proper way to *play* church!

How precious it is when we see young children imitating worship, but imitation is not acceptable to God when we are mature and accountable for our actions. We can look spiritual and recite scriptures from Genesis to Revelation, but God looks right past our façade and goes straight to the heart. He knows whether we're for *play* or real.

In Revelation 3:1–2 (NLT), Jesus sent a message to the church in Sardis saying, "You have a reputation for being alive—but you are dead. Wake up! Strengthen what little remains, for even what is left is almost dead. I find that your actions do not meet the requirements of my God."

It's not the person who can pray the longest or shout the loudest who delights the Father. It's the one who has a heart for Him and strives to live faithfully by His Word. It's the one who is repentant when mistakes are made. It's the person who is honest with God.

Playing church as a little girl may have brought a twinkle to my Father's eyes, but He requires much more of me now.

> "May the words of my mouth and the med-
> itation of my heart be pleasing to you, O LORD,
> my rock and my redeemer" (Psalm 19:14 NLT).

DOORKEEPER

Revelation 3:7 (NLT) describes Jesus as "The one who has the key of David. What he opens, no one can close; and what he closes, no one can open." I love that! The Lord opens doors that no one on earth can close. No power above or below can shut the door of blessing, the door of opportunity, the door of escape, or the door that leads us to purpose and fulfillment.

When the Lord opens a door for us, we should enter boldly with thanksgiving. When the Lord closes a door, we should be grateful that He is watching out for us. A closed door can be just as much a blessing as an open one. Those who have walked through forbidden doors know how devastating it can be when we're in the wrong place, or in the wrong relationship, or outside the will of God.

Philippians 4:6 (NLT) says, "Don't worry about anything; instead, pray about everything." When we surrender everything to our Father, He can open the door of miracles! He can open a door that catapults us to the next level of our Christian journey, our next assignment, a deeper relationship with Him.

When we abide in Him, our Father will keep us safe and secure. This may mean closing a door that leads us in the wrong direction. He may slam the door in the enemy's face saying, "That's enough, satan!" putting a halt to his schemes.

Got a need? Take it to the *doorkeeper*!

LUKEWARM

I always liked my coffee hot, so you can keep your *lukewarm* cup. To me, it's not fit to drink! I recently switched to tea, and I like to drink it hot as well. My mother had one of those old campfire coffee pots that could be used over a fire or on a stove. Now that pot would make some hot coffee! It's amazing to me how good something can taste when it's hot and how awful it is when it cools down to *lukewarm* temperature. How do you feel when you are hot and thirsty, and grab a bottle of water only to find it *lukewarm*?

In Revelation 3:16–17 (NLT), Jesus sent a message to the church in Laodicea saying, "But since you are like lukewarm water, neither hot nor cold, I will spit you out of my mouth! You say, 'I am rich. I have everything I want. I don't need a thing!' And you don't realize that you are wretched and miserable and poor and blind and naked." Our devotion to Christ was never meant to be *lukewarm*.

Father, You deserve top spot in my life. Help me to disengage from busyness that drains my passion, joy, and focus. Forgive me when I put anything else above You. I desire to worship You with all that is in me, for anything less is not worship at all (Romans 12:1–2).

RICH

How much does it take to be *rich*? Psalm 112:3 says those who fear God and keep His commandments will be wealthy. The Old Testament introduces us to many men and women who had great *riches*, but Jesus says in Luke 12:15 (NLT), "Life is not measured by how much you own." Then he told a story about a man who placed his security in his croplands. In verse 21 (NLT), Jesus says, "Yes, a person is a fool to store up earthly wealth but not have a rich relationship with God."

I believe God wants us to work hard, produce abundantly, and be good stewards. We know God owns everything and can honor His children with material wealth, but His priority is for us to have a *rich* relationship with Him. The *richness* of our relationship is far more important than the size of our bank account.

God has promised to supply our needs (Philippians 4:19), but the abundance He desires to pour out on us cannot be measured in digits and dollars. The *richness* He desires for us to pursue is measured by His character deposited in our hearts. The treasury of our heart should be measured by the abundance of love, joy, peace, patience, kindness, goodness, and faithfulness.

When we pursue a *rich* relationship with our heavenly Father, we will recognize the abundant blessings we receive and understand how incredibly wealthy we are. That, my friend, is what it takes to be *rich*!

Word for the Day

RESTORATION

Adear friend of mine spoke the word of *restoration* over my children several months ago, when my son and his wife lost their home in Hurricane Florence. I have been holding this word in reserve for the day that *restoration* is completed. But for some reason I have not been able to get away from this word today. Perhaps there is someone out there who needs to know *restoration* is on the way.

My mind drifts back to Joseph, a young man who had his whole life in front of him. Joseph was betrayed by his own brothers, sold into slavery, and wrongfully placed into prison. I also think about Job who lost his wealth, his livelihood, and his children—all in the same day. Sometime after that, he lost his health. Both Joseph and Job endured suffering for a period of time, but God *restored* their lives with more than they had before tragedy struck them.

What has the enemy stolen from you? Have hard times and long waiting periods calloused your beliefs and confidence? Has a severed relationship crushed your spirit? Perhaps you've been robbed of your health. Maybe the enemy has stolen the hearts of your children. Perhaps you've made bad choices and are reaping the consequences. If we cling to our hope in Christ, our heavenly Father will *restore* what the enemy has taken. We may feel like we've lost everything, but we've only lost everything when we lose our faith.

"Your righteousness, O God, reaches to the highest heavens. You have done such wonderful things. Who can compare with you, O God? You have allowed me to suffer much hardship, but you will restore me to life again and lift me up from the depths of the earth. You will restore me to even greater honor and comfort me once again" (Psalm 71:19–21 NLT).

Pray for *restoration*. Trust God for it. Expect it!

TRANSPLANT

History records the first human heart *transplant* in 1967, but heart *transplants* were being performed long before then. In Ezekiel 36, the Lord says He gives His people a heart *transplant*. He says in verses 26 and 27 (NLT), "I will give you a new heart, and I will put a new spirit in you. I will take out your stony stubborn heart and give you a tender, responsive heart. And I will put my Spirit in you so that you will follow my decrees and be careful to obey my regulations." I'm glad I received a *transplant*, aren't you?

Even now I need regular checkups to ensure my heart is operating as the Lord intended. While a growing relationship should bring excellent checkups, sometimes my heart needs adjustments. I fail to feed it properly with the Word. Sometimes I get slack in exercising what I know to do. My Maker jumpstarts the heart and catapults me forward. Sometimes He uses the Word. Sometimes the Holy Spirit tugs my heartstrings. Sometimes my Father allows a trial to get my attention. Other times He sends a powerful message by song, sermon, or friend. It doesn't take much, because I've already received a *transplant*.

The prognosis? If I believe in Him, I will not perish but receive everlasting life (John 3:16).

Father, I am eternally grateful for the *transplant*. I yield to regular checkups, because I desire a tender, responsive, healthy heart. I pray you "Create in me a clean heart…and renew a steadfast spirit within me" (Psalm 51:10 NKJV).

Word for the Day

INTENTIONS

I believe good *intentions* are looked favorably upon by our heavenly Father. David told his son, Solomon, "The LORD searches all hearts and understands all the *intent* of the thoughts" (1 Chronicles 28:9 NKJV). With a fierce and passionate love for us, the Lord looks for the good. I believe He is longsuffering with our good *intentions*, giving us continuous opportunities to act on them.

It's when our *intentions* never produce, never materialize, never develop, that speak the truth. Our Father knows the difference between heartfelt *intentions* and heart-soothing *intentions*. Do we?

The enemy doesn't mind us having good *intentions* as long as he can deceive us into thinking *intentions* are for tomorrow, not today. We can pray tomorrow. We can read the Word tomorrow. We can serve the Lord tomorrow. His ploy is to use *intentions* as a means to soothe our conscience for doing nothing today.

"Examine me, O LORD, and prove me; Try my mind and my heart" (Psalm 26:2 NKJV). Give me the courage to act on every good *intention*. Forgive me when I fail. May I sincerely examine my *intentions* to ensure they are steering me to give You my best today. Tomorrow may never come.

Word for the Day

HERO

I don't recall growing up with a favorite *hero*, but I believe anyone who inspires us to be our best is a *hero*. Whether our *heroes* are parents, teachers, cartoon characters, or our own imaginary friends, they portray the character and images we desire to model.

The Bible introduces us to many people who were spiritual giants—Daniel being one of them. When Daniel was thrown into a den of aggressive lions, the Lord sent an angel to close the mouths of the lions and protect him. Talk about a *hero*! Daniel was lifted out of the den without a single scratch! Did he sleep any that night? I know I wouldn't have! Daniel's life was in jeopardy more than once, but God always rescued him.

Daniel was a gifted man, a powerful man, and a wise man. He was singled out for his loyalty to his God, promoted for his integrity and work ethics, and sought out by kings for his wisdom. He definitely meets the criteria of a *hero*, but it's worthwhile to remember Daniel endured challenging times, hard choices, times where his destiny was solely in the hands of God. He was born into captivity, taken from his family, and required to train for the king's service. He had powerful moments of triumph among seasons of difficult times. Those times prepared him for the *heroic* victories that would make history.

You may not consider yourself a *hero*, but you never know who's watching your life. You may never know how the worst of times is preparing you for the triumphant peaks that will make a difference in a life, in your community, perhaps the world. It is those glorious moments that make all those teaching days priceless.

> "The more we suffer for Christ, the more God will shower us with his comfort through Christ" (2 Corinthians 1:5 NLT).

TOLERANT

I've been reading through the books of the minor prophets. The Lord delivered message after message warning His people of the punishment coming for their disobedience. While the driving message seems harsh, I believe our Father was passionately pleading with His children, giving them every chance to repent. God isn't, never has been, nor ever will be *tolerant* of sin, but He is immediately moved with compassion when we come to Him with a repentant heart.

Today the same message is being preached, and the response is equally concerning. So many people want to ignore the commandments, believing God is a god of love, and He is! It doesn't matter how far we've gone. He is ready to forgive when we repent, and He will remove our sins as far as the east is from the west! (Psalm 103:12). However, our Father is also righteous, and He will judge the world solely on His Word. There are no favorites, no exceptions, no extenuating circumstances. Fiercely loving each one of us, He has made the way to heaven plain and simple: "Repent of your sins and turn to God, for the Kingdom of Heaven is near" (Matthew 4:17 NLT).

Don't be fooled into thinking there's any other way. We may live in a *tolerant* culture, but make no mistake: God will not *tolerate* sin! Judgment is coming.

Word for the Day

LIGHT

My appetite for *light* has grown over the past few years. I prefer a room that lets in the greatest amount of light. My optometrist says it's an age thing—that as my eyes age, they don't let in as much *light*.

Just as I crave physical *light*, I believe seasoned Christians—those who have grown in their relationship with the Lord—have an appetite for spiritual *light*. Our relationship catapults to a new level when we seek God above all else. No longer are we doing just enough to get by. We are not flirting with the boundary lines of darkness. We stay well clear of the shady areas that can lure us away from the *light*.

I may have to settle for dimmer eyesight these days, but thank God I don't have to settle when it comes to spiritual sight! Our spiritual vision can get better with age (spiritual maturity). "For once you were full of darkness, but now you have light from the Lord. So live as people of light! For this light within you produces only what is good and right and true. Carefully determine what pleases the Lord. Take no part in the worthless deeds of evil and darkness; instead, expose them" (Ephesians 5:8–11 NLT).

Word for the Day

PROVE

John the Baptist was not a man to mince words. He had one message, and he spoke it wherever he went, to whoever he was around. He didn't blend in with the crowd, and his message didn't change to please a crowd. Matthew 3:1–2 (NLT) says, "His message was, 'Repent of your sins and turn to God, for the Kingdom of Heaven is near.'" When the "religious" folks gathered at a baptismal service, John said, "Prove by the way you live that you have repented of your sins and turned to God" (Matthew 3:8 NLT).

His message is just as relevant to us today as it was in his day. We are not saved by our works, nor can our works *prove* righteousness. The indwelling Spirit drives the outward actions to manifest the light of Christ in us. Together faith and works *prove* who we are in Christ. One without the other is empty. I want to be like James who says, "I will show you my faith by my works" (James 2:18 NKJV).

Father, I pray my words glorify You and my everyday living mirrors my talk. Christian living is more than confession and profession. It's living with a repentant heart and living intentionally by the Word of God.

> "Do not be conformed to this world, but be transformed by the renewing of your mind, that you may prove what is that good and acceptable and perfect will of God" (Romans 12:2 NKJV).

Word for the Day

ALL

This three-letter word is small but carries great significance! Matthew 4:23 (NLT) says Jesus began sharing the Good News in Galilee and "healed every kind of disease and illness." Verse 24 (NLT) says, "People soon began bringing to him all who were sick. And whatever their sickness or disease, or if they were demon possessed or epileptic or paralyzed—he healed them all."

Not one left the presence of Jesus disappointed. He may not have healed everyone he met, but I believe Jesus healed *all* who asked Him and believed. Then He went to the cross to make healing for soul, mind, and body available to us *all*.

We must continue to profess *all* that Christ has done for us so that it may be done in us, refusing to let the enemy steal our blessing, our hope, our healing. What Jesus did for *all* includes you and me, our children, our neighbor, the homeless, the helpless. May the Word of God become the power of God in us so that He is able to do more than we can ever ask or think (Ephesians 3:20)!

WALL

My sister and I wrote a short poem for my mother. It was meant to be a joke. Later on, we framed it as a gift for her. The poem simply went like this: "Mother, Mother, on the wall... What you doin' up there?" We thought it was profound!

Ever feel like someone drives you up the *wall*? Ever feel like you are up against a *wall*? Ever feel closed in or shut out? Maybe you feel a *wall* is destroying your relationships. Maybe you're hiding behind a *wall*. I think most of us have a *wall* or two that need to come down.

Joshua 6 records the fall of Jericho. The town was on lockdown. The *walls* were secure. No one could enter or exit. Having promised the children of Israel the town of Jericho, the Lord told them to march around the town for six days, marching in silence as the priests blew horns. The priests carried the ark of the Lord's covenant, which signified the Lord's presence. On the seventh day, they were told to march seven times until the priests sounded a long blast. The people were then instructed to let out a shout, and the *walls* came tumbling down!

Not one single person could take credit, for it was the Lord's army who crushed the *walls*. The Word of God can crumble our *walls*! We may have to walk it out in silence. We may have to wait for God's timing, but the Word of God becomes the power of God that brings victory. When the Word speaks and collides with our faith, the *wall* will tumble! It's not by my hand or yours (Zechariah 4:6). We must do what the Word says and then watch the Word go to battle for us. "For the word of God is alive and powerful...cutting between soul and spirit" (Hebrews 4:12 NLT).

Will you join me in praying for *walls* to fall?

Word for the Day

CALLED

Without hesitation, I can say the Lord didn't choose me because of who I am. He chose me in spite of who I am. Jesus said, "Healthy people don't need a doctor—sick people do... For I have come to call not those who think they are righteous, but those who know they are sinners" (Matthew 9:12–13 NLT). We cannot come to God with a repentant heart until the Holy Spirit reveals our sins. The foundation of serving is to understand where we were headed and where grace now takes us.

The Lord doesn't *call* us to serve Him because He needs us. He *calls* us to have relationship with Him. He places us within the body of Christ to serve where He chooses. When we feel unsure of ourselves, the least qualified to serve, that's when God can do the most. In our weakness, we are compelled to depend on our heavenly Father.

If we think we have all the moves and all the answers, we may be like Simon, described in Acts 8, who offered to buy the Holy Spirit from the disciples so he could lay hands on people too. Our Father has *called* us to love Him and love others. We do that best when we understand how great He is and how incredibly blessed we are.

> "You are a chosen generation... His own special people, that you may proclaim the praises of Him who called you out of darkness into His marvelous light" (1 Peter 2:9 NKJV).

OPPORTUNITY

Matthew 10 records Jesus commissioning the twelve disciples. He gives them the authority to heal sickness and cast out evil spirits. He empowers them to do the same work He is doing. He also warns them of the challenges that will follow their ministry. In verses 16 through 18 (NLT), Jesus says, "Look, I am sending you out as sheep among wolves… You will stand trial before governors and kings because you are my followers. But this will be your opportunity to tell the rulers and other unbelievers about me."

We may take our religious freedom for granted, but be aware the powers of evil are working diligently to destroy them. I don't know if our faith will become challenged by the laws of the land as in other countries, but I do know it is challenged by the enemy.

What Jesus tells His disciples is relevant to you and me. We will meet challenge; we are already there! It may be through those closest to us. It may be through sickness. It may be through loss. It may be through a blanket of mind battles that war deep and relentless in the soul. We must be ready to defend our faith. Whatever the challenge, we need to know we have the name of Jesus to flip the battle into *opportunity* to show the world who God is! Our God is greater—that says it all (1 John 4:4)!

Father, I pray I turn every challenge into *opportunity* for You to be glorified. You've already said challenges will come. Thank you for giving us the authority to meet them head-on, in the name of Jesus!

Word for the Day

DISCIPLESHIP

Church is more than a place we spend on Sundays for a couple of hours. It's a community of people who form a unique bond that doesn't sever over time or distance. It's a place of support, a place of accountability, and a place of *discipleship*. A believer without a church is like a wanderer without a roof over his head or a family to come home to.

Jesus speaks a parable in Matthew 13, which describes the absence of *discipleship*. There are "those who hear the message about the Kingdom and don't understand it. Then the evil one comes and snatches away the seed that was planted in their hearts" (Matthew 13:19 NLT). There are "those who hear the message and immediately receive it with joy. But since they don't have deep roots, they don't last long" (Matthew 13:20–21 NLT). There are "those who hear God's word, but all too quickly the message is crowded out by the worries of this life and the lure of wealth" (Matthew 13:22 NLT). Lastly, Jesus says there are "those who truly hear and understand God's word and produce a harvest" (Matthew 13:23 NLT).

Discipleship develops believers into fruitful Kingdom workers. The church helps us to understand the Word, become rooted, establish priorities that will grow our spiritual health, and help *disciple* others. We all need *discipleship*, and we all need each other. Get connected; you'll be glad you did! (If you don't have a church, contact me. I'd love to save a seat for you!)

AWAY

Don't you love getting *away* from time to time? Getting *away* from our normal routine allows us to slow the pace (or pick it up) to enjoy moments we typically don't experience every day. We get to set aside routines, agendas, and exchange stress for relaxation, enjoyment, and renewal. Unfortunately, vacation time doesn't come often enough for most of us. However, there is an alternative. We can find ways to get *away* without leaving home or traveling across country.

For me, it's sitting down to a dose of dark chocolate and hot tea. It's sitting on my porch in the late evenings. I find the small daily things I do help keep me healthy. Mostly for me, it's establishing alone time with my heavenly Father. Getting *away* with Him prepares me for the day, offers strength as I carry out my tasks, and allows me to unload to the one who not only listens but empowers me to conquer!

Jesus often got *away* with the Father. After hearing about the death of John the Baptist, Jesus went to a private place to be alone. After feeding the five thousand men (plus women and children) Jesus went up into the hills to get *away* with the Father. What the Lord can do in a few moments is far more valuable—far more reviving—than traveling the world. The greatest times of refreshing come from the presence of the Lord (Acts 3:19–20).

If you need to get *away*, don't wait till your next vacation. Steal *away* every day to connect with God. You may be surprised what God can do in moments! "Be transformed by the renewing of your mind" (Romans 12:2 NKJV).

Word for the Day

LIVING

We watch a lot of westerns at our house a lot—over and over! There are no surprises. Each time, the movie goes the same way. And yes, we watch our share of Hallmark movies too. When you've seen one, you've seen them all, right? It's the same story with different towns and faces. But there's one story that never gets old.

The Bible can be read from cover to cover, over and over, and the reader can gain new insight every single time. Why? The Word of God is *living*! "All Scripture is inspired by God and is useful to teach us what is true and to make us realize what is wrong in our lives. It corrects us when we are wrong and teaches us to do what is right. God uses it to prepare and equip his people to do every good work" (2 Timothy 3:16–17 NLT). The Word of God becomes the power of God working in us.

Father, open my eyes to the wonderful truths in Your Word. Your truths are nuggets of wisdom that breathe life. Knowing just what I need, You open my eyes to truths that transform every layer of my being. May Your *living* Word bring me just what I need today.

Word for the Day

EXPONENTIALLY

Has anyone ever said, "You're full of it!" Sometimes the remark is said to me in jest (I think). I'm not sure what I'm full of, but I know what I want to be full of—the Word of God. I realize the Word of God has the power to change me—change the way I think, the way I look, the way I talk, and the way I do life.

Psalm 119 defines the value of God's Word:

Our steps are directed by it (verse 133).

Our hope is in it (verse 147).

The Word establishes truth so that we don't have to rely on human feeling (verse 160).

We are blessed when we live by it (verse 2).

The Word breathes life in us (verse 50).

It opens our eyes to truths we could never see or experience on our own (verse 130).

To be filled *exponentially* with the Word is to discover the greatest treasure of all (verse 162)!

How do we get filled *exponentially*? Matthew 5:6 (NKJV) says, "Blessed are those who hunger and thirst for righteousness, for they shall be filled." When we get hungry for food and drink, we make it a priority to get our fill. For most of us, we do it every day—multiple times a day. Feeding our stomachs doesn't happen by chance. We pursue it, prepare, and ingest with anticipation.

I desire to ingest the Word with the same fervor and consistency as I feed my natural body. Then the Word of God will become the power of God that works *exponentially* in me (Ephesians 3:20)!

Word for the Day

USE

Jesus shares a parable about three servants who were entrusted with investing money for their master. The money was divided among the servants according to their abilities. Two of the servants were successful in returning the monies with profit. One servant did nothing with the money he was given. Jesus finalizes the story in Matthew 25:29 (NLT), by saying, "To those who use well what they are given, even more will be given, and they will have an abundance. But from those who do nothing, even what little they have will be taken away."

The enemy is relentless when it comes to attacking Kingdom work. He tries to minimize, in our eyes, the abilities God has given us. He places thoughts of inadequacy in our minds and prompts us to compare ourselves to others. On the other hand, he can inflate our ego, our importance, so that we become territorial. The truth is we all have abilities; yet none of us are indispensable. It is the Lord who gives and takes away.

Father, my abilities belong to You. Help me to recognize what You have given me and *use* them to bless You!

Word for the Day

SHEEP

By nature, *sheep* are a prey species, having little ability to defend themselves. *Sheep* are also naturally inclined to follow a leader and tend to congregate close to each other. In fact, they can become stressed when separated from one another. It's no wonder that our heavenly Father refers to us as *sheep*. Psalm 100:3 says we are the Lord's people and the *sheep* of His pasture.

Jesus says He is the Good Shepherd; He knows His *sheep*, and they know Him. As *sheep*, we may appear vulnerable, but the Shepherd's rod and staff protects and comforts us in the dark places (Psalm 23:4). The Lord is always watching and ready to intervene on our behalf.

We enjoy strength in numbers as we congregate together, but we become prey when we fail to stay connected to the family of God. If we should stray too far, the Shepherd cares enough to come looking. The Lord doesn't give up on us (Matthew 18:12–13).

Father, thank You for watching over me. Thank you for the constant care You provide and for gently nudging me when I tend to stray. Thank You for surrounding me with a body of Christian believers I call family. We all have our own personalities and ways, but we need each other…and we all belong.

Word for the Day

FOLLOWER

To be a good leader, one needs to be a good *follower*. First Kings 19 records the calling of Elisha to assume the work of Elijah. Elisha shadowed Elijah's ministry, learning everything he could from his mentor. Nearing his ascension, Elijah tried to leave Elisha behind, but Elisha insisted on *following* him.

Second Kings 2 records the miraculous ascension of Elijah and how Elisha received a double portion of Elijah's spirit. He received what he asked for because he *followed* Elijah to the moment of his ascension. Elisha could have become distracted for one moment and missed the anointing. Instead he *followed* hard after Elijah and received a double portion of God's power. Elisha became a great leader because he *followed* a great leader.

Every believer has been called to lead the lost to the cross. To effectively lead, we must *follow* God with all our heart, soul, and mind. When we fail to *follow*, we fail to lead people to Jesus. Our witness becomes dim, and if we're not careful, we may find ourselves *following* the wrong things, the wrong people. Though we may not even be aware, we may be leading others to a path of destruction. Someone is watching. Someone will *follow*. Where are we leading?

"Thus I will bless You while I live… My soul
follows close behind You" (Psalm 63:4, 8 NKJV).

Word for the Day

HOLE

Isn't it frustrating to discover a *hole* in your pocket? Really, what good is a pocket with a *hole*? It's worthless! In the Gospels, Jesus often talks about the value of riches. In Luke 12:15 (NLT), He says, "Life is not measured by how much you own." In verse 21, He says, "A person is a fool to store up earthly wealth but not have a rich relationship with God."

In verse 32, Jesus says giving us the Kingdom brings great happiness to the Father. He acknowledges our need for material things and promises to give us everything we will ever need, but He tells us to seek the Kingdom of God first (verse 31). When we seek Him first and foremost, our life pieces fall into place—finances, careers, happiness, and success. When we pursue life pieces above God, however, we may be consequently wearing a *hole* in our pockets. The relentless hours we work may never produce enough. Even if we were to gain wealthy status, it will only last a season. All the wealth in the world cannot buy the peace of God or the riches of heaven.

The Word promises abundance to you and me for the purpose of blessing others in need (2 Corinthians 9:8). When we give to others, we are giving to God. Jesus says, "This will store up treasure for you in heaven! And the purses of heaven never get old or develop holes" (Luke 12:33 NLT). We may not get the red carpet rolled out here, but every deed, every cup of water, every love blessing, given in the name of Jesus, is ringing "Cha-ching" in heaven!

IMPORTANT

If you were to ask me what is most *important*, my answer would probably differ from my response ten years ago. Our values and priorities tend to shift as we enter different stages of life. I'm reminded today that the most *important* relationship we can have is with our heavenly Father. He has created us in His image, giving us strong minds and bodies to be at our best: people of integrity, successful, and influential ambassadors for Him.

For every good thing our Father gives, however, the enemy attempts to manipulate it against God's purpose. If he can, satan will make us feel the need to choose relationship over God. If he can, satan will convince us to put career first until we have the things we want. If he can, satan will flood our minds with what we have or what we lack. If he can, satan will mercilessly drown us in unforgiveness and heartbreak over past and present circumstances. If he can, he will!

Thank God, our victory has already been won for us, and we have the authority to call his bluff! Our Father loves each of us as much as He loves His own Son. What's *important* to you is *important* to God, but nothing or no one can trump His *importance*! "Seek the Kingdom of God above all else, and live righteously, and he will give you everything you need" (Matthew 6:33 NLT).

Father, I resolve to maintain my focus on You. When I do that, I don't have to succumb to fear of losing or never achieving things that are *important* to me. I will live a blessed life, knowing You will rescue me from every trap the enemy lays before me. As long as my heart and mind stay on You, I will "live in the shelter of the Most High" and "find rest in the shadow of the Almighty" (Psalm 91:1 NLT).

Word for the Day

ASSOCIATION

Have you ever met someone of great status? Now that isn't a fair question! If you are a born-again believer, you have status! You are a child of the Most High! There are people who think they qualify for heaven, based on their *association*. Perhaps they attend church every Sunday. Perhaps they give regularly to local charities. Perhaps their parents are God-fearing Christians.

Judas Iscariot was a disciple of Jesus. He lived with Him as the other eleven disciples did and, by *association*, was thought to be a devout follower of Christ. His *association*, however, did not make him a believer. The good things people do will never take them to heaven. God saves us when we repent of our sins and believe in Jesus Christ. Contrary to the movies, we can't earn our wings! Redemption is a gift from God (Ephesians 2:8). The redeeming grace of God changes us from the inside out. Don't miss it by thinking *association* is sufficient.

Association got Judas recognition as one of the twelve; but in the end, he lost his soul. God made salvation simple enough for a child. "If you openly declare that Jesus is Lord and believe in your heart that God raised him from the dead, you will be saved. For 'Everyone who calls on the name of the LORD will be saved'" (Romans 10:9, 13 NLT).

Don't settle for *association*. Go for transformation!

Word for the Day

POWER

Nearing the end of His ministry on earth, Jesus says to His disciples, "I don't have much more time to talk to you, because the ruler of this world approaches. He has no power over me, but I will do what the Father requires of me" (John 14:30–31 NLT).

This verse really pricked my heart today. If satan has no *power* over Jesus, then he has no *power* over the believer! Why? God the Father, Jesus, and the Holy Spirit are one. Having lived *with* them, Jesus tells the disciples that the Father will send the Holy Spirit to live *in* them.

The Holy Spirit was promised to come live in us so that we can have the Spirit of God leading, teaching, and protecting us. Satan, the ruler of this world, has no *power* over Jesus, and he has no *power* over the Holy Spirit of God living in us. Make no mistake: he attacks in full force and runs his bluff! We cannot overcome by force or by our strength, but we overcome by the Holy Spirit living within us (Zechariah 4:6)!

Father, thank You for sending Your Son to bring life to us. Thank You for sending Your Holy Spirit to live in us. I do this day in confidence, knowing the Holy Spirit, who abides in me, is greater than the ruler of this world (1 John 4:4)!

FRUIT

Have you ever felt scalped from a haircut? I have a wonderful hairdresser! All you ladies know just how important that is. (How many of you guys will admit you are just as peculiar about your "head-do?") Before I met my current hairdresser, I had my share of squirrelly cuts!

In John 15:1–2 (NLT), Jesus says, "I am the true grapevine, and my Father is the gardener. He cuts off every branch of mine that doesn't produce fruit, and he prunes the branches that do bear fruit so they will produce even more." This verse gave me flashbacks of my squirrel days! My Father has done a lot of cutting on me over the years. I mean a lot! Now I'm realizing what a good thing this is. Jesus says we can't be *fruitful* apart from Him. He goes on to say, "If you remain in me and my words remain in you, you may ask for anything you want, and it will be granted! When you produce much fruit, you are my true disciples. This brings great glory to my Father" (John 15:7–8 NLT).

Do you know what *fruit* does? It protects the seed. When the seed matures, the *fruit* helps spread the seed. Being connected to the Word of God protects our soul, our purpose, our destiny. As our spiritual fruit matures, the Word is dispensed where God sends it. As the Word goes forth, it doesn't return void but accomplishes what it was sent to do (Isaiah 55:11). Jesus says, "I appointed you to go and produce lasting fruit, so that the Father will give you whatever you ask for, using my name" (John 15:16 NLT).

The next time I get scalped by my Father, I will thank Him for the blessing that's coming!

PASS

Isn't it amazing how stories and events can alter as they are *passed* on from one person to another? I wish I were a better listener. Maybe I would communicate better. I'm guilty of assuming and interpreting instead of asking and validating.

In John 16:13–15 (NLT), Jesus says, "When the Spirit of truth comes, he will guide you into all truth. He will not speak on his own but will tell you what he has heard. He will tell you about the future. He will bring me glory by telling you whatever he receives from me. All that belongs to the Father is mine; this is why I said, 'The Spirit will tell you whatever he receives from me.'"

Aren't you glad Jesus asked the Father to send the Holy Spirit to us? Holy Spirit, I invite you to speak truth into me that I might *pass* it on! I am fallible, but You are not! You *pass* the living Word—the Word that is "inspired by God and is useful to teach us what is true and to make us realize what is wrong in our lives. It corrects us when we are wrong and teaches us to do what is right" (2 Timothy 3:16 NLT).

I may fail to interpret correctly, but if I continue to seek and search with all my heart, soul, and mind, my Savior will reveal the truth of His Word through the Holy Spirit of God. What He reveals is worth *passing* on!

Word for the Day

CONNECT

Have you ever met a stranger who changed your outlook for the day? Perhaps they spoke an encouraging word to you. Perhaps you did something for them that brightened their day. Psalm 37:23 (NKJV) says, "The steps of a good man are ordered by the LORD." I believe He *connects* us to others and others to us. It is a divine orchestration with purpose.

An excellent example is Peter and Cornelius, as recorded in Acts chapters 10 and 11. Peter was a Jew, and Cornelius was a Gentile. Jewish custom would never have *connected* their paths, but God prepared Cornelius to seek salvation and sent Peter to his house to tell him how to get saved. Both men encountered a vision that would change their lives. Peter's vision prepared him to open the gospel door outside his circle of ministry. Cornelius's vision prepared him to accept the gospel and pioneer Christianity to the Gentiles.

We never know whom God will place in our paths. Father, I want You to order my steps. Help me to have an open heart, eyes, and ears to *connect* with those you place in my path. Forgive me when I have been so busy or self-focused that I missed the *connection*. I don't want to miss another opportunity to make a difference. I don't want to miss the opportunity to have my life influenced by relationship You've orchestrated. Guide me today in every way (Proverbs 3:6)!

Word for the Day

EXALT

The book of Acts records the fates of three individuals who found themselves in the spotlight. One person was King Herod Agrippa. Chapter 12 describes how the people of Tyre and Sidon literally worshipped him in exchange for food provisions, calling him a god. The other two individuals were Paul and Barnabas. Chapter 14 describes their mission trip to Lystra. Amazed at the healing of a lame man, the crowd began to call them gods and made preparations to offer sacrifices.

How did the men react to their circumstances that cast them in the spotlight? Herod Agrippa accepted the people's worship. Paul and Barnabas did not. In fact, Paul and Barnabas tore their clothing in horror and said, "Friends, why are you doing this? We are merely human beings—just like you! We have come to bring you the Good News that you should turn from these worthless things and turn to the living God" (Acts 14:15 NLT).

What were the fates of these three men? Acts 12:23 (NLT), says, "Instantly an angel of the Lord struck Herod with a sickness, because he accepted the people's worship instead of giving the glory to God. So he was consumed with worms and died." Acts 14:19–20 (NLT) says the Jews "stoned Paul and dragged him out of town, thinking he was dead. But as the believers gathered around him, he got up and went back into the town."

Jesus says, "For those who exalt themselves will be humbled, and those who humble themselves will be exalted" (Luke 14:11 NLT).

SEARCH

We are surrounded by mountains of knowledge. Quick answers are at our fingertips. Does anyone remember the libraries of encyclopedias now shelved in dust? I wonder if younger generations know they exist! Got a question? Today we just google it or ask any smart device. How blessed we are to have facts and figures instantly available.

While we're flooded with information, we're not always provided truth. Information that changes to adapt to our lifestyles or our thinking patterns does not meet the definition of truth. That's what makes the Word of God so beautiful. The words inspired by the Holy Spirit thousands of years ago are relevant to every person, tribe, and generation today. The Bible's contents are complex and yet simple enough for a child.

In Acts 17, Paul and Silas visited a place called Berea and preached the gospel message. The people listened and "They searched the Scriptures day after day to see if Paul and Silas were teaching truth. As a result, many Jews believed, as did many of the prominent Greek women and men" (Acts 17:11–12 NLT).

It's imperative we *search* the Scriptures! At the end of the day, it really doesn't matter what I think or feel—nor you. We are fallible, but the Word of God is not. The Word not only provides us the roadmap to heaven but lays foundational truths for successful living, right here and now! Ask the Holy Spirit to open your eyes and ears to the Word. Prepare to be amazed as truth is revealed and you are enlightened!

> "And you will seek Me and find Me, when you search for Me with all your heart" (Jeremiah 29:13 NKJV).

Word for the Day

STAY

Why is it that a dog can be trained to *stay* at command, but someone like me has difficulty with it? Acts 27 describes a storm at sea as Paul is being transported to Rome. The storm lasted for fourteen nights, and the sailors decided to abandon ship. Having heard from the Lord, "Paul said to the commanding officer and the soldiers, 'You will all die unless the sailors stay aboard'" (Acts 27:31 NLT).

Hurricanes are common to our region and last longer than most storms, but even these storms never last fourteen days! By this time, the sailors had to be exhausted, and were expecting the worst. They were ready to jump overboard and take matters into their own hands.

Life storms can wear us down like that, but just as Paul received assurance from the Lord, we too have His Word. He has promised to never leave us and instructs us to *stay* strong in the power of His might (Ephesians 6:10). If we abandon His plan and take matters into our own hands, we will fail and flail! How do I know? I've been there; done it!

Let me encourage you to *stay* put, *stay* on course, *stay* in the Word. When you can't see the end of the storm, *stay* still. Arm yourself with Psalm 91 as your survival plan. Pray it back to the Father, making each verse personal. Read it as often as it takes to *stay* where you are until God moves you out of the storm. (And He will!)

Father, may my testimony be, "My steps have stayed on your path; I have not wavered from following you" (Psalm 17:5 NLT).

PRIVILEGES

M ost of us enjoy *privileges* because they make us feel special. If we can afford it, we'll pay a bit extra to acquire the benefits of the premium package. We like extra discounts, bonus points, upgrades, rewards, special parking, and first-class seating. Romans 5:2 (NLT) says, "Because of our faith, Christ has brought us into this place of undeserved privilege where we now stand, and we confidently and joyfully look forward to sharing God's glory."

This great and glorious *privilege* is totally undeserved. It cannot be purchased or earned but is a gift from our heavenly Father. When we allow the devil to make us feel less than who we are in Jesus Christ, we are living beneath our *privileges*. We are who the Word says we are—redeemed, whole, adopted into royalty, destined for heaven, loved unconditionally, blessed beyond measure, and more than a conqueror! "His great love…made us alive together with Christ…and made us sit together in the heavenly places" (Ephesians 2:4–6 NKJV).

Indulge in His *privileges* today with a heart of gratitude. This delights our Father!

Word for the Day

ONE

Is there *one* particular thing that brands you, any particular physical or behavioral characteristic for which you are known? Maybe it's the way you walk or laugh. Maybe it's a phrase you use frequently. My dad branded us with high cheek bones and squinty eyes! That's the Brisson's physical signature!

Even more important is that *one* characteristic that tells the story of every believer—the love of Jesus Christ! God's love in us changes everything about us. It's who we are in Christ that leaves an honorable legacy. How do you want to be remembered? Think about the first man, Adam. He was a good gardener and caretaker, but the *one* thing history remembers about him is that he's the guy who ate forbidden fruit, blamed it on his wife, and was forced out of the Garden of Eden.

Romans 5:18 (NLT) says, "Yes, Adam's one sin brings condemnation for everyone, but Christ's one act of righteousness brings a right relationship with God and new life for everyone." It's that *one* selfless act that brings life to every man, woman, boy, and girl. Through Jesus Christ, we're branded by the cross and marked for the glory of His righteousness!

Father, may Your character be the *one* thing that others see in me.

> "Those who are righteous will be long remembered" (Psalm 112:6 NLT).

Word for the Day

INTERCEDE

In my growing up years, sometimes I would ask my mother to talk to Dad for me when I wasn't sure he would say yes. I needed someone close to him to *intercede* on my behalf. This is what the Holy Spirit does for us. According to 1 John 5:14–15, God hears us and gives us what we ask when the request aligns with His will. Our Father has given us His Word to define His will and the Holy Spirit to guide us in living His will.

The Holy Spirit prays for us when we don't know the will of God. In Romans 8:26–27 (NLT), Paul says when we don't know what to pray, the "Holy Spirit prays for us with groanings that cannot be expressed in words. And the Father who knows all hearts knows what the Spirit is saying, for the Spirit pleads for us believers in harmony with God's own will."

Holy Spirit, thank you for *interceding* to the Father for me—for taking my needs, my concerns, my circumstances, and my desires to my Father. I will live in confidence that You are working all things for my good (Romans 8:28).

Word for the Day

USELESS

Here's a question for you homemakers: Do you ever wonder why you spend hours cleaning your house only to start the whole process over the next week? We realize what we do is not going to last very long—maybe not even the day! Sometimes all the effort seems *useless* when the results disappear before our eyes in a matter of minutes!

We often spend time trying to do all the right things to please others. At the end of the day, sometimes we score, and sometimes we don't. First Corinthians 15:58 (NLT) says, "Nothing you do for the Lord is ever useless." We may not see the benefits of everything we do, but God does.

What we do for His glory will continue beyond our lifetime. Psalm 112 says our good deeds will last forever. The Kingdom work we do today may not feel important. It may not make headlines or turn a head, but it catches the eye of God and will be used by Him to accomplish His plan. I don't know of anything else in which I can invest my time, effort, and heart that will render such dividends. Think about it: nothing we do for the Lord is ever *useless*! Doesn't it make you want to rethink today's agenda?

Word for the Day

ADVICE

With every milestone in life comes an influx of *advice*—want it or not. Graduation, dating, college, career, marriage, parenting—there's plenty to be shared. Over the years I have received some good *advice*. Unfortunately, I've not always heeded words of wisdom. Other times, I have listened to the wrong words at the wrong time.

In 1 Corinthians 16:13–14 (NLT), Paul gives great *advice* worth soaking in: "Be on guard. Stand firm in the faith. Be courageous. Be strong. And do everything with love." Paul's *advice* will help us make it to heaven and promote success in our journey getting there.

"Be on guard." When we let our guard down, we make ourselves vulnerable to the attack of the enemy. Make no mistake—the devil is always watching for an opportunity. Demons spring into action when our guard is down.

"Stand firm in the faith." Either we believe or we don't. We must get into the Word and get the Word into us so that we will know the truth and choose to stand on it.

"Be courageous. Be strong." Relying on self makes us vulnerable to failure. We must live in the strength and boldness of the Holy Spirit, knowing His power works best in our human weakness (2 Corinthians 12:9).

Lastly, if we "do everything with love," our testimony stands unmatched. It only takes one unlovable action to destroy a thousand sweet words.

Paul's *advice* can only make a difference if we put it into practice. I can't think of better *advice* to jumpstart my day!

Word for the Day

NOT

This word often carries a negative connotation. If we focus on the *not*-haves and the *not*-fairs we will find ourselves depressed, depleted, and deflated. Isn't it beautiful how the Scriptures can take the same word and deliver a powerfully, dynamic message of encouragement?

Second Corinthians 4:8–9 (NLT), says, "We are pressed on every side by troubles, but we are not crushed. We are perplexed, but not driven to despair. We are hunted down, but never abandoned by God. We get knocked down, but we are not destroyed."

Paul was describing his life experiences. I believe we can relate, but Paul faced persecution beyond what most of us have ever encountered. Perhaps my difficulties pale to yours, but it's not necessary to compare our "boo-boos." We all have struggles, but in Jesus Christ, we are more than conquerors (Romans 8:37)! If He speaks it, we can tread on water (Matthew 14:28–29)! We can run against a troop and leap over a wall (2 Samuel 22:30)! The Lord never said we would be exempt from trouble, but He did promise to be with us and deliver us (Psalm 91:14–15).

Do you recall ever playing with an inflatable punching figure? No matter how hard you hit it, the inflatable toy would spring back. This is who we are in Christ Jesus! We are *not* crushed. Our troubles do *not* drive us to despair. We are *not* abandoned, nor destroyed! When troubles knock us for a loop, we can spring back by the powerful name of Jesus! Aren't you glad you know Him?

IMITATE

Do you enjoy watching children *imitate* adults? Their motions can be quite entertaining while they're babies, but the cuteness dissipates when children get a little older. The words, expressions, tone, and actions quickly transition into behavioral patterns that make parents want to crawl under a table. We wonder where in the world did little Johnny pick up such behavior. Sometimes little Johnny is simply *imitating* the adults in his world. Ephesians 5:1 (NLT) says, "Imitate God, therefore, in everything you do, because you are his dear children."

I wonder if the Lord rolls His eyes sometimes when my character is showing off and not His. If I learn to *imitate* Him, the world will take notice. I want every gesture, every word, and every action to reflect His character. This means learning the nature of God through His Word and asking myself, "What would Jesus do?" The more we *imitate* His nature, the more His nature becomes who we are.

Father, may others see more of You and a little less of me.

Word for the Day

SECRET

I recall hearing a message about the *secret* place that changed my prayer life. Jesus says in Matthew 6:6 (NKJV), "But you, when you pray, go into your room, and when you have shut your door, pray to your Father who is in the secret place; and your Father who sees in secret will reward you openly."

I don't think Jesus was referring to a specific location—rather, the *secret* place is anywhere we get alone with God. Shutting the door—that is, getting in the *secret* place with God—actually opens the door for God to change us and change our circumstances. It's where we pour our hearts out to Him about anything and everything. It's where the Lord delightfully receives our praise. It's where He hears our concerns and our heart's desires. It's where the Lord speaks His heart to us, grows our faith, and pours His peace into us. It's the place where miracles are conceived.

Our heavenly Father is always delighted to meet us in the *secret* place—day or night. He's never too busy or too far away to see us enter the *secret* place. Our schedules, distractions, exhaustion, and emotions will interfere, but how can we neglect going to the *secret* place when we know our Father is waiting? We may not feel His presence every time we enter the *secret* place, but be assured God is faithful to meet us there. What better way to start the day, or end it, having met with our heavenly Father?

FAULT

If you're around me long enough, you will probably discover a *fault* or two. We all have our ways. One of my major *faults* is picking out others' *faults*. I doubt we'll ever be perfect in each other's eyes, but I'm so grateful that our heavenly Father sees us differently. Colossians 1:22 (NLT) says, "Yet now he has reconciled you to himself through the death of Christ in his physical body. As a result, he has brought you into his own presence, and you are holy and blameless as you stand before him without a single fault."

The idea of standing before my Father is so humbling. Being totally exposed, I'm keenly aware every *fault* and weakness is showing. Instead of seeing my *faults*, however, He sees my potential. Instead of focusing on my weaknesses, He pours His strength into every crevice of my being. Standing totally exposed before Him, He sees me as holy, blameless, and without a single *fault*, because He sees Christ in me!

We will never measure up to everyone's expectations—may never be perfect in anyone's eyes—but how priceless is it to know the God of the universe sees His Son in us and loves us as His own. We are the apple of His eye!

Word for the Day

TREASURES

Imagination is a wonderful gift given by our heavenly Father. Exploring with imagination begins before we ever learn to read and write. Most of us have hunted for *treasure*, played with *treasure* chests, and buried *treasures* of our own. Books, amusement parks, and movies appeal to our imagination by making our quest for *treasure* feel delightfully real.

While these types of *treasures* are fueled by the imagination, God has much to say about real *treasure*. In Deuteronomy 7:6, God's chosen people are defined as a special *treasure* to Him. Imagine that! The Creator of all the universe *treasures* us! Owning everything, He labels us uniquely valuable to Him.

Matthew 6:19–21 encourages us to pursue the things that build *treasures* in heaven, not here on earth. How we live and what we do for Him reaps *treasures* that will exceed and outlast anything we can accumulate for ourselves. Colossians 2:3 says all the *treasures* of wisdom and knowledge lay hidden in Jesus Christ. These *treasures* reveal God to us and are available for the asking (James 1:5). Psalm 119:162 (NLT) says, "I rejoice in your word like one who discovers a great treasure."

Hidden within the pages of His book, we find truth, life, purpose, power, and destiny. *Treasures* conceived by the imagination are seldom trumped, but we can never dream bigger than God! "No eye has seen, no ear has heard, and no mind has imagined what God has prepared for those who love him" (1 Corinthians 2:9 NLT).

Word for the Day

WORK

S ome people are fortunate enough to love their job and get paid for it at the same time. Others simply *work* for the paycheck. I don't know if there is such a thing as a perfect job, but Colossians 3 gives us great insight on how to be successful in our careers. This is one of the things I love about the Word. It not only teaches us how to get to heaven, but it provides great life skills for living successfully here and now.

Colossians 3:23 (NLT) says, "Work willingly at whatever you do, as though you were working for the Lord rather than for people." Our *work* ethics should mirror our Christian name. We have been called to share the gospel with those around us. Our character preaches a sermon before we ever open our mouths. When we give an honest day's *work*, our principles, character, and integrity will open the door for others to see Christ in us.

We may not always be recognized for the *work* we do, but know God is watching and has the final record. If you're feeling the *work-day* blahs, take on Colossians 3:23 and make it a productive day!

MOTIVES

Have you ever wondered why people say the things they say and do the things they do? First Thessalonians 2:4 (NLT) tells us that God "alone examines the motives of our hearts." Aren't you glad our heavenly Father knows us that well? When others don't understand, He does. God sees past the outward person and goes straight to the heart.

We can do all the right things and still not have the right *motive* behind it. Sometimes we may do the wrong things, yet God knows we meant well. When our *motives* are not pure, the Holy Spirit will reveal it to us so that we can make things right. "Search me, O God, and know my heart; test me and know my anxious thoughts. Point out anything in me that offends you, and lead me along the path of everlasting life" (Psalm 139:23–24 NLT).

Father, may everything I say and do be *motivated* by You. When it's not, may I quickly respond to the Holy Spirit and confess my wrongdoing so that I may grow in Your likeness. As I align my *motives* to Your Word, my desires will mirror Yours and my regrets will be few.

Word for the Day

GAP

In 1 Thessalonians, Paul writes a letter to the church in Thessalonica. Chapter 3 really captures my heart as it describes a beautiful bond between Christians. The letter describes the encouragement Paul, Silas, and Timothy receive from the church and their desire to return to Thessalonica so they can pour into the church family. Paul says, "We have been greatly encouraged in the midst of our troubles and suffering…because you have remained strong in your faith. It gives us new life to know that you are standing firm in the Lord" (1 Thessalonians 3:7–8 NLT).

In verse 10 (NLT), Paul goes on to say, "Night and day we pray earnestly for you, asking God to let us see you again to fill the gaps in your faith." That's what Christians do for each other. We stand in the *gap* when one is sick, discouraged, or emotionally beaten down. When there is a *gap* in our faith, we have a host of believers filling the *gap* for us.

I may not always know who is praying for me, but I know the Lord whispers my name to others when I need reinforcements. How do I know that? Sometimes, the Lord whispers your name to me. Love you all! You're family!

Word for the Day

GENUINE

We are all born with a measure of faith. From there it's up to us to grow great faith. I love what Paul says to Timothy: "I remember your genuine faith, for you share the faith that first filled your grandmother Lois and your mother, Eunice. And I know that same faith continues strong in you" (2 Timothy 1:5 NLT).

I am grateful for my spiritual heritage, but I know *genuine* faith goes beyond family name. *Genuine* faith can't be handed down or imitated. *Genuine* faith is bred in us when we get into the Word and get the Word into us. *Genuine* faith teaches us to rely solely on the Word of God, not emotion. *Genuine* faith encourages us to remain steady and not base our convictions on what we see or feel. *Genuine* faith doesn't block our human tendencies, but it will empower us to bring "every thought into captivity to the obedience of Christ" (2 Corinthians 10:5 NKJV).

Positive thinking and self-discipline have limitations, because they are based on human strength. *Genuine* faith has no limitations, because it is God-breathed into us when we pursue His living Word.

Father, I can't make it or fake it. *Genuine* faith only comes through Your Word. May every letter of Your Word capture and transform my mind, heart, soul, and spirit so that my faith bears fruit.

Word for the Day

CHASE

At a very young age, we are often asked what we want to be when we grow up. That dream may change many times. I believe our Creator has instilled giftings within us that should be identified as we *chase* our dreams. Opportunities are birthed from dreams. The important thing is that we *chase* God so that our dreams align with God's plans for us. The giftings He has placed within us are designed for His purpose and pleasure.

Second Timothy 4:3–4 (NLT) says, "For a time is coming when people will no longer listen to sound and wholesome teaching. They will follow their own desires and will look for teachers who will tell them whatever their itching ears want to hear. They will reject the truth and chase after myths." By world standards, we may reach success *chasing* our own dreams, but there will still exist an emptiness that only the Creator can fill. How sad it would be to live an entire lifetime and miss God's plan.

Proverbs 3:6 (NLT) says, "Seek his will in all you do, and he will show you which path to take." The beautiful thing about God's plans is that they don't expire or exclude anyone. We are never too young or too old, too rich or too poor. Our assignments may change as we enter different seasons, but God is never through with us. If we choose to *chase* God, our lives can exceed our greatest dreams (Ephesians 3:20).

KEPT

Everyone loses something sometime. As children, we sometimes lose our favorite toys. We lose our baby teeth. We lose the baby face as we grow into that awkward stage. Then we start losing homework! Next it's the car keys. The list can go on and on. By the time we reach our senior years, we more clearly understand loss is a part of life, and we realize there is a season for everything (Ecclesiastes 3:1).

Every day is an opportunity to enjoy God's provisional blessings; however, life lessons teach us how quickly earthly accumulations can vanish. The strongest vault cannot safeguard our valuables. The financial wizards of Wall Street cannot secure wealth, but salvation in Jesus Christ guarantees us an inheritance. First Peter 1:4 (NLT) says, "We have a priceless inheritance—an inheritance that is kept in heaven for you, pure and undefiled, beyond the reach of change and decay."

The best is yet to come! Our inheritance is *kept* for us so that we can enjoy it forever. It can't be taken, shaken, or mistaken! It's in the best hands! Your inheritance awaits!

Word for the Day

REAL

Did you ever play the "I like you, do you like me?" game? This is where one writes a note and inserts a box for the recipient to check. If the box was checked yes, the flirting began. If the box was checked no, the game was over. We grow out of this childish game as we mature, but we often play an adult version of it. We're willing to throw a little bait to see if we get a bite. If the other person doesn't respond, we dismiss them as a potential friend.

Aren't you glad our Father is not this way? First John 4:9–10 (NLT) says, "God showed how much he loved us by sending his one and only Son into the world so that we might have eternal life through him. This is real love—not that we loved God, but that he loved us and sent his Son as a sacrifice to take away our sins."

He loved us and sacrificed His Son for each one of us before we were ever born. He loves us when we don't love back. Our love is conditional. His love is regardless. That's *real* love!

CONFIDENT

Life experiences have a way of building *confidence* and crushing it, helping us to achieve a dream and sometimes never pursuing it. Where our *confidence* is founded makes all the difference. *Confidence* in ourselves, others, material assets, and the status quo are shakable, but when our *confidence* is in God and His Word, we celebrate life's goodness and overcome its hardships.

First John 5:14–15 says, "We are confident that he hears us whenever we ask for anything that pleases him. And since we know he hears us when we make our requests, we also know that he will give us what we ask for" (NLT). If God's Word says it's ours, we can depend on it. Sometimes we have to wait for it, but as Hebrews 10:35 (NLT) says, "Do not throw away this confident trust in the Lord. Remember the great reward it brings you!"

We can also take our desires not specifically addressed in the Word to our Father and be *confident* that He will withhold no good thing (Psalm 84:11). When our *confidence* is founded in Jesus Christ, the baggage attached to hardships will fade in our faith.

Suffering may be used to catapult us to another level in our Christian journey. Then we can become a source of help to others. Be strong by taking *confidence* in the Lord!

Word for the Day

AWAY

What makes us want to explore a no-trespassing zone? What makes us want to touch a surface when a "don't touch—wet paint" sign is posted? What is so intriguing with keep-out areas? There's just something about our human nature that is compelled to test the boundaries.

We display these tendencies from early childhood. We don't teach our children to challenge the rules; human nature does. Then we must teach our children the consequences. First John 5:21 (NLT) says, "Keep away from anything that might take God's place in your hearts."

God's wisdom warns us against our wayward nature. According to Genesis 2:9, God placed the tree of life and the tree of the knowledge of good and evil in the middle of the garden He made for Adam and Eve. God specifically warned Adam to stay *away* from the tree of the knowledge of good and evil. The serpent convinced Eve to eat the forbidden fruit, and she persuaded Adam to eat it; thus, the will to test the boundaries was born into the human race.

The Bible doesn't itemize every possible danger, but 1 John 5:21 (NLT) says it all and is worth repeating: "Keep away from anything that might take God's place in your hearts."

Holy Spirit, my heart is to please the Father, but my nature tends to flirt with boundaries. Thank You for nudging me when I stray past the safety zone. Keep my heart tender toward Your guidance. I don't want anything or anyone to take God's place.

Word for the Day

EXCUSES

We all have *excuses* for why we do things and why we don't. *Excuse* is a cousin to the "blame game." Adam and Eve played it in the Garden of Eden. The Bible only names one restriction they were given: don't eat the fruit from the tree of the knowledge of good and evil. There was no logical reason for their disobedience. They enjoyed a daily abundance of delicious fruit from all the other trees in the garden. The fruit from the tree of life would have kept them vibrant forever. Adam and Eve simply chose to ignore God's warning.

Their *excuses*? "The man replied, 'It was the woman you gave me who gave me the fruit, and I ate it.' Then the LORD God asked the woman, 'What have you done?' 'The serpent deceived me,' she replied. 'That's why I ate it'" (Genesis 3:12–13 NLT). Even though Adam directly blamed Eve, he also said it was "the woman you gave me" (speaking to God). Eve blamed the serpent whom God created. It's almost as though Adam and Eve wanted to blame God. Does this sound familiar?

What's the life lesson in this? The sooner we can accept responsibility for our shortcomings, the sooner we can learn from them and move forward. Our Father is not interested in our *excuses*, but He is always ready to forgive. *Excuses* can become toxic and keep us in bondage. Repentance, however, can separate us from the things that weigh us down.

Father, I don't want to be rutted in *excuses* for my shortcomings. I realize my *excuses* are birthed by pride. Empty every part of me that is unlike You. I repent of my failures, for those things I do that displease You, and for the things that I fail to do. Thank You for forgiving me and setting me free today!

Word for the Day

TRUST

If I were to ask if you *trust* in God, I would imagine you would say, "Sure!" Allow me to ask the same question, but leave out the word *in*. Do you *trust* God? For me, there is a substantial difference. I believe we can *trust in* God and yet struggle to *trust* God.

Trusting God is much more personal. To say, "I *trust* God" means I know He will take care of every situation concerning me, even when I'm facing the worst. To say, "I *trust* God" means I believe He loves me as much as He loves His Son, Jesus. To say, "I *trust* God" means refusing to believe anything else but what He says, even when others think my faith is fanatic. To say, "I *trust* God" means I continue to confess what God has done for us when I have yet to experience every promise.

This kind of *trust* can only be birthed by relationship with the Father. This kind of *trust* is built when we allow the Word to transform our thinking. This kind of *trust* grows as we surrender ourselves to Him. This is the kind of *trust* I'm working on as I pray this scripture: "Let me hear of your unfailing love each morning, for I am trusting you. Show me where to walk, for I give myself to you" (Psalm 143:8 NLT).

I quote from one of my favorite hymns: *"Oh for grace to trust Him more."*

Word for the Day

SEE

I'm glad no one can read my mind, although my sisters come close to it! Only our heavenly Father can do that. He *sees* the good and the ugly. He's witnessed our greatest moments and our worst. Psalm 139:1 (NLT) says, "O LORD, you have examined my heart and know everything about me."

The amazing thing is He still loves us! I imagine He rolls His eyes when we avoid talking to Him about certain things, as though we can hide it from Him. While He *sees* our failures and faults, our Father also looks "deep within the mind and heart" to *see* His Son in us (Psalm 7:9 NLT). Every shortcoming pales when He *sees* His Son's righteousness.

What we *see* in the mirror is superficial. It's who God *sees* in us that defines us as His beloved children. There are no secrets with Him—no need to pretend. He already knows, so go ahead and share your deepest thoughts. Spill your pressing troubles that no one else can understand or do anything about. Express your most passionate desires. Whatever is important to you is important to Him.

Word for the Day

PROVIDE

Have you ever been asked what you're going to do in a dire situation? Abraham was faced with that difficult question. Genesis 22 tells how God tested his faith. Imagine hearing God say, "I want your child. I gave him to you, and now you must give him back to Me."

The scripture doesn't record backtalk or Abraham's attempt to run away from God's instructions. Abraham left the next morning with his son to carry out God's plan. Understanding they were going to make sacrifice, Isaac asks his father a question that must have pierced Abraham's heart. "'We have the fire and the wood,' the boy said, 'but where is the sheep for the burnt offering?'" (Genesis 22:7 NLT). Abraham must have gathered every ounce of faith to respond, "God will provide" (Genesis 22:8).

Today there are people who feel they have lost everything. Maybe you're one of them. May God's peace drape you in courage, strength, and faith to believe God will *provide*. Jesus says, "The thief does not come except to steal, and to kill, and to destroy. I have come that they may have life, and that they may have it more abundantly" (John 10:10 NKJV).

So what are you going to do? What's a good plan of action? Trade your "ashes for beauty" and your "mourning for the oil of joy" (Isaiah 61:3). Let me be transparent. This is not easy, but if we live by the Word and intentionally put on the "garment of praise" in difficult times, we set ourselves up for God's intervention. Our gracious Father will not ignore our obedience or our worship. Speak praise and praise Him more! Praise Him in every situation. As you praise, watch your faith soar and watch God *provide*.

Word for the Day

KNOWLEDGE

Since the days of Adam and Eve, mankind has had an appetite for *knowledge*. Magnificent minds have produced medicines, electricity, transportation, modes of communication, and so many other remarkable inventions. God created our intelligence and is well aware of our capabilities, as well as our flawed thinking. He created mankind in His image, providing everything man would ever need.

The serpent convinced Eve that the tree of *knowledge* was not what God said; rather eating fruit from the forbidden tree would be empowering and would make Adam and Eve like God. Since then, human ego has thrived on human intelligence. Having *knowledge* of truth, we are still compelled to look intelligent in the world's eyes.

According to 1 Corinthians 2:14 (NKJV), "The natural man does not receive the things of the Spirit of God, for they are foolishness to him; nor can he know them, because they are spiritually discerned." This means the world will label godly values as foolish myths. Only the Lord can open the heart of man to His truth. We simply must speak and practice truth in love—being content with knowing "the foolishness of God is wiser than men" (1 Corinthians 1:25 NKJV).

We cannot live by our own opinions, nor can we follow the crowd. Our Father has given us His Word and His Spirit. Successful Christian living requires us to align our core values with what the Word says—then be conformed to live and defend it. Truth, coupled with God's wisdom, will not be the world's philosophy, but it should always be ours.

Word for the Day

HIGH

My devotional time today took me to a favorite psalm of mine: Psalm 27. Verses 5 and 6 (NLT) say, "He will place me out of reach on a high rock. Then I will hold my head high above my enemies who surround me."

My mind flashes back to my childhood when everything was so much bigger and everyone looked so much taller than me. To get hoisted on the shoulders of my older siblings or my father was like breathing fresh air. I remember getting caught once in the ocean's rip current and my older brother swimming underneath me, lifting me above the waterline. That first gulp of air was priceless!

Sometimes we can feel smothered by the pressures of everyday living. Our problems can tower over us and attempt to drain the life out of us. The good news is problems cannot keep us suppressed when we call out to our heavenly Father. He responds to our faintest whisper and our resounding cry. He is our Rock! When we call out to Him, our Warrior God shows Himself strong (2 Chronicles 16:9)!

Are you needing a breath of fresh air? Drench your soul in the Word. Focus on the nearness of a big God. Be persistent and intentional on things that are praiseworthy (Philippians 4:8). Let your Father set you *higher*—out of reach from the enemy's lies. God's blanket of peace can revive your spirit, as though you're receiving your first breath of fresh air.

Word for the Day

FOLLOW

Most of the time when I think of the word *follow*, I picture myself in the rear. I usually think about who or what I am *following*. Today my mind wanders in the opposite direction. What *follows* me?

God promised blessing to the children of Israel if they *followed* Him. Leviticus 26 and Deuteronomy 28 promise the umbrella of blessing: abundance, security, peace, rest, victory, and the favor of God. Notice these promises are intangible and priceless, and they are passed on to each believer. What more can a person want?

The blessing cannot be earned or purchased; neither can it be stolen from us. The only way we lose the blessing is when we choose to walk away from the path of God's Word and *follow* our own desires.

A host of promises *follow* the righteous. Life as we know it has its struggles, and believers are not exempt. We can, however, take on assurance that goodness and mercy will *follow* us all our days (Psalm 23:6). *Follow* the Word of God and expect the umbrella of blessing to *follow* you!

Word for the Day

THANKFULNESS

Do you have days when gratitude pours out of you? Days when praise erupts in hallelujah tears, flowing down your cheeks? *Thankfulness* that tickles your heart so that you burst into song and laughter?

What about other days when you are wearing heaviness? We all have them. Those are the times when *thankfulness* must be performed intentionally. That's when the Lord gives us "the garment of praise for the spirit of heaviness" (Isaiah 61:3 NKJV). Psalm 50:14 (NLT) says, "Make thankfulness your sacrifice to God." In verse 23 (NLT), the Lord says, "Giving thanks is a sacrifice that truly honors me."

In Exodus 23, the children of Israel were instructed to celebrate three festivals. The first was the Festival of Unleavened Bread, celebrating their departure from Egypt. The second was the Festival of Harvest, requiring them to give the very best of their first crops to the Lord. The third was the Festival of the Final Harvest, celebrating the end of the season.

The festivals provide a model of *thankfulness* for us. As believers, we should remember where we came from, celebrating the newness of life that Christ brings to all who confess, believe, and repent. We sacrifice in *thankfulness* when we offer our best, not our leftovers. As we exit seasons, we give glory to our heavenly Father for the best of times and for bringing us through the worst. He guides us through each season of our lives.

We all enjoy the hallelujah moments, but it's the sacrificial *thankfulness* that moves the heart of God and develops us into vessels of honor.

REJECT

I tend to *reject* foods based on presentation. If it doesn't look appealing or if it has a peculiar smell, I'm not willing to try it. I'm sure I've missed out on some scrumptious dishes over the years. I've missed out on other things beside food. I've *rejected* new experiences, relationships, and adventures to stay within my comfort zone.

I've also been on the receiving end of *rejection*. I imagine you have too, but no one knows *rejection* better than our Savior. Jesus was *rejected* by the very people He came to save. He continues to be *rejected* every single day. The amazing thing? He willingly gave His life for ours, knowing mankind would *reject* what He made possible for us through the cross. His love is that fierce for every man, woman, boy, and girl! No matter what we've done, no matter how many times we come to Him for forgiveness, our loving Savior will gladly meet us with mercy and grace. The enemy may say you've gone too far, but we can *reject* his lies and receive the Word of truth.

"You will not reject a broken and repentant
heart, O God" (Psalm 51:17 NLT).

Word for the Day

LONG

Is anybody good at waiting? Not me! Waiting takes me out of my comfort zone, but it's something we all are required to do—like it or not. How we wait sets us up for the circumstances that follow. Exodus 32:1 (NLT) says, "When the people saw how long it was taking Moses to come back down the mountain, they gathered around Aaron. 'Come on,' they said, 'make us some gods who can lead us. We don't know what happened to this fellow Moses, who brought us here from the land of Egypt.'" Big mistake! The children of Israel paid a price for their failure to wait, as Moses and God had instructed.

Isn't it interesting how history repeats itself? We've been hearing all our lives that Jesus is coming back. The *long* wait has covered generations of lifetimes and has left many skeptical. We live our lives as though Jesus will not return—at least in our generation. Some professing "believers" don't even believe Jesus is coming back at all! Don't let the *long* wait fool you!

> "For you know quite well that the day of the Lord's return will come unexpectedly, like a thief in the night. So be on your guard, not asleep like the others. Stay alert and be clearheaded" (1 Thessalonians 5:2, 6 NLT).

PRESENCE

The Lord assigned Moses the task of freeing over a million people out of Egypt and leading them to another country. They were to live and possess a land that was already inhabited by others. This assignment was more challenging than what our country's best military forces can accomplish!

Moses could have let his first success go to his head, but Exodus 33 (NLT) indicates Moses knew the source of his help and strength. Moses prays to God in verse 13, "If it is true that you look favorably on me, let me know your ways so I may understand you more fully and continue to enjoy your favor." I love God's reply in verse 14: "I will personally go with you, Moses, and I will give you rest—everything will be fine for you." It's Moses's response in verse 16 that really pricks my heart today: "How will anyone know that you look favorably on me—on me and on your people—if you don't go with us? For your presence among us sets your people and me apart from all other people on the earth."

Father, it's Your *presence* in us that brings value and purpose to life. I don't want to do a day, I don't want to do an hour, without You! It's Your *presence* that divinely anoints, empowers, loves, and equips us with all we'll ever need to live—to make Your mark in this world.

I ditto the words of Moses: "How will anyone know that you look favorably on me—on me and on your people—if you don't go with us?"

WATCH

In Leviticus chapter 24, the Lord instructs Moses to keep the lamps in the tabernacle burning continuously. Verses 3 and 4 (NLT) say, "This is the lampstand that stands in the Tabernacle, in front of the inner curtain that shields the Ark of the Covenant. Aaron must keep the lamps burning in the LORD's presence all night. This is a permanent law… and it must be observed from generation to generation. Aaron and the priests must tend the lamps…continually in the LORD's presence."

As I was reading this, my mind flashed to Matthew, 25. Jesus tells a story about bridesmaids taking lamps to meet the bridegroom. Some of them brought extra oil for their lamps. The bridesmaids fell asleep as they waited. Consequently, their oil was depleted by the delayed arrival of the bridegroom. Upon hearing the news of his arrival, those who had extra oil quickly replenished their lamps and met the bridegroom. Those who failed to bring extra oil with them missed the rendezvous.

I don't know if the scriptures in the Old and New Testaments connect in meaning. The Old Testament describes a law God established for the Israelites. In the New Testament, Jesus conveys a parable describing the kingdom of heaven. However, I believe both Testament passages signify the importance of keeping *watch*. The Old Testament described the means of keeping *watch* over the ark of the covenant and the very presence of the Lord. The New Testament parable serves as a reminder to keep *watch* for the return of Jesus Christ.

Keeping *watch* involves daily commitment and constant readiness. I don't want to get side-tracked or numbed by the long wait, do you? Our destiny depends on it!

Word for the Day

IF

How can such a small word have so much power? The *if* word can set the path for dreams or destruction. The *if* word can teach or terrorize. It's not always good, and it's not always bad. It's what we do with the *if* word that makes or breaks us.

Today I was reading Numbers 14, where the children of Israel were punished for their continuous rebellion. They were ready to set foot on the land God had promised them. They had made it! This could have been a hallelujah time for the Israelites, but their continuous disobedience sent them back to the wilderness to wander for forty years. What *if* they had revered God instead of rebelling? What *if* they had trusted instead of taking matters into their own hands? What *if* they had chosen to follow God's plan?

It's easy for us to see how they could have had everything; yet we are often blinded when making our own choices. Perhaps we should implement the *if* word before we make decisions. What will God do for me *if* I surrender my life to Him and live according to His Word? For starters, check out Psalm chapters 91 and 112. These promises are ours *if* we belong to Christ, the Savior.

Every promise in the Word has a premise. Hindsight always asks what would have happened *if* we had chosen differently. Wouldn't it be wonderful *if* we could ask the important questions before we take a step?

"Guide my steps by your word, so I will not
be overcome by evil" (Psalm 119:133 NLT).

Word for the Day

ABOUT

Have you ever spoken a cross word or showed your intolerance to an undeserving person or thing? Bless my husband's heart! I'm guilty! It's really not *about* him at all. Unfortunately, he's in the range of fire.

Today I am reading Numbers 20, where Moses received a blow to his reward. Once again enduring the complaints of the people and their lack of respect and gratitude, Moses was instructed to speak to a rock and the Lord would provide water for the entire camp. Being human, tired, and frustrated with the people's attitudes, Moses struck the rock with his staff instead of speaking, as the Lord had commanded. God honored his attempt and provided the water, but He corrected Moses for his failure to follow exact instructions. Verse 12 (NLT) says, "Because you did not trust me enough to demonstrate my holiness to the people of Israel, you will not lead them into the land I am giving them!"

Moses was human, yet he is a hero to me. He carried the burden of leadership as our pastors do. He endured the complaints and fingers pointed at him when hardships came. He stood in the gap multiple times when the Lord was ready to destroy His people for their arrogance and disobedience. What makes him a hero to me is what Moses did thereafter. He didn't quit! He accepted correction and continued to lead the people until the Lord was ready to take him. He was an amazing leader and a shining example for us.

I'm learning it's not always *about* me! It should always be *about* Him.

Father, help me to have a humble, teachable spirit and surrender to Your ways and Your timing. Your correction is never comfortable, but it's always for my good.

Word for the Day

REMEMBER

As I age, I find it challenging to *remember* everything. Amid the clutter of overload, sometimes I need to hit the purge button, delete, and reformat! Seriously, when the bad stuff controls our thinking, it's time to do something about it. Do you find bad memories linger in high definition? If we were able to dissect the memories in our brain, I believe most of us would have a greater stack of good memories versus the bad. So why is it that we are consumed with the bad ones?

The devil likes to magnify the ugliness in our lives, rehearse the painful memories of the past, and make us feel like our dirty laundry is displayed on Broadway! Here's one thing we all need to *remember*: when we repent of our sins, the ugliness of the past is removed as far as the east is from the west (Psalm 103:12)! First John 1:9 (NKJV) says, "If we confess our sins, He is faithful and just to forgive us our sins and to cleanse us from all unrighteousness."

If we are good with the Creator, then we must learn how to be good to ourselves and to others. We must start filling our minds with good (Philippians 4:8). "Remember the wonders he has performed, his miracles, and the rulings he has given" (Psalm 105:5 NLT).

When we are intentional with what we *remember*, our hearts and minds will be guarded and kept safe in the hands of our loving Father.

Word for the Day

LISTEN

When someone asks a question, what makes us say, "Huh?" Sometimes we don't hear; perhaps we just speak before our brain processes what we hear. In any case, *listening* takes skill, and I could certainly benefit from developing my *listening* skills! I think the children of Israel could have too.

In Numbers 13, God told Moses to send out scouts to explore the land of Canaan—the land He was giving them. The scouts spent forty days checking it out. The land was everything God said it would be. They witnessed the beautiful, fertile country, but they also saw giants living in the land. The giants impressed them more than the words spoken by the Lord.

God had already told them He was giving them this land, but fearful thoughts, formed by the sight of giants, drowned out the words of the Lord. Their failure to *listen* cost them greatly. They spent forty days filling their mind-sets with impossibility and forty years wandering in the wilderness.

Father, help me hold on to every word You have spoken so that my circumstances don't drown out Your voice. Though my eyes may see impossibility and my circumstances appear as giants, may I choose to *listen* to Your Word.

> "Therefore do not cast away your confidence, which has great reward" (Hebrews 10:35 NKJV).

COMPARE

Why do we sometimes struggle to trust God? Perhaps we size Him up by human standards. Numbers 23:19 (NLT) opens our eyes to a great God. "God is not a man, so he does not lie. He is not human, so he does not change his mind. Has he ever spoken and failed to act? Has he ever promised and not carried it through?" Our God's faithfulness cannot be *compared*!

People's intentions can exceed their ability to make it happen, but our Father is all-powerful, and He cannot fail. He is able to do more than we can even ask or think (Ephesians 3:20). Our words may change with circumstances, but God's Word lasts forever (Psalm 119:89). Human promise may fade, but every promise in the Word stands firm—generation after generation. "He always stands by his covenant—the commitment he made to a thousand generations" (Psalm 105:8 NLT).

God is greater than what the human mind can conceive. "To whom can you compare God? What image can you find to resemble him?" (Isaiah 40:18 NLT). We often box our faith to what we know, feel, or see. God is so much bigger!

Father, help my faith soar far beyond what I can *compare*!

Word for the Day

HISTORY

While it was never my favorite subject in school, I have come to appreciate *history* and realize how important it is to our future. Psalm 107 (NLT) recites the *history* of our Father's faithfulness to His children. Verse 7 says He led His people to safety. Verse 14 says the Lord "snapped their chains." When the children of Israel cried for help, verse 20 says the Lord "sent out his word and healed them."

Our Father provides these same blessings to us through His Son, Jesus. In John 17:15, Jesus asked the Father to keep us safe from His and our enemy. In Galatians 5:1 (NLT), we are told that "Christ has truly set us free" and it's up to us to live in His freedom. First Peter 2:24 says we are healed by the stripes Jesus bore for us. Matthew 8:26 tells us that even the winds and waves obey Jesus Christ. The last verse of Psalm 107 (NLT) says it best: "Those who are wise will take all this to heart; they will see in our history the faithful love of the LORD."

When challenging times come, look back. Know "Jesus Christ is the same yesterday, today, and forever" (Hebrews 13:8 NLT). He is forever faithful!

Word for the Day

WISDOM

It's not necessarily the smartest cookie who is successful. Knowledge without *wisdom* has as much potential as a balloon without air. Our Father is the author of both, and He designed them to complement each other. We gain knowledge by developing our God-given abilities. Learning is a lifelong process, and most of us just scratch the surface.

James 1:5 (NLT) says, "If you need wisdom, ask our generous God, and he will give it to you. He will not rebuke you for asking."

Psalm 111:10 (NLT) says, "Fear of the LORD is the foundation of true wisdom. All who obey his commandments will grow in wisdom."

Having a reverent, sacred understanding of who God is puts us on the path to *wisdom*. America has removed itself from pursuing God's *wisdom*. It's no wonder our leaders can't agree on anything. Mass shootings have become common, and teachers lack respect in the classroom. This is what man produces. True *wisdom* doesn't come from within. It comes from above.

Father, You have told us that we can ask for Your *wisdom*, and it starts by living in Your Word. Open my eyes to Your greatness as My Creator, Righteousness, Healer, Defender, Provider, and Judge. May Your *wisdom* keep me on a righteous path that honors You.

Word for the Day

DAY

Psalm 118:24 (NLT) says, "This is the day the LORD has made. We will rejoice and be glad in it." Being one of the most popular verses in the Bible, we are taught it at an early age and often sing it in worship. So what is so special about this *day* that the Lord has made?

For starters, it's a clean slate.

We can't change yester*day* and tomorrow may never come, but to*day* is full of opportunity—a chance to love God with all our heart and love others.

To*day* opens the door to forgive someone who has left our spirit toxic.

To*day* we can choose to realign our priorities so that God orders our steps.

To*day* we can surrender our worries to the Lord and trust He is on it!

To*day* we can partner with our Father to make it the best one yet!

Let me be transparent: my *day* doesn't always go the way I plan. Sometimes I finish my *day* with regrets, but nothing catches my Father by surprise. He's already been there and will see me through my heartache. Lord willing, He brings a new *day* filled with His mercy and blessing.

"Choose for yourselves this day whom you will serve" (Joshua 24:15 NKJV). Your choice will make the biggest difference! Have a great *day*!

Word for the Day

PLENTY

America is blessed with *plenty*. Sadly, there are many right under our noses who do not know what it's like to have a full belly, a warm place to sleep, and a roof over their heads. If we all shared our abundance, our country would look differently. Don't misunderstand me, I fully support capitalism. The government cannot do what Christ has called us to do.

Moses warned the children of Israel of their human tendencies to forget the Lord when living in the land of *plenty*. He says in Deuteronomy 8: "When you have become full and prosperous and have built fine homes to live in…and your silver and gold have multiplied along with everything else, be careful! Do not become proud at that time and forget the LORD your God… Remember the LORD your God. He is the one who gives you power to be successful" (Deuteronomy 8:12–14, 18 NLT).

Christ commands us to love God with all we have and love others (Matthew 22:38–39). Some may have more to give, but it should never be compared; nor is it always about money. Sometimes it's a kind word, a thoughtful deed, or a listening ear.

Father, help me to realize I am living in *plenty* and that You provide the abundance—not just for me, but for those You set in my path. I pray I never get too busy or too wrapped up in my own *plenty* to miss an opportunity to share. As Your Word says, You will provide so generously that we will always have what we need and "plenty left over to share with others" (2 Corinthians 9:8 NLT).

SLUMBER

Psalm 121:2–3 (NLT) says, "My help comes from the LORD, who made heaven and earth! He will not let you stumble; the one who watches over you will not slumber."

My mind flashes to the garden of Gethsemane where Jesus asked three of His disciples to accompany Him as He prayed, just prior to His arrest and crucifixion. Knowing what was coming brought great distress to Jesus, as He told the disciples, "My soul is crushed with grief to the point of death. Stay here and watch with me" (Matthew 26:38). Jesus walked a bit farther and prayed. When he returned to the disciples, Jesus found them sleeping. He said, "Couldn't you watch with me even one hour?" (Matthew 26:40 NLT). Jesus went off to pray again, and when He returned, the disciples had fallen asleep again.

I'd like to think I would have been there for my Lord, but the truth is I have my own shortcomings. I find myself being lulled to sleep by my own weaknesses. I'm just so grateful for a heavenly Father who keeps constant watch over every single day of our lives. He never gets distracted or weary. When the busyness of the day and the pleasures of life seek to lull us into spiritual *slumber*, our Father will send the appropriate nudge to get our attention.

Father, I pray we never refuse your gentle nudges. They will keep us spiritually healthy and vibrant. Thank you for watching over us as we come and go—today and forever (Psalm 121)!

AGAIN

Repetition is an effective teaching tool. For me, doing something over and over makes it click and stick!

The children of Israel witnessed the miraculous parting of the sea when they marched out of Egypt. You would think an event of this magnitude could only happen once in a lifetime. But God parted the Jordan River for His children to enter into the land He had promised them. Joshua 3 describes how our God parted the waters *again*!

The Word shares God's faithfulness from cover to cover. There's an old chorus I grew up singing that says, *"It is no secret what God can do. What He's done for others, He'll do for you!"* He demonstrates His unmatched love *again* and *again*. He keeps watch over us when we lay our heads on the pillow, and He wakes us each morning. We don't have to wonder if He is there. Our heartbeat reminds us that He is! If we need mercy, He'll meet us with open arms. He's healed before; He'll do it *again*! "When the enemy comes in like a flood, the Spirit of the LORD will lift up a standard against him" (Isaiah 59:19 NKJV). What He does for us *again* and *again* is out of unfathomable love and teaches us to trust Him.

Father, Your blessings are beyond my ability to record. Each day brings blessing. Forgive me when I fail to recognize Your presence and Your goodness. You continue to teach me just how faithful You are. When I am less than faithful, I can come to You with a repentant heart to experience Your grace and mercy *again*. How can I not trust You?

"The faithful love of the LORD never ends!
His mercies never cease" (Lamentations 3:22 NLT).

Word for the Day

CHANGED

"There was a woman." Since the fall of Adam, there's always been a woman! In the book of Proverbs, Solomon warns men of immoral women and their destructive path. In Proverbs 21:19 (NLT), Solomon says, "It's better to live alone in the desert than with a quarrelsome, complaining wife." But can I tell you about one immoral woman whose life was *changed* and whose life *changed* history?

Her name was Rahab. She was a prostitute—the kind of woman that men used and abused. Joshua 2 tells how a couple of men were sent to check out the city of Jericho. Having learned of their coming, the king sent men to apprehend them. Fearing their God, Rahab hid the two men from the soldiers and protected their lives. The Lord helped Joshua and the Israelites destroy Jericho. What happened to Rahab? Joshua 6:25 (NLT) says, "So Joshua spared Rahab the prostitute and her relatives who were with her in the house, because she had hidden the spies Joshua sent to Jericho. And she lives among the Israelites to this day."

Here's the best part: Matthew 1 records the ancestors of Jesus Christ. Guess who's listed—Rahab! The day she showed favor on the two Israelite men (God's chosen) *changed* everything! The day we ask Jesus Christ to forgive us of our sins and invite Him to live as Lord and Savior in our hearts *changes* everything! Our past is over, and we begin living *changed* lives (2 Corinthians 5:17)! We forsake our destitute ways and become sons and daughters of the Lord God Almighty! We are called to love and serve Him with all our heart—to tell our story so that others can be *changed* too.

We may not recognize it, but our lives are *changing* history—our own and those around us. Everyone needs the mercy and grace of Jesus Christ. Everyone has a story. Share your story with the world and watch the world *change*!

Word for the Day

KIND

I have a sweet tooth. Over the past few years, I've tried to integrate healthier sweeteners, like honey, in my diet. Proverbs 16:24 (NLT) says, "Kind words are like honey—sweet to the soul and healthy for the body." The right word at the right time is priceless. Proverbs 25:11 (NKJV) says, "A word fitly spoken is like apples of gold in settings of silver."

I don't have to tell you the impact our words have. We've all been lifted up by an encouraging word and torn down by less than *kind* words. I confess I've produced hurtful words that I so regret. Some were not intentional, and unfortunately, some were. The Holy Spirit convicts me when I'm less than *kind*, and I seek forgiveness from my Father and from the receiver.

We must take ownership of our words and actions, if we are going to live the way Christ teaches. Saying "This is just the way I am" is unacceptable to our Father. He made us in His image, and that's not the way He is! And for the record, sweet words are empty calories when they are not supported by the heart. People can see through our sugar-coated talk. If they choose to digest it, they will eventually recognize the words don't match the actions.

Father, keep my heart pure and let my words be *kind*. Give me the wisdom to speak words of life. Give me the wisdom to know when to be silent. Draw my focus to others and not myself. I'm made in Your image. Now help me live in it.

Word for the Day

REMOVE

I detest clutter! I prefer everything have a home. That's not to say my life is clutter-free. Wouldn't that be a dream? God birthed a dream, in the Israelites, of a land that would be theirs for the taking. He promised to go before them and win battle after battle. He also warned them He would *remove* His favor if they failed to follow His instructions.

Joshua 7 describes such an event. God had specified that everything in Jericho was to be destroyed; only things made of silver, gold, bronze, and iron were to be spared and brought into the treasury. One man violated God's instructions and kept a little for himself. The consequence was deadly. The next battle ended in defeat for the Israelites. When Joshua asked God why He had abandoned them, God said, "Hidden among you, O Israel, are things set apart for the LORD. You will never defeat your enemies until you remove these things from among you" (Joshua 7:13 NLT).

These words pricked my heart today. The Lord reminds me that our bodies are His temple—we belong to Him. Unforgiveness, pride, selfishness, rebellion, and hopelessness (among other things) do not belong in His temple. These things take up His space, and He detests our clutter! Our Father wants us to *remove* these things to experience the freedom and favor that comes with a clean heart.

We can *remove* our clutter, but if we distance ourselves from our heavenly Father and His Word, these things will return and nest in our spirit again. How do we stay clutter-free? We must get into the Word daily and get the Word into us! The Word and the Holy Spirit will provide day-to-day maintenance and reveal what needs to be *removed*. Then it is up to us.

> "Search me, O God, and know my heart; test me and know my anxious thoughts. Point out anything in me that offends you, and lead me along the path of everlasting life" (Psalm 139:23–24 NLT).

Word for the Day

HEALTH

We don't have control of everything that affects our bodies and minds, but we should make *healthy* deposits. Our Creator wonderfully made our bodies to heal, regenerate, and filter toxins, but if we never feed it with *healthy* things, repetitive abuse eventually brings consequence. The Bible offers advice for *healthy* living.

In Proverbs 4:20–22 (NLT), Solomon says, "Listen carefully to my words. Don't lose sight of them. Let them penetrate deep into your heart, for they bring life to those who find them, and healing to their whole body."

Proverbs 14:30 (NLT) says, "A peaceful heart leads to a healthy body; jealousy is like cancer in the bones."

In Ecclesiastes 6:9 (NLT), Solomon says, "Enjoy what you have rather than desiring what you don't have."

In chapter 11, verse 10 (NLT), he says, "So refuse to worry, and keep your body healthy."

God's Word is filled with *healthy* advice, and it doesn't even cost a copay! The path to abundant living is outlined in the Scriptures. No wonder the psalmist refers to the Word as great treasure (Psalm 119:162). Our bodies will not live forever, for they are subject to the curse. But when we accept Jesus Christ as Savior and live according to His Word, we will one day trade our corruptible body for an incorruptible one and experience perfect *health* in every way. Is this not reason enough to follow the Word every day, as prescribed by the Creator?

Here's to your *health*! May God's Word bring blessing all your days on earth and bring perfect *health* in eternity!

Word for the Day

CHOICE

Have you ever made a wrong *choice* and then wanted to kick yourself for it? Life is full of *choices*. We may not always understand the consequences, and that's why it's so important to seek the wisdom of our heavenly Father. Sometimes the path is marked with warning, and we *choose* it anyway. This is what the children of Israel did (in 1 Samuel 8) when they asked Samuel for a king. They rejected the King of kings for a mere mortal man.

Who in their right mind would *choose* human strength over power of the Almighty God?

People do it every day. Our culture teaches us to look inside instead of looking up, believe in ourselves instead of believing in the Savior, trust our instincts instead of God's Word. If only people could see what they are giving up for self-gratification.

Father, I don't want to miss heaven for the world! I *choose* You! Give me wisdom to make godly *choices*. Give me eyes to see Your path and then give me courage to walk it. Give me strength to follow Your ways when the enemy entices me to follow him. Give me faith to trust Your way is best. Open my eyes to every blessing along the way, as You walk this journey with me.

What does our Father say? "Today I have given you the choice between life and death, between blessings and curses. Now I call on heaven and earth to witness the choice you make. Oh, that you would choose life, so that you and your descendants might live!" (Deuteronomy 30:19 NLT).

Word for the Day

WALL

Y ou may not have roused from your sleep to ponder the intricacies of a *wall*, but I spent a portion of the night doing so. To some people, a *wall* may suggest hopelessness, while others see it as a challenge. A *wall* can separate us, or it can shield us. It can defend us or defeat us—it all depends on how we look at it, right?

Isaiah 38 tells the story of King Hezekiah's sickness and recovery. After being told he was going to die, Hezekiah "turned his face to the wall and prayed to the LORD" (verse 2 NLT). Moved by his prayer and tears, God added fifteen more years to Hezekiah's life. There was nothing supernatural or divine about the *wall*, but I sensed the presence of the Lord in my spirit when I read how the king turned his face to the *wall* and poured his heart out to God. For me, the *wall* signifies getting into the secret place with God—unloading burdens, concerns, and needs to my heavenly Father.

Psalm 56:8 (NLT) says, "You have collected all my tears in your bottle. You have recorded each one in your book."

Psalm 126:5 (NLT) says, "Those who plant in tears will harvest with shouts of joy."

I don't know what you may be facing, but I encourage you to turn your face to the *wall* and leave your cares in the hands of the capable, Almighty God. What is important to you is important to Him. He has more than enough power to tear down the *walls* that bind you and build *walls* that sustain you.

Word for the Day

CHANGED

Isn't it fun to browse through old photo books and reminisce? Our family pages are full of hilarious hairdos, bugs bunny teeth, signature clothing, one-of-a-kind expressions, and awkward poses that invoke tearful laughter. My sister and I were known as "the girls with the hair." I think our hair was permed once a week! We already had natural curl, and the perm would quadruple the poof! Thus, we were "the girls with the hair." Looking back, I can chuckle at the photos and feel grateful that things *change* from time to time.

We all go through *changes*, but none can equal the inward *change* that Christ makes in us.

First Samuel 10 describes Saul being anointed as ruler over Israel. Samuel tells Saul, "The Spirit of the LORD will come powerfully upon you, and you will prophesy… You will be changed into a different person" (verse 6 NLT). Verse 9 (NLT) says, "As Saul turned and started to leave, God gave him a new heart, and all Samuel's signs were fulfilled that day."

I'm glad Jesus gave me a new heart. The initial *change* that happens at the moment we accept Jesus as Savior *changes* everything—our heart, our destiny, our story. While salvation is an instantaneous experience, we continue to be *changed* daily by His Spirit. Second Corinthians 3:18 (NLT) says, "The Lord—who is the Spirit—makes us more and more like him as we are changed into his glorious image."

As described in 1 Corinthians 15:51–52 (NKJV), ultimately, we shall all be *changed* "in a moment, in the twinkling of an eye, at the last trumpet." I sure don't want to miss that, do you? *Change* isn't always comfortable, but it's necessary. I pray my Father looks on with delight as He assesses the *changes* He is making in me. I am a work in progress!

SHAME

One of my favorite scripture verses says, "Those who trust in me will never be put to shame" (Isaiah 49:23 NLT). Our heavenly Father will always come through for us, will always do the right thing, will work fiercely to produce His best in us!

This doesn't mean we have a genie god in our back pocket that grants every wish and jumps at our command. If we know Jesus Christ as Savior, we have much more than that! We have the Almighty God as our Father, Redeemer, Provider, Defender, and Teacher. Our Father cherishes our trust, and He will never put it to *shame*.

I'm reminded of a strange story recorded in 1 Samuel 19, where Saul becomes envious of David and wants to kill him. Saul sends troops to capture David, but God places His Spirit over the soldiers, and they begin to prophesy! No murdering David today! Saul sends two additional sets of troops, and each time the soldiers are slain in the Spirit! Saul sets out for David himself. Guess what happens to him? The Almighty God drops his Spirit over Saul, and Saul lays "naked on the ground all day and all night, prophesying" (1 Samuel 19:24 NLT).

When Saul came to himself, I wonder how foolish he must have felt! I wonder how many of the townspeople watched and laughed. David's God is our God. He honors our faith and will never allow the enemy to prevail when we trust Him.

> "Therefore, I have set my face like a stone,
> determined to do his will. And I know that I will
> not be put to shame" (Isaiah 50:7 NLT).

Word for the Day

BEFORE

D o you know someone so well, you can predict their next move? My sister and I can look at each other and laugh, without saying a word, because we know what the other is thinking. Usually my son and I can accurately predict what his dad will say about a subject *before* he ever utters a word.

We learn a lot about the people we're around, but no one knows us like the Creator. He knows our thoughts *before* we think them and our words *before* we speak them (Psalm 139:1–4). He knows every intricate detail of our body, because He created it (Psalm 139:14). He knows how many days we have left on this earth, because He's numbered them (Psalm 139:16). He knows what's ahead and how to prepare us for it (Psalm 139:8–10).

The Lord told Jeremiah, "I knew you before I formed you in your mother's womb. Before you were born I set you apart and appointed you as my prophet to the nations" (Jeremiah 1:5 NLT).

Imagine that? God plans our life story *before* we are born! *Before* we mess it up, isn't it wise to ask Him to take charge?

Word for the Day

SAKE

I wish I had a dollar for every time I've said, "For goodness' *sake!*" While I use this phrase often, I really don't believe goodness just happens. God's mercy is not coincidental. Divine mercy constantly intercedes for your *sake* and mine. First Kings 15:4–5 (NLT) says, "For David's sake, the LORD his God allowed his descendants to continue ruling… For David had done what was pleasing in the LORD's sight and had obeyed the LORD's commands throughout his life."

When we live for God and follow His Word to the best of our ability, goodness follows us (Psalm 23:6). Just as God blessed David's descendants, He will bless our children for our *sake*. When paths of destruction grip your children, know your Father does not abandon them. It doesn't matter whether the path is chosen by them or for them. He continues to pour mercy on them for your *sake*, and He pursues them even harder for His name's *sake!* Be encouraged today—know God is working even when paths take your children to forbidden places.

Father, I pray for every parent who has a heavy heart for their children. We desire to spare our precious sons and daughters the pain and tears that come with life lessons, but we know these tests refine and birth purpose into them. Thank You for reminding us today that You are watching over them for our *sake*, and You are fiercely pursuing them for Your name's *sake*. Amen.

Word for the Day

ETERNAL

I gave Molly, my grand-dog, a squeaky toy for Christmas. I knew the toy wouldn't last long—maybe for a day (or less). Molly thinks she's a surgeon, and the squeaky thing needs to come out! She has fun with it for a little while, and that's what counts.

Life as we know it today is temporary. Frankly, we're better off to embrace it this way. When life gets hard, we can be thankful to know the trouble is temporary. When everything is going well, we can be grateful for the season and allow the Lord to prepare us for life's next jolt.

We have very little control over what happens tomorrow, but if we know Jesus, we know the one who controls it all—the one who made it all. There is nothing too hard for Him (Jeremiah 32:17)! He has given us an advocate who will never leave us (John 14:16). That's an *eternal* promise! As David quotes in 1 Chronicles 17:27 (NLT), "When you grant a blessing, O LORD, it is an eternal blessing!"

There's an old hymn that says, "*This world is not my home. I'm only passing through*." What the world offers is temporary, and that's a good thing. What our heavenly Father offers is *eternal*, and that's everything!

Word for the Day

SINK

Ezekiel 2 describes the calling and commission of Ezekiel to take the Lord's message to the people of Israel. The Spirit of the Lord warns Ezekiel the people are rebellious; nevertheless, he should relay the Lord's messages, whether they listen or not. The message would be hard, because the people's hearts were hard. In chapter 3, verses 10 and 11 (NLT), the Lord tells Ezekiel, "Let all my words sink deep into your own heart first. Listen to them carefully for yourself. Then go to your people in exile and say to them, 'This is what the Sovereign LORD says!' Do this whether they listen to you or not."

God has given us His Word for the world. Some will listen, and some will not. But first, just as the Lord told Ezekiel, we must allow His Word to *sink* deep within us. That's when our testimony becomes effective. The Word must prepare us before we can attempt to prepare others. If we fail to get rooted in the Word ourselves, the world can justifiably say, "Hypocrite! First get rid of the log in your own eye" (Matthew 7:5 NLT).

Father, may Your Word *sink* into the deepest core of our beings. It's Your Word hidden in our hearts that keeps us on a righteous path (Psalm 119:11) and prepares us to be a light to the world (Matthew 5:16).

344

KNOW

One consistent phrase that God speaks throughout His Word is, "Then you will know that I am the Lord." From the beginning, our Creator has desired us to *know* Him. The Bible is filled with miracles and supernatural events pointing us to the Almighty God. Throughout history, the Lord has lavished His goodness and executed His judgment on mankind so that we would *know* He is Lord!

I'm reminded of the wise advice David gives his son, Solomon: "Learn to know the God of your ancestors intimately. Worship and serve him with your whole heart and a willing mind. For the LORD sees every heart and knows every plan and thought. If you seek him, you will find him. But if you forsake him, he will reject you forever" (1 Chronicles 28:9 NLT).

Solomon went on to seek the Lord and ask for wisdom. Moved by his sincere request, the Lord made Solomon the wisest man ever. Our Father will use circumstances to move us toward Him—to show us He is LORD. He pursues us in every good thing and in every hard thing. What must He do to get our attention?

Father, help us to seek You in every part of our lives, withholding nothing. Thank you for pursuing me, as I'm prone to wander. You *know* everything about me, and amazingly, You still pursue me with Your fierce affection. Open my eyes to Your Word and Your ways, that I might *know* You more intimately every day. There are so many who desperately need You! Show Yourself strong! When You do what no one else can do; when You do the unexplainable, the world will take notice. Then they will *know* who You are!

Word for the Day

WEARY

If we make a donation to a worthy cause, we can expect to receive an influx of appeals from others. If we spend quality time with a child, they will want to spend time with us. If we feed a hungry animal, it may return for another meal. Why? Living things respond to goodness.

Once we open our hearts and give, generosity becomes our signature. Sometimes we can get *weary* doing good things. What's the remedy? Pause to reflect on the goodness that's been shown to us. Gratitude will take care of the attitude. I'm reminded of David's prayer, recorded in 1 Chronicles 29:14 (NLT), "But who am I, and who are my people, that we could give anything to you? Everything we have has come from you, and we give you only what you first gave us!"

Our health, our strength, our resources, and our talents come from the Creator. Our abundance is given to share. We all have something to give. My gifts may pale to yours, but when I give from the heart, others will be blessed and so will I. There is nothing we can give that the Lord has not given us first, so "let us not grow weary while doing good" (Galatians 6:9 NKJV).

Word for the Day

ME

Life is all about *me*—at least my flesh thinks so. As Psalm 139:14 (NKJV) says, "I am fearfully and wonderfully made; Marvelous are Your works, And that my soul knows very well." The part that is all about *me*, however, is not God-made. This devotional may be just for *me*, so if you stop reading here, that's okay.

The *me* word can be haunting, and my Father has brought His Word full-face today to address the *me* thing. In 2 Chronicles 1, God appears to Solomon and asks him what he wants, telling Solomon He will give him whatever he asks. There's no doubt my response would have been different from Solomon's. I'm sure I would have asked for things that would have made my life more comfortable. Solomon, however, asked for wisdom to lead God's people.

What was God's response to Solomon? "Because your greatest desire is to help your people, and you did not ask for wealth, riches, fame, or even the death of your enemies or a long life… I will certainly give you the wisdom and knowledge you requested. But I will also give you wealth, riches, and fame such as no other king has had before you or will ever have in the future!" (2 Chronicles 1:11–12 NLT).

Our Creator can give us anything, but He wants us to desire Him over everything. Sometimes this requires suffering, patience, and all the side effects that come with growing an intimate relationship with the Lord. Is it worth it? Absolutely! Either He is Lord of all or really not Lord at all.

Father, I want You to be Lord of my life. I confess the *me* part doesn't always reflect the obedience and honor You deserve, but thank You for looking past the surface of my selfishness. Thank You for continuing to work on *me* with gentleness and patience. How can I do life without You?

Word for the Day

CLOUD

I'm a sunshine girl! The sun fuels my energy, mind-set, and often drives my activity for the day. A *cloudy* day is surely not my favorite, as it has an opposite effect on me. You might say it *clouds* my thinking (pardon the pun!).

Favorite or not, the *clouds* nurture life. Without them, there would be no rain and living things would soon parch to become extinct. If we had no *clouds*, we would never experience the beauty of the rainbow. It takes the *clouds* to appreciate the sun.

Do you ever feel like you're living on top of a *cloud* or living under one? Our Father is the creator of both. We are designed to thrive under their influence. I'm no longer speaking of the physical elements. I'm referring to seasons that create God's character in us. Our Father allows us to spend some time under the *cloud* to learn how to appreciate His goodness, to cultivate growth, and blossom into His likeness. It's there that we get rooted and grounded in His truth.

The season does not last forever. We are not destined nor meant to dwell indefinitely under the *cloud*. Our Creator wants us to thrive. If you're living under a *cloud*, I want to encourage you to dig into God's Word and soak in all you can. As often depicted in the Scriptures, you'll find the Lord there. God is preparing you for the next season, so don't plan on setting up house under the *cloud*! God has more for you.

"When troubles of any kind come your way, consider it an opportunity for great joy. For you know that when your faith is tested, your endurance has a chance to grow. So let it grow, for when your endurance is fully developed, you will be perfect and complete, needing nothing" (James 1:2–4 NLT).

REMEDY

The worldwide web provides a *remedy* for just about everything. What works for one doesn't work for all, but sometimes they're worth a try. Do you need a *remedy* for worry? The most effective one I know is this: Trust God. The *remedy* is simple, but its practice is challenging.

How do we develop trust? We must first understand trusting God is a process that is connected to spiritual growth. When we are in a growing season, we are in a trust-building season. While there is a wealth of benefits to be gained, this season takes us out of control and away from our comfort level. A trust-building season will test our endurance and leave us feeling weak. None of us enjoy being there, but that's how we learn to lean on our Father's strength, not our own.

How do we develop trust? Next, we get into the Word and get the Word into us. We cannot rely on feeling; instead, we must practice what the Word says. Worry will always send us in the wrong direction if we follow our emotions. The Word of God is more than ink on paper. It is living and powerful and has the ability to change us and change our circumstances (Hebrews 4:12).

How do we develop trust? We choose to practice intentional behavior. We say what the Word says, until we can do what the Word says. We combat every hell-sent thought with the Word. We cannot control the thoughts that enter the mind, but we can control what we do with them. "If there is anything praiseworthy—meditate on these things" (Philippians 4:8 NKJV).

The *remedy* is simple. Putting it into practice is the challenging part, but oh the rewards that await us.

Word for the Day

STILL

Second Chronicles 20 describes how God's people find themselves surrounded by attacking nations. King Jehoshaphat calls for the people to fast. The Spirit moves on a man to tell the people what they must do. "This is what the LORD says: Do not be afraid! Don't be discouraged by this mighty army, for the battle is not yours, but God's...you will not even need to fight. Take your positions; then stand still and watch the LORD's victory" (2 Chronicles 20:15, 17 NLT).

The odds were greatly against Judah, but they followed the Lord's instructions and watched Him win the battle. Verse 24 (NLT) says, "Not a single one of the enemy had escaped." The men of Judah showed great courage to stand *still*. They stood *still* when everything inside them screamed to run for their lives and hide. It took more courage to stand *still* than fight to the bitter end.

What they could do on their own would never have saved them. Perhaps you are surrounded by situations that are draining the life out of you. Are you running from one person to the next for advice? Maybe your impulses are dictating your next move. May I encourage you to seek God and His Word to determine your next step. Matthew 7:7 (NKJV) says, "Seek, and you will find."

Your Father may tell you to move forward when you see nothing but the Red Sea in front of you. He may tell you to stand *still* when everything inside of you is ready to strike. Action requires courage and courage requires faith. God knows best. We must get *still* before the Lord to get His leading so that every step moves us to victory. Trust Him! You'll be glad you did!

Word for the Day

FIRST

There's something special about the word *first*. Can you think about all the *firsts* in your life? The stories might be comical, or there may be details you'd rather not share. We all love the feeling of winning *first* place. What about the *first* date, the *first* kiss? Of all the memorable *firsts*, none will compare with the *first* day we spend in heaven.

The moment we slip into eternity, our loved ones will be there and the sights will be spectacular. We'll have a glorified body absent from the weight of mortality. I don't know what a glorified body will be like, but I believe every inch and every layer will be perfect. Can you imagine living in a body like that? Try recalling the greatest day on earth and magnify it a hundred billion times! Dazzling lights will display streaks of brilliant colors we've never experienced. Then we see Jesus!

As I am writing this devotion, my precious mother-in-law just spent her *first* day in heaven. I wish I could read her *first* journal entry. Jesus said, "I am the resurrection and the life. Anyone who believes in me will live, even after dying" (John 11:25 NLT).

What will our *first* day in heaven really be like? Only heaven knows! The important thing is to know our names are written in the Book of Life (Revelation 3:5) so we may someday experience the *first* of forever!

Word for the Day

SORRY

Reading 2 Chronicles 21 (NLT), I came across a sad phrase in verse 20: "No one was sorry when he died." The phrase was describing Jehoram, king of Judah. Jehoram's father was remembered as a good king, pleasing the Lord. Unfortunately, Jehoram didn't follow the legacy of his father. He killed his own brothers and led the people of Israel to worship idols. Verse 19 (NLT) says, "His people did not build a great funeral fire to honor him as they had done for his ancestors."

How sad is it to come to the end of life and find no one with a kind word? How awful it would be to have these words recorded: "No one was sorry when he died." Second Corinthians 9:6 (NLT) says, "Remember this—a farmer who plants only a few seeds will get a small crop. But the one who plants generously will get a generous crop."

Father, I desire my daily living to please You. What I do in my home should honor You. What I do for my neighbors should reflect You. What I do for the least should mirror You. I desire to plant generously in Your character. I won't please everyone, but when I am living Your character, I will spread generosity. When my actions come short of Your character, teach me to be *sorry*. A repentant heart brings change on my part and forgiveness by You and others. Teach me to live Your character today and every day, to do what I can while I can. I quote a phrase of an old song from my childhood days, "*Then my living shall not be in vain.*"

PRESS

I love to *press* buttons. Give me a calculator and a row of figures to add, and I'm entertained for hours! I am deliberately using the word *press* instead of *push*. For me, they carry different connotations. I don't like to push buttons, as this usually invokes conflict.

To settle conflict in our own lives, I believe it's critical to find healing by *pressing* forward. There are hurtful situations we may never forget, but the hurt will infect our deepest core if we choose to dwell in it. When we choose to *press* forward, we can transform our test into a testimony. We can learn from the past and be equipped to make better decisions for the future. Our scars can become trophies of victory, instead of images of victimization.

Hurt is personal. I may not understand yours and you may not understand mine, but there is a Savior who has experienced more hurt than you and I can fathom. He understands when no one else does. He has given us an action plan in His Word to implement healing. If we follow His Word and *press* forward, we can comfort others who are going through difficult times. Second Corinthians 1:4 (NLT) says, "He comforts us in all our troubles so that we can comfort others."

We can embrace patience and purpose for our troubles, or we can *press* the "back button" to rehearse them over and over, as our days are squandered away. I wouldn't dream of demeaning your troubles, but I can tell you there is a Savior who's been there and cares. I believe He wants us to *press* forward today and allow Him to make the most of who we can be in Him.

If you find yourself living in your hurtful past, ask the Lord to show you His plan in the Word. Then choose to live it every day. God will give you the steps and the strength to *press* forward. "I focus on this one thing: Forgetting the past and looking forward to what lies ahead, I press on to reach the end of the race and receive the heavenly prize for which God, through Christ Jesus, is calling us" (Philippians 3:13–14 NLT).

Word for the Day

PRESCRIPTION

I support natural wellness. I believe our Creator supplied us with healing supplements in the earth's soils, plants, and waters to help our bodies heal themselves. Given the proper environment, our bodies are miraculously sustainable. However, there may be times when we need more. Thank God for physicians and nurses who have dedicated their lives to aid the healing process. I've often told my family there's no need in seeing a doctor, if we're not going to follow orders and take what is *prescribed*.

The Word provides an array of *prescriptions* for the soul, body, and mind. Take fasting, for example. The Old Testament is full of accounts where people fasted, prayed, and received God's mercy. Jesus fasted, and He gives us instructions for doing the same. Fasting is one of many Bible-taught principles that matures us spiritually, but did you know fasting can be physically beneficial?

The *prescriptions* provided to us in His Word not only heal the soul but bring healing to us physically and emotionally. Our Creator connected the body, soul, and mind to feed each other. When we obey His Word, healing comes to all three.

Do you have an ailment? His *prescription* for you may involve forgiveness. His *prescription* may require a heavy dose of intentional praise. His *prescription* may instruct you to take a soaking in the Word. The *prescriptions* we need are readily available, but we must follow the Great Physician's orders. "Trust in the LORD with all your heart; do not depend on your own understanding. Seek his will in all you do, and he will show you which path to take. Don't be impressed with your own wisdom. Instead, fear the LORD and turn away from evil. Then you will have healing for your body and strength for your bones" (Proverbs 3:5–8 NLT).

Word for the Day

BUILD

Have you read the book of Nehemiah? It's a great read! Nehemiah has a beautiful testimony that brings encouragement and an action plan to those who face challenges. Nehemiah describes how he goes to Jerusalem to help his people *rebuild* the city wall. Returning from captivity, the Jews come home to a desecrated city. The wall has been torn down and the gates burned. They leave a land of wealth and come home to a city of ruins.

Feeling compelled to help, Nehemiah seeks favor from the Lord. He asks for a leave of absence, from King Artaxerxes, to go to Jerusalem and help *rebuild* the city. Furthermore, he asks for letters authorizing the work and requests *building* materials. In chapter 2, verse 8 (NLT), Nehemiah says, "The king granted these requests, because the gracious hand of God was on me."

Nehemiah brings hope and a plan to his people. (We see people hurting every day—hopeless and helpless. As believers in Christ, we have a hope to share. This hope involves more than a quick prayer and a pat on the back). Let me get back to the story. As the people of Judah begin to *build* the wall, they meet opposition from their enemies. In Nehemiah 4:14 (NLT), Nehemiah tells them, "Don't be afraid of the enemy! Remember the Lord, who is great and glorious, and fight for your brothers, your sons, your daughters, your wives, and your homes!" They strap weapons by their sides and continue to *build*. A trumpeter is on call to signal an alarm when the enemy approaches. Together, they assemble to defend their families and their city.

Maybe you feel your life is crumbling around you and you need help *building* a wall of protection around your home. You don't have to do it alone! The Lord will strategically place believers in your path. *Building* from ruins requires seeking the *direction* of God, obtaining the *favor* of God, sharing the *hope* of God, uniting by the *love* of God, and fighting with the *power* of God.

Yes, this is how we *build* a protective wall around our homes. The community of believers must come together to protect what is ours. Unified with God leading us, we can *build* the Kingdom: one soul at a time, one family, one city, our nation, even our neighbors across the globe. This is how we save the world with the message of salvation!

SERVE

One of my favorite verses in the Old Testament is Joshua 24:15 (NLT), "But as for me and my family, we will serve the LORD." These are some of Joshua's final words to the Israelites. He instructs the children of Israel to *serve* the Lord wholeheartedly—to *serve* God and Him alone.

Jesus says in Matthew 6:24 (NLT), "No one can serve two masters." Either Jesus is Lord of all or not really Lord at all in our lives. God doesn't share His throne. Just as the children of Israel struggled with idol worship, our human desire for relationship, security, and acceptance can be dictating. Our Father doesn't impose lordship. He doesn't have to, because He is Lord—always has been, always will be! Rather, He freely gives us the opportunity to choose Him as Lord.

I made my choice at the age of five years old, and my heavenly Father has been longsuffering with all my fumbles throughout the years. It doesn't matter if we are five years old or ninety-five. What really counts is making the choice to *serve* Christ now while we can and knowing He is our Lord and Savior when we take our final breath.

Word for the Day

MOMENT

Waiting is not in my comfort zone, and I don't like it! I want to see action the *moment* I ask for it. My heavenly Father is teaching me, however, that my "wants" nor my timing always line up with His best for me. There are other times my desires and prayers are His delight.

In chapter 9, Daniel offers a prayer of sincere repentance for his sins and those of his people. Moved with compassion, the Lord immediately sends His angel, Gabriel, to Daniel to deliver this personal message: "The moment you began praying, a command was given. And now I am here to tell you what it was, for you are very precious to God" (Daniel 9:23 NLT).

Our Father hears our prayers the *moment* we speak them. Psalm 147:15 (NKJV) says, "He sends out His command to the earth; His word runs very swiftly." First John 5:14–15 (NKJV) says, "Now this is the confidence that we have in Him, that if we ask anything according to His will, He hears us. And if we know that He hears us, whatever we ask, we know that we have the petitions that we have asked of Him."

Our heavenly Father is always listening! We must trust He is deliberate, precise, just, and loving with every command He gives on our behalf. "Listen! The Lord's arm is not too weak to save you, nor is his ear too deaf to hear you call" (Isaiah 59:1 NLT).

Word for the Day

WORD

Who gets the last *word* in your household? In mine, I suppose it depends on the subject and the passion behind it. Have you ever thought about the impact our *words* have? Proverbs 15:4 (NLT) says, "Gentle words are a tree of life; a deceitful tongue crushes the spirit."

Our *words* can bring blessing or curse on us and those around us. "The tongue can bring death or life; those who love to talk will reap the consequences" (Proverbs 18:21 NLT). This makes me want to watch my *words*. I desire to make my *words* few (Ecclesiastes 5:2) and make my *words* count (Proverbs 22:17–21).

Unfortunately, *words* of regret cannot be erased. We can make amends, and we should; however, a spoken *word* is irreversible. There is only one whose *words* are always wise, precise, appropriate, and worthy of following: our Lord and Savior, Jesus Christ. His *Word* sets us free, brings healing to soul, body, and mind, changes us from the inside out, and sets our destination to heaven. At the end of the day, my opinion really doesn't matter. Only His *Word* counts! Following the trend may generate popularity, but following His *Word* makes us prosperous in every way.

Father, teach me to live by Your *Word* daily. I resolve to seek Your *Word* for direction, understanding, wisdom, and clarity. Your truth not only guarantees my success in getting to heaven, but Your *Word* gives me all the life lessons I need to become the person You've created me to be. May You always have the last *word* in my heart and in everything I say and do!

CAN

As a child, I remember reading the book entitled *The Little Engine That Could*. It's a delightful classic fairytale that motivates us to reach our potential. What we do in life starts with what we think we *can* do. The higher we raise the standard of potential, the more we accomplish.

What we *can* do, however, is not founded in a classic fairytale; rather, our potential lies in the Creator. Philippians 4:13 (NKJV) says, "I can do all things through Christ who strengthens me." From cover to cover, the Bible is filled with ordinary people who conquered, persevered, and did extraordinary things.

Let's name a few. Noah built a boat, of extraordinary proportions, that would save his family and every kind of animal from global flood.

David slew a giant who significantly towered him in size, strength, armor, and battle experience.

Daniel camped overnight in a den of ferocious lions.

Peter stepped out of a boat, in the middle of a storm, and walked on water.

Paul triumphantly endured beatings, stoning, being shipwrecked, and imprisoned.

Let's not forget the women! Deborah served as a judge to Israel for forty years, leading with impeccable faith and wisdom.

Hannah gave the Lord a child, for which she had persistently prayed, modeling the stature of a prayer warrior and demonstrating total surrender.

Then there's Mary—the young woman created to mother the Son of God! Could there be a greater calling? With exceptional honor came exceptional suffering. How could she explain the pregnancy? How could Mary bear to witness the horrific torture and death of her son?

Yes, these women and men were extraordinary, making their mark in history. Being human—just like you and me—these individuals (and so many more) allowed the Creator to take charge. If we do the same, we *can* be all God intends. Otherwise, the world will never know the person we could have been.

SECRET

Can I tell you a *secret*? We don't have a single one! According to Psalm 139, there's not an action taken, a word spoken, or thought entertained, that our Creator doesn't know. Only God has *secrets* (Deuteronomy 29:29 NLT).

When I think about my Father knowing everything I've ever done, said, or thought, I'm amazed that He still loves me. I quickly get people-intolerant from what I can observe, and I don't know the half of it! Oh, how blessed we are to have our Father's love—to know our repentance moves His heart, to know He sees the righteousness of His Son, Jesus, in us instead of our failures. He sees us as His sons and daughters. Of course, He isn't blind to our faults. He's well aware of every *secret* sin, but He's also delighted with our desire to please Him. He hears beyond our spoken words and sees past our shelled exterior.

Our Father discerns the cries from our souls and sees who we really are. We may fool others and even ourselves, but the Creator "knows the secrets of every heart" (Psalm 44:21 NLT). He knows our individual weaknesses. That's why He has given us the Holy Spirit to show us a right path and correct us when we stray from it. Sometimes we try to ignore the Holy Spirit when He reveals a *secret* sin, but because of His love for us, the Spirit will continue to tug at our heart. Because of our love for Him, we choose to obey, face our denial, and lay it at the feet of Jesus. We may not enjoy the purging process, but the healing is totally worth it!

When we face a *secret* sin and allow the blood of Jesus to cover it, that sin is forgiven—never to be revealed or remembered by our

Father. "He has removed our sins as far from us as the east is from the west" (Psalm 103:12 NLT). We have no *secrets*! Trying to harbor one can be toxic, putting our spiritual, physical, and emotional health in danger. We must take it to the Lord. He already knows!

Word for the Day

MESSAGE

Have you ever tried to tell someone something, and they just don't get it? God gave Malachi a *message* for the children of Israel. The Lord starts with "I have always loved you" (Malachi 1:2 NLT). He reminds His children that they have always been the apple of His eye, but He goes on to describe how they have failed to love Him in return. The *message* God gives Malachi is clear and precise. Just in case the Israelites are not aware, the Lord spells out the error of their ways.

They are giving Him their leftovers. Instead of offering unblemished animals for sacrifice, they are using animals that are not fit for anything else. The Lord's *message* also addresses the priests of that day. They have strayed from the truth and are causing people to practice false doctrines. The Lord continues by saying, "You cry out, 'Why doesn't the LORD accept my worship?' I'll tell you why! Because the LORD witnessed the vows you and your wife made when you were young. But you have been unfaithful to her, though she remained your faithful partner, the wife of your marriage vows" (Malachi 2:14 NLT). Then the Lord accuses His children of cheating Him by failing to pay their tithes and give offerings. Lastly, the Lord reminds them that justice is coming.

Reading Malachi's *message* from the Lord hits home!

The Lord deserves more than my leftovers.

My daily living will be measured by the Word of God, for which I will be accountable—nothing more or less.

Vows are sacred, and I must be faithful to them.

My Father deserves my first fruits. When I give Him the first fruits of my time, talents, and resources, He will bless the rest!

Yes, Lord, the *message* is for me too, and I get it!

Word for the Day

GOOD

Have you ever had too much of a *good* thing, like indulging at the table and turning a wonderful meal into an evening of indigestion? Exodus 16 describes how God supplied the children of Israel with manna in the mornings and quail in the evening. The Lord provided instructions on how much manna was to be collected daily. The people were told not to save any of it for the next day.

Being natured as people are, some tried to keep the manna anyway, only to discover it would rot by morning. Furthermore, the Lord instructed the children of Israel to collect twice the amount as usual on the sixth day so that the seventh day would be a day of complete rest. And being natured as people are, some tried to go out on the seventh day, but they found no manna.

God has a plan for us. When we follow it, the *goodness* of God follows us (Psalm 23:6). When we skirt around God's plan, we leave the umbrella of His blessing and protection.

Father, forgive me for my stubborn ways. Thank you for nudging me back on track when I begin to pursue my own direction. I desire to live according to Your Word. Your plan is always best and has my *good* in mind.

> "For the LORD God is a sun and shield; The LORD will give grace and glory; No good thing will He withhold From those who walk uprightly" (Psalm 84:11 NKJV).

WORK

I have a question for you. If you knew you were going to meet your Maker tomorrow, what would you do differently today? That's a loaded question, isn't it? Maybe we would blow our diets and eat everything in sight! (I confess the thought crosses my mind!) Maybe we would take one last shopping spree. Perhaps we would call a friend or a family member and attempt to resolve a dispute.

I wouldn't be packing a suitcase, but I'm confident I would be packing my soul with the Word, asking God to clean up my heart (Psalm 51:10) and making one final attempt to get others ready to go! When it comes to Kingdom *work*, I tend to procrastinate, and that's not even my personality!

We know our Savior's return is soon, and we know our personal days are numbered, but the uncertainty of the "day" numbs its urgency. When we're young, we think we will have more time when we're older. Then when we're older, we think our window of time has passed and the younger folks can do it better.

My Father reminds me today that our *work* for Him is far more valuable than anything else we put our hands and minds to—young or old. What we achieve here stays here. Our houses, our bank accounts, our "things" won't go with us, but our Kingdom *work* will continue to matter. Our Kingdom *work* will affect our children and our children's children. Our Kingdom *work* may change the destiny of a family member, a neighbor, a stranger, even a community. Our *work* may be in seed form—small and hidden from view—but God's Word will bring it to fruition at His appointed time. "It is the same with my word. I send it out, and it always produces fruit. It will accomplish all I want it to, and it will prosper everywhere I send it" (Isaiah 55:11 NLT).

At the end of the day, what do my accomplishments look like? Who cares? Our Father does! "Always work enthusiastically for the Lord, for you know that nothing you do for the Lord is ever useless" (1 Corinthians 15:58 NLT).

ONLY

The writer of Psalm 80 (NLT) repeats this verse three times: "Make your face shine down upon us. Only then will we be saved." The writer is appealing to the Lord for help. He acknowledges that the children of Israel have made life about everything else except God. It's easy to find ourselves in the same predicament, especially when life is going well.

As we consume our time with life's pleasures, our time seeking the Lord often dwindles. We begin to venture away from God's umbrella of protection. Before long, the enemy entangles us in our own web. Our Father waits patiently as we attempt to wrestle our way out. Exhausted and broken, it's then we cry out for help, knowing God is the *only* one who can save us. We look up and find God. He's right there. He's been there the whole time—ready, willing, and capable. *Only* God loves us this much!

Father, I confess I am prone to wander. Thank You for Your faithfulness when I am less than faithful. I desire to seek You daily so that Your face shines graciously upon me. *Only* You are God (Deuteronomy 4:39)! *Only* You are the way, the truth, and the life (John 14:6)! You sent Your *only* Son into the world so we can live with You eternally (1 John 4:9). If that were the *only* thing you ever did for us, it would be more than we could ever repay—more than we would ever deserve!

NAME

O ur *name* can be a powerful possession. While it's not an accurate measure, we are often judged by our *name*. It has the power to label us—be it good or bad. Our *name* may open doors for us or close them, turn heads or go unnoticed. Have you ever been in a crowd and hear your *name* called? It gets your attention, doesn't it? But there is one *name* above all! There's something about the *name* of *Jesus*!

When we speak the *name* of Jesus, our Father is drawn to His *name*! I can only imagine how angered He must become when His Son's *name* is spoken with no regard for the respect it deserves. I can only imagine how delighted He becomes when His Son's *name* is breathed in praise, honor, and worship. I love to visualize our Father's response to the *name* of Jesus as we cry out for help.

Because Jesus has given us His *name*, we can go to the throne of grace for anything—everything. No other *name* can do that! No other *name* can move heaven and earth on our behalf. We are surrounded by family and friends and blessed with shelter, food, and so many comforts. These things bring value to our lives, but they can never bring the one thing the *name* of Jesus brings: relationship with the Father. May the most honorable *name* of Jesus be forever cherished in my heart, soul, and mind.

> "There is salvation in no one else! God has given no other name under heaven by which we must be saved" (Acts 4:12 NLT).

Word for the Day

STUMBLE

Are you one of those people who like to shop Black Friday? I tried it a couple of times, and it didn't work for me! I don't like being pushed, prodded, and poked. And patience? Well, it takes all the patience I have, and then I'm left with none for the rest of the week! I guess I'll stick to shopping Black Friday online.

Psalm 105 describes the incredible things God did for the children of Israel. Verse 37 (NLT) says, "The LORD brought his people out of Egypt, loaded with silver and gold; and not one among the tribes of Israel even stumbled." Reading this, my mind flashes back to Black Friday shopping. The shopping crowd can't compare to the exodus crowd! The number of people who walked out of Egypt that day is reported to be thousands to millions. In any case, the number is vastly higher than a Black Friday shopping day!

The children of Israel were loaded with silver, gold, and possibly some provisions, yet the scripture says not even one *stumbled*! This miracle could have only been accomplished by the Lord's hand. Psalm 119:165 (NKJV) says, "Great peace have those who love Your law, And nothing causes them to stumble."

The enemy wants us to think we're walking this journey alone, but our Warrior God has equipped us with everything we need to stand our ground. His Word imparts the knowledge and wisdom we need to stay upright. Proverbs 3:21–23 (NKJV) says, "Keep sound wisdom and discretion; So they will be life to your soul And grace to your neck. Then you will walk safely in your way, And your foot will not stumble."

When temptation is walking on your heels, find confirmation and strength in the Word. Ask the Lord to empower you to do what the Word says. When you feel like you're walking alone, know the Holy Spirit never leaves you. He knows your next step and will prepare you. Our Father led an army of people out of Egypt without one accident or incident. Surely, He can guide us in our journey.

Word for the Day

PROMISE

We often view movies depicting the simple life of earlier years, where a man's word was enough. His word was binding and respected as much as a written contract. I believe there are honorable men today whose handshake and word are enough. That being said, the breaking of a *promise* is not just a product of this generation. *Promises* have been broken since the fall of Adam.

I believe we are all susceptible to breaking a *promise*—be it intentional or out of our control. The only one with a perfect record is our heavenly Father, Creator, and Savior. Psalm 138:2 (NLT) says, "Your promises are backed by all the honor of your name." I just love that! When God says it, we can believe it! Why? It's God saying it! All of heaven is behind His Word (2 Chronicles 18:18)!

He never comes up short of His Word. Nothing is ever out of His control. All eight thousand plus *promises* He has made are sure and dependable; furthermore, they are for you and me! Psalm 146:6 (NLT) says, "He made heaven and earth, the sea, and everything in them. He keeps every promise forever."

> "Abraham never wavered in believing God's promise. In fact, his faith grew stronger, and in this he brought glory to God. He was fully convinced that God is able to do whatever he promises" (Romans 4:20–21 NLT).

Are you fully convinced? "Let us hold tightly without wavering to the hope we affirm, for God can be trusted to keep his promise" (Hebrews 10:23 NLT).

JOY

You may remember the story of Samson and Delilah—the infamous story in the Bible about Delilah's quest to discover the source of Samson's supernatural strength. His enemies could not conquer him until Delilah tricked Samson into sharing his secret. Delilah pulled out all her tricks we ladies sometimes use. She poured on the charm, persistently nagged him, and pouted when Samson teased her with false concoctions about his strength. Samson eventually confided in Delilah, telling her his strength came from his uncut hair. Being dedicated to God as a Nazirite from birth, no scissors had ever touched his head. As long as Samson remained loyal to the Nazirite custom, God's strength would be with him.

I remember learning this story as a young girl. Here I am so many years later, and the Lord reminds me of the source of my strength: *joy*. Nehemiah 8:10 says it's the *joy* of the Lord that is our strength. You know who else knows our source of strength? The enemy knows. He knows the Word as well as you and I do. The devil quoted the Word to Jesus as he was tempting Him in the wilderness (Matthew 4).

So what do you think the devil continuously attacks? You guessed it—our *joy*. He puts trouble in our paths to steal our *joy* and replace it with worry and confusion. If we don't fight for our *joy*, continuous struggles can eventually wear us down. How do we fight for *joy*? I know you've heard the old cliché that spells the word *joy*: *J*esus first, *o*thers second, and *y*ourself last. Old as it is, this is a good action plan.

Maintain your relationship with Jesus, first and foremost. Get into His presence by getting into His Word. Ask for what you need in the name of Jesus (John 16:24). Then turn your expectation to receiving what you've asked for. Combat every thought of "what-if" with "what I have" and "whose I am." Go ahead and turn on your favorite praise music. Step up your praise game and allow gratitude to shift the attitude.

Do something for someone else. When you attempt to bless others, you'll find a blessing coming right back at you "in full—pressed down, shaken together to make room for more, running over, and poured into your lap" (Luke 6:38 NLT).

It's okay to take care of yourself too! Find some "me" time. Some people enjoy alone time while others prefer buddy time. Whether alone or with others, make time to do something fun and enjoyable. Proverbs 17:22 (NLT) says, "A cheerful heart is good medicine, but a broken spirit saps a person's strength."

> "I pray that God, the source of hope, will fill you completely with joy and peace because you trust in him. Then you will overflow with confident hope through the power of the Holy Spirit" (Romans 15:13 NLT).

Final Word for the Day

TESTIMONY

Twenty-one months after experiencing disaster, I am absolutely giddy to share how our family's test is becoming our *testimony*. In September 2018, my son and daughter-in-law purchased their first home and watched helplessly as Hurricane Florence took it away within days of moving in their belongings. They lost everything. Damage was substantial, and the house was condemned. We knew the following four to six months would be difficult. We never dreamed the recovery would actually take twenty-one months.

There were days when we thought our kids would have to walk away and give up everything they had invested. There were days when we were so discouraged, we simply wanted to give up and walk away. For every step of progress we made, another complication would arise and take us three steps back. Damage was substantial and required that the house be elevated above flood level before restoration could begin. Elevation costs were not covered by insurance and were way beyond our means to pay. Early on, my husband and I realized this was too big for us to fix. It would have been hard enough had this happened to us, but to happen to our children…

When our son was just a tot, we could Band-Aid the booboos and kiss away the hurts. All was better. This catastrophic event, however, took the ability to fix things completely out of our hands. It's then we had to solely rely on a faithful God with a mighty outstretched hand!

I won't try to divulge the complications and challenges that have been a part of this process, as it would fill the pages of a book. What I do want to convey, however, is the faithfulness of my God.

Just as our test is reaching its completion, yours will too. What's left is the *testimony*—the best part of the story. The *testimony* allows us to comfort others, sharing lessons learned and wisdom gained. Most of all, the *testimony* allows us to share the changes, not only in our circumstances, but more importantly, the inward transformation our Father makes in us.

There are many people who became the hands and feet of Jesus, moving us to our *testimony*. We are forever grateful and changed, desiring to move forward with a serving heart. I'm praying for you if you're in a testing season. Your test may differ from mine, but I'm well aware of how consuming the test can be. When you've gone as far as you can, know your Father will strengthen, sustain, and even carry you when you're ready to give up. The Holy Spirit intercedes for you, and the Father whispers your name to His prayer warriors. Help is on the way. You will be able to tell all about it in *your testimony*!

> "He comforts us in all our troubles so that we can comfort others. When they are troubled, we will be able to give them the same comfort God has given us" (2 Corinthians 1:4 NLT).

Special Days

BIRTHDAY

FLOURISHING

My husband and I celebrate our birthdays the same week. That's a good thing! He doesn't forget my birthday.

We celebrate more than age. We celebrate the promises of our heavenly Father. I don't multitask as well as I once did. I'm not defying gravity as well as I have in past years. And yes, I wish the mirror were a little kinder these days, but my get-up-and-go has not gone!

I'm trading the stress that busyness brings for quiet time with my Father. I am finally grasping how inadequate my understanding is and how unsearchable are the vast riches of His knowledge.

I am releasing the addiction of perfection to being content with who I am in Christ. I'm letting go of things that once captivated my attention so my energies can now be spent on what really matters.

I cherish the health I have and am more committed to nurturing it. Not by any stretch am I wiser, smarter, or have reached the "utopia" (whatever that is). In fact, I realize more than ever how quick I can create a mess! The years are mellowing me to bear my endless faults.

I may not pass the benchmarks of success in our culture. I do find it easier to laugh at myself these days, especially when I mimic actions of my parents. I'm proud to flash my AARP and AMAC cards. No, my get-up-and-go is far from being depleted.

My personal strength exhausted itself long ago, but I have God's promise that I can do all things through Him. I'm not done growing, sowing, and working until God's done with me.

"Those who are planted in the house of the LORD Shall flourish in the courts of our God. They shall still bear fruit in old age; They shall be fresh and flourishing" (Psalm 92:13–14 NKJV).

Special Days

NEW YEAR

Word for the Day

WHOLEHEARTED

Have you ever participated in something when your heart wasn't in it? Others can usually tell. Sometimes we get labeled as "party poopers." Been there; I'm guilty! In Deuteronomy 6, Moses told the children of Israel, "The LORD is our God, the LORD alone. And you must love the LORD your God with all your heart, all your soul, and all your strength. And you must commit yourselves wholeheartedly to these commands that I am giving you today. Repeat them again and again to your children. Talk about them when you are at home and when you are on the road, when you are going to bed and when you are getting up. Tie them to your hands and wear them on your forehead as reminders. Write them on the doorposts of your house and on your gates" (Deuteronomy 6:4–9 NLT).

Jesus refers to these words in Matthew 22:37–38 as the first and greatest commandment. My New Year's resolution is to love God *wholeheartedly*! This must become a daily thing. My heart has to be in it. My love for Him must come from way down deep in the soul, and I must *wholeheartedly* commit to pursuing Him with all I am and all I have!

My prayer for you this year? "The LORD bless you and keep you; The LORD make His face shine upon you, And be gracious to you; the LORD lift up His countenance upon you, And give you peace" (Numbers 6:24–26 NKJV). Happy New Year!

Word for the Day

EXERCISE

Holiday traditions can bring on a few extra pounds. Thankfully, the new year often brings the motivation to work them off. Any way you look at it, *exercise* is an action verb that requires us to get up and get going. All the wishful thinking cannot jumpstart our metabolism or get us in shape. We have to put wishful thinking into motion. Our faith works the same way. The Creator endows each one of us with a measure of faith. Then it's up to us to feed and *exercise* it.

Second Kings 4 describes a poor widow woman who asked help from Elisha when creditors were threatening to take her sons. Elisha asked her what she owned, and the woman told him all she had was a flask of olive oil. Elisha instructed her to borrow as many jars as she could and fill them with the oil. The widow woman went into action mode. She directed her sons to get all the jars they could while she began to fill them. The oil lasted as long as the jars kept coming. She had enough oil to pay off her debtors and live on what was left over.

If the widow woman had only collected one jar, I believe the oil would have depleted with the one container. The results hinged on her actions. She and her sons collected all the jars they could find, even though she knew the olive oil in her flask was not sufficient to fill even one container. She *exercised* her faith, and she received all she could contain.

As the new year rolls in, I will probably be one of those who will attempt to jumpstart my physical fitness; but even more than that, I'm so ready to rev my faith into action mode! I'm praying this will be a year overflowing with miracles and breakthrough for those who prepare to receive!

Word for the Day

2020

I'm not sure I can count 2020 as a word, but it speaks volumes to me! As we approach the coming of Christ, our culture continues to deteriorate, and one must wonder just how far evil will take those who are not guarded or guided by the Lord God. For those of us who are, we do not have to fear or frown. Our Father is in control! Instead of feeling anxious, we can feel assured all is well.

I'm praying this year will be a year of light—that 2020 will explode in us and around us. May the light of His love and salvation shine in this dark world. May the gospel spread from the flicker of His love in our hearts. May the world's eyes be opened to the goodness and mercy of our Lord, Jesus Christ. May our faith guide us to higher heights and deeper depths. May the Lord open our eyes to His Word and His will.

I'm so grateful for this set of eyes the Lord has given me. They rock! They continue to be tops on the best pair list, even though they have experienced some wear and tear over the years. From a natural perspective, I may never have perfect vision, but my desire goes far beyond natural limitations. My focus for 2020 is spiritual vision.

Father, my prayer for this year is, "Open my eyes to see the wonderful truths in your instructions" (Psalm 119:18 NLT). May the revelation of Your words burn within my heart and be shared with those who cross my path.

Word for the Day

CITIZEN

As we come into the new year, many will begin preparing tax returns. In Matthew 17, a tax collector comes to Peter and asks if Jesus pays the temple tax. Jesus instructs Peter to go fishing. "Open the mouth of the first fish you catch, and you will find a large silver coin. Take it and pay the tax for both of us" (Matthew 17:27 NLT).

Jesus modeled good *citizenship* for us. First Timothy 2:1–3 instructs us to pray for all those who are in authority. Titus 3:1–2 says to submit to government and its officers and be ready to do what is good. Romans 13:7 says to render to all their due, whether it be taxes, customs, reverence, or honor. First Peter 2:13–17 (NKJV) says to submit to the ordinances of man, "For this is the will of God, that by doing good you may put to silence the ignorance of foolish men."

America needs our prayers! America needs us to be good *citizens*. "I pledge allegiance to the Flag of the United States of America, and to the Republic for which it stands, one Nation under God, indivisible, with liberty and justice for all." God bless America!

Special Days

VALENTINE'S DAY

MORE

Today is Valentine's Day! For some, this day will bring smiles and feelings of value. For others, today may bring tears and feelings of exclusion. At some time, we may experience disappointment in friendship and relationship. Something or someone may not meet our expectations, but isn't it comforting to know that God is *more* than enough? Our value, purpose, and fulfillment can never be stripped from us if we place these things in Christ.

First Kings 4 speaks of the blessings God granted to Solomon when he asked for wisdom to lead the nation of Israel. God gave Solomon *more* wisdom than all other men. (I can't see where the Scriptures says Solomon had *more* wisdom than women. Just saying!) Verses 32 through 34 (NLT) say, "He [speaking of Solomon] composed some 3,000 proverbs and wrote 1,005 songs. He could speak with authority about all kinds of plants… He could also speak about animals, birds, small creatures, and fish. And kings from every nation sent their ambassadors to listen to the wisdom of Solomon."

Not only did God grant Solomon wisdom above all men, but God also made him rich and gave his kingdom peace with its neighbors. Ephesians 3:20 (NLT) says, "Now all glory to God, who is able, through His mighty power at work within us to accomplish infinitely more than we might ask or think."

We may not always understand the works of God, but we can place our trust and hope in Him. When our desires line up with His will and our faith marries with His Word, our Father will lavish *more* blessing than we can ever imagine!

I hope Valentine's Day brings you *more* than you expected and *more* of God's goodness than you can grasp!

Special Days

EASTER

Word for the Day

NAILED

Being Easter week, we often think about Jesus being *nailed* to the cross for our sins. We speak of the *nail* prints in His hands, which serve as a reminder of the punishment our Savior took for us. Today, however, Galatians 5:24 (NLT), speaks tenderly to my heart: "Those who belong to Christ Jesus have nailed the passions and desires of their sinful nature to his cross and crucified them there."

What Christ did on the cross was more than enough to pay the sin debt of every man, woman, boy, and girl. I wasn't there to see Him bear my sin, but the moment I asked for forgiveness, my Savior received me in all my brokenness. I *nailed* my sin passions to His cross and crucified them right then and there, to receive a transformation that would forever change my life.

Repentance is more than saying, "I'm sorry." Godly sorrow includes crucifying our old desires and allowing our Savior to fill us with new ones. I'm glad I *nailed* the old Kathy to my Savior's cross. The day I gave my heart to Jesus, I actively participated in His crucifixion. From this day forward, when I think of my Savior on the cross, I will visualize my own hands *nailing* my sin passions to His cross while He willingly took the spikes. Just as He spoke to the man next to Him the day He was crucified, I can envision my Savior looking at me, saying, "You are forgiven, child. I have a place for you in paradise."

Word for the Day

GLORY

With the crucifixion approaching, I can only imagine the thoughts on Jesus's mind and the heaviness He must have felt. Jesus says, "Now my soul is deeply troubled. Should I pray, 'Father, save me from this hour'? But this is the very reason I came! Father, bring glory to your name" (John 12:27–28 NLT).

Jesus modeled a great prayer for us. God can be *glorified* in our sufferings just as He was *glorified* in the sufferings of His Son, so we wait in faith for His *glory*. He can be *glorified* in our everyday living, so we choose to walk according to His Word. God can be *glorified* in our success, so we give Him credit for our accomplishments.

Just as Jesus expressed His desire for the crucifixion to pass from Him, we can share our desires with our heavenly Father. "The LORD will withhold no good thing from those who do what is right" (Psalm 84:11 NLT).

Modeling after Christ, we must yield to the will of our Father, first and foremost. This is how we receive abundant life in Him and how others witness the *glory* of God in us. Our lives will bring *glory* to our Father if we are willing to chase after Him and not our own desires (1 Peter 4:2). As Romans 12:1 (NLT) says, "This is truly the way to worship him."

Word for the Day

ABANDONED

Mark 15 describes the final hours of Jesus as He hangs on the cross. Verses 33 and 34 (NLT) say this: "At noon, darkness fell across the whole land until three o'clock. Then at three o'clock Jesus called out with a loud voice, 'Eloi, Eloi, lema sabachthani?' which means 'My God, my God, why have you abandoned me?'" Why would He say that?

The very moment Jesus took on the sins of the world, He was banished from the presence of God. The beatings, the thorns pressed into His head, the splitting of His skin as spikes were driven into His hands and feet, the gasping of every breath—the pain must have been excruciating. Isaiah 52:14 (NLT) says, "His face was so disfigured he seemed hardly human, and from his appearance, one would scarcely know he was a man." But the unbearable part was having the Father turn away from Him, because sin could not abide in the presence of God.

Think about it—the Son of Man, who never knew sin, simultaneously bore the sins of every man, woman, boy, and girl. The stench, filth, and shame of our unrighteousness must have been suffocating—inhumane. Christ suffered the agonizing separation from the Father so we don't have to, so we can enjoy His eternal presence. "For the wages of sin is death, but the free gift of God is eternal life through Christ Jesus our Lord" (Romans 6:23 NLT).

Word for the Day

SILENCE

Friday—that most horrible day—finally ended. Jesus, the one His followers came to believe to be the Messiah, had been crucified and was dead. We can only imagine how His followers felt as the crowds disbursed.

Silence must have filled the hearts of those who loved Him—a *silence* that deafened their senses. No one wanted to talk about what happened. What was there to say? The Messiah they had believed in was gone. They would wake up on Saturday morning hoping it was all a terrible nightmare, only to experience flashbacks of yesterday's occurrence. The *silence* of death would once again paralyze their minds, crush their hopes, and leave them suffocating with emptiness.

If only they had known what joy was coming in the morning!

SATURDAY

The day after Jesus was crucified—the day before He arose in all His glory—was *Saturday*. It was a day of uncertainty. Anyone who had believed Jesus was the Messiah woke up to a *Saturday* of emptiness. Wishing they didn't have to rehearse the previous day, the graphic details of the crucifixion replayed itself over and over. Wondering what to do now left a blank stare in the eyes of His followers.

Feeling abandoned and foolish for believing Jesus was the Messiah, the people went about their daily routine aimlessly. But Sunday came and changed everything! Jesus walked out of the tomb, conquering death, hell, and the grave! The great news spread, and hope was ignited again!

You may be living in transition where the worst has happened. You wake up hoping it's all a nightmare, only for reality to settle in as the calendar marks *Saturday*. Your *Saturday* may last for a day, a month, or even years. Can I tell you Sunday is coming? God was there through your tragedy. While you are feeling alone to pick up the pieces, your heavenly Father continues to work behind the scenes to bring deliverance and healing. We aren't excluded from adversity, but we are promised Sunday if we don't give up.

"Weeping may endure for a night, But joy comes in the morning" (Psalm 30:5 NKJV).

Word for the Day

HOPE

What if Resurrection Sunday had never occurred? History would remember Jesus merely as a martyr. *Hope* in a Savior would have dissipated forever, but thank God for Resurrection Sunday!

This event separates Christianity from all other religions. Jesus sacrificed His life for our sins and was placed in the grave, but God's resurrection power raised Him on the third day, conquering death, hell, and the grave! Our Savior is not a memory from the pages of history, but a risen Lord—a living Lord!

The same resurrection power that raised Jesus from the grave lives in every believer and seats us with Him in the heavenly realms (Ephesians 2:6). Paul prayed that the Ephesian Christians would grasp the incredible greatness of God's power. When we allow His resurrection power to work in us, our Father can accomplish more than we can even imagine (Ephesians 3:20).

Jesus's followers thought *hope* was buried on Good Friday, but Resurrection Sunday came and *hope* was reignited! Blessings to you this Easter! May Jesus be your living *hope*!

Special Days

MOTHER'S DAY

Word for the Day

WORTH

The value of a gift is not always about the price tag. What makes a gift special is the thought behind it—the sentiment revealing the giver's insight. As a child, I remember making a Mother's Day gift at school. Each student was given three square boards varying in size. I painted all three white. The boards had no design, no flowers or bows. I simply painted them white (bless my heart).

I was so proud of those boards! I wrapped them in tissue and tied them with a pretty pink bow. I could hardly wait for Mom to open my gift on Mother's Day. It was only after my siblings started snickering, as my mother opened her gift, that I realized just how plain my boards were. My siblings laughed and asked what the boards were for, but my mother just raved about how wonderful her gifted "pot holders" were! She gave my gift *worth*, because she looked past the plain boards and saw my heart.

It's not what I can do for my Father that impresses Him. It's what He sees beyond my best attempts and biggest blunders that brings Him pleasure. He sees my heart for Him, and that brings Him delight. It's His delight that brings *worth* to every stutter of praise and every act of worship.

> "Let the words of my mouth and the meditation of my heart Be acceptable in Your sight, O LORD, my strength and my Redeemer" (Psalm 19:14 NKJV).

Special Days

MEMORIAL DAY

Word for the Day

SACRIFICE

There are those who *sacrifice* every day to put food on the table. There are those who *sacrifice* their time and energies to care for children and the elderly. There are those who *sacrifice* for our country, leaving their homes and loved ones behind. There are mothers and fathers, spouses and siblings, who share in the *sacrifice* so their family member can serve in foreign lands. Some return; some don't.

Today we remember those who have given the ultimate *sacrifice*. Words are inadequate to recognize those who have given their lives for our freedom. There aren't enough words to heal the hearts of the grieving spouses, the broken mothers and fathers, the loneliness of children who are missing their mama or daddy.

Our heavenly Father can comfort like no one else, because He knows all about *sacrifice*. His Son paid the ultimate price on the cross so every man, woman, boy, and girl can have everlasting freedom. Our heavenly Father is also the author of victory, and the same resurrection power that raised Jesus from the dead lives in the believer! First Corinthians 15:42 (NLT) says, "Our earthly bodies are planted in the ground when we die, but they will be raised to live forever."

While our words may be few and our gratitude inadequate, we say to those who remain, we remember, we care, we pray for you. Perhaps each of us can find a way to honor the fallen. Share a word, a meal, a moment with those who have experienced loss.

> "Love each other with genuine affection, and take delight in honoring each other" (Romans 12:10 NLT).

408

Special Days

FATHER'S DAY

FATHER

This day comes with mixed emotion as we celebrate Father's Day. Some people, like me, charge their success in life to their *father*, while others charge their failures to the lack of a supporting *father*. Some carry memories they will cherish forever, while others try desperately to forget. Some people hope to be just like their dad, while others sadly end up just like theirs. You may have the best *father*; you may not.

The good news is this: our Creator desires to be our *father*. He created us in His image. It doesn't matter how scarred we are. He will take our mangled mess and make us new—removing our transgressions from His sight, as though they never happened. From the moment we repent of our sins and believe in the Lord Jesus, we are adopted by Him and loved unconditionally.

That, my friend, should make this Father's Day a blessed one!

(I hope you get to spend today with a man like my dad, who is truly a giant of impeccable character, faith, and godly wisdom. He is a treasure in my eyes and yours too, if you know him!)

Special Days

INDEPENDENCE DAY

Word for the Day

CELEBRATE

How do you choose to *celebrate* Independence Day? There will be picnics and barbecues, fireworks and flags, movies and memorials, music and dancing with family and friends. Just what does independence mean? Doing only what we want? I don't think so. Can you imagine the chaos of living in a country with no rules, no boundaries?

I think the idea of independence denotes breaking away from one influence to be joined to another. In 1776, our nation declared freedom from Britain and declared its thirteen colonies united as free states. We became independent from Britain, not each other. Wouldn't it be great if we all could set aside our differences to *celebrate* our heritage? As a nation, we are blessed (Psalm 33:12). We have every reason and right to cherish and *celebrate* our independence.

As individuals, we are fearfully and wonderfully made (Psalm 139:14). Unique as we are, "We the People" are all created in the image of our heavenly Father and share a bond as fellow citizens. We *celebrate* our nation and its history with pride and gratefulness.

As born-again believers, we are united into the family of God and should *celebrate* freedom every day! We don't *celebrate* the right to do what we want; rather, we *celebrate* our freedom won at Calvary. As a born-again believer, I have the most to *celebrate* this Independence Day.

I salute my country and fellow citizens who stand "indivisible, with liberty and justice for all." I humbly bow to Jesus Christ, my Lord and Savior, who reigns over all, bringing ultimate freedom to anyone who will believe in Him (John 3:16)!

Special Days

REMEMBERING 9/11

UNITE

Isn't it interesting how the worst of times can bring out the best in us? Crisis brings community. Disaster jolts us to quick defense. Tragedy births a will for triumph. Flashing back to an unthinkable 9/11 drives us to *unite* our thoughts and prayers for families who suffered loss on that horrific day.

This day we set aside our politics, our prejudices, and agendas to remember our losses, honor our heroes, and respect our beloved America. We stand side by side, resilient, never to forget, ready to defend. We stand *united*.

Father, we lift every first responder, every military family, every medical team, our social workers, our teachers, and our leaders. Comfort those who experienced loss on this tragic day. Drape them in Your blanket of perfect peace. We pray for one another, as we all have a duty to love our neighbor. Keep us strong and quick to defend our freedom. May we maintain our dignity by maintaining Your commandments. Help us to love You with all our heart, soul, and mind. "This is the first and greatest commandment. A second is equally important: 'Love your neighbor as yourself'" (Matthew 22:37–39 NLT). Continue to pour Your mercy and blessings upon this nation. We pray in Jesus's name.

Special Days

VETERAN'S DAY

Word for the Day

GUARD

I don't know what it's like to hear bombing in the distance and wonder if the next blast will desecrate my home. I don't know what it's like to flee, leaving everything behind in search of safety. I don't go to bed in fear of my life, and I don't wake to the dreadful realization that I am living in a war zone. Why? Men and women from all corners of this nation have dedicated their lives to *guard* ours.

At a moment's notice, they are ready to do what it takes to keep this country—you and me—safe and secure. Because they do their jobs so well, we often go about our day without giving it a thought, until the calendar rolls around to days like this: Veteran's Day.

Today, we acknowledge the freedom we enjoy comes at a cost by the men and women who *guard* it. They serve time away from their families so that we can be with ours. They put their lives on the line so that we are free to pursue our dreams. While such holidays are sparse, our gratitude shouldn't be.

Father, thank you for those who are serving or have served our country. Your Word says, "There is no greater love than to lay down one's life for one's friends" (John 15:13 NLT). May Your grace and favor go with them, Your wisdom and protection sustain them, Your healing and presence shadow them. *Guard* them as they *guard* us, in Jesus's name.

Special Days

THANKSGIVING

Word for the Day

PRE-THANKSGIVING

Most of us love the holidays. (At least we say we do.) Do our families see the same person we post on Facebook? If we peel away the public image, who are we? I want to be real around the people I know. I desire the love of God to show, shine, and share in the best of times and in the worst—when my turkey turns out perfect and when it doesn't.

I desire to give with thanks—give my family and friends the love and attention they deserve. I desire to give my time and resources to make new memories—giving thankfully though I'm tired and feel like going to bed. I want to give without grumbling and complaining about the messy kitchen and the tight schedule.

What am I trying to say? I just want *thanksgiving* to be about cherishing all God has given me. I post this *pre-thanksgiving* devotional today with resolve to make tomorrow's holiday the best ever!

Father, "I will offer to You the sacrifice of thanksgiving" (Psalm 116:17 NKJV).

THANKSGIVING

Luke 17 describes an incident where ten lepers cried out to Jesus for help. They were required to stand at a distance because of their horrible disease. Having compassion, Jesus told them to go show themselves to the priest. As the ten men walked, the disease yielded to the authority of Jesus, and their bodies were made whole! One of them returned to give thanks. Jesus asked, "Didn't I heal ten? Where are the other nine?" (paraphrased).

Thanksgiving is one of my favorite holidays. I love family time and adding a bit extra to the table meal. I want to celebrate this day by giving thanks to my heavenly Father. He adopted me, and I am loved and cared for as His own. My life is in Him; my purpose, my peace, and my passions are wrapped up in my heavenly Father.

I celebrate this day by giving thanks to my Lord and Savior, Jesus Christ. His blood was shed and His body was broken so that we might have new life, inheriting the promises of His Word. I celebrate this day by giving thanks for family and friends who bring immeasurable richness to me.

Thanksgiving is more than a holiday; it is a way of life. Gratitude changes attitude! It heals our hearts and spirits. It changes our demeanor and helps us become the best person we can be—the person God designed. It's no wonder 1 Thessalonians 5:18 (NKJV) says, "In everything give thanks; for this is the will of God in Christ Jesus for you."

Happy *Thanksgiving*!

Special Days

CHRISTMAS

BLESSING

Mary, the mother of Jesus, was *blessed* above all women. But in her *blessing*, she probably suffered as much as any woman. Mary suffered among those closest to her (like Joseph) and her peers. The Lord gave her the greatest gift of all, and she is forever *blessed* among women. But in her *blessing*, she had to trust God to restore her relationship with Joseph and standing with her community.

God's *blessing* is over you too! With it comes intentional trust on your part for restoration, healing, and wholeness. The *blessing* is a promise to God's children. "You go before me and follow me. You place your hand of blessing on my head" (Psalm 139:5 NLT). But with every promise in God's Word, there is a premise: to obey His Word.

Yes, there will be seasons of suffering, but the *blessing* will be worth it! Profess His *blessing* over your life and thank Him for every good thing that comes to you—even through suffering.

Word for the Day

VIRGIN

The *virgin* birth of Jesus was not just a miracle of that era but the miracle of the ages! Really, what can top that?

Learning Mary was pregnant and knowing they had not been sexually intimate, Joseph must have loved her dearly. He didn't want any harm to come to Mary, but to believe her story—well, that's asking more than a man can do. An angel of the Lord came to Joseph in a dream and said, "Do not be afraid to take Mary as your wife. For the child within her was conceived by the Holy Spirit" (Matthew 1:20 NLT).

According to one survey, 66 percent of Americans say they believe Jesus was born to the *Virgin* Mary. I am most eager to be included in the 66 percent and declare my unshakable belief in the *virgin* birth! I stand firmly with those who will never be convinced that the *virgin* birth is a whimsical tale.

Jesus Christ is truly the Son of God and the Son of Man! His birth, His life, His death, His resurrection, is God-planned and God-orchestrated. The *virgin* birth brings the miracle of life to us all. "Look! The virgin will conceive a child! She will give birth to a son, and they will call him Immanuel, which means 'God is with us'" (Matthew 1:23 NLT).

Word for the Day

IMMANUEL

The Son of God came to live among us. John 1 says Jesus Christ existed with God from the beginning. "He came into the very world he created, but the world didn't recognize him" (John 1:10 NLT).

He left behind His royal place in heaven to be born in a cave-like barn, filled with the stench of animals. He left His royal place in heaven to become a man who had no place to lay His head. He left His royal place in heaven to be rejected, even by His own people. He left His royal place in heaven to become our Savior, bearing the sins of every man, woman, boy, and girl. "He was...crushed for our sins...beaten so we could be whole...whipped so we could be healed" (Isaiah 53:5 NLT).

The Son of God left His royal place in heaven so that He could be with us—experience our struggles, understand our pain, know our deepest hurts and disappointments. He left His royal place in heaven to provide us a royal home with Him. He understands us because He became flesh, lived among us, and experienced the frailties of human life. The story of Christmas lives in us! Isn't that the greatest gift of all?

> "The virgin will conceive a child! She will give birth to a son and will call him Immanuel (which means 'God is with us')" (Isaiah 7:14 NLT).

Word for the Day

MANGER

The *manger* is a familiar icon. One instantly recognizes it as a symbol of the Christmas story. However, the *manger* is more than a Christmas logo. It not only tells the Christmas story, but it tells Jesus's life story.

Jesus left His royal deity in heaven to begin His life in the lowest of human conditions—a feeding trough for animals. His birthplace serves as a reminder that "Though he was rich, yet for your sakes he became poor, so that by his poverty he could make you rich" (2 Corinthians 8:9 NLT).

The *manger* served as a feeding trough—a place where food was available to the animals. Jesus said in John 6, verses 33 and 35 (NLT), "The true bread of God is the one who comes down from heaven and gives life to the world. I am the bread of life. Whoever comes to me will never be hungry again. Whoever believes in me will never be thirsty."

The *manger* was a sign to the shepherds. Luke 2:12 (NLT) says, "And you will recognize him by this sign: You will find a baby wrapped snugly in strips of cloth, lying in a manger." Some believe the angel visited Levitical shepherds who used swaddling cloths to protect lambs for sacrifice. Perhaps the swaddling bands point to Jesus, the Sacrificial Lamb. While the strips of cloth were the attire of all newborns in that day, the definitive sign that pointed them to the Savior was the *manger*. Jesus said in John 14:6 (NLT), "I am the way, the truth, and the life. No one can come to the Father except through me."

The *manger* was the epitome of Jesus's life—from beginning to end. He willingly traded His royalty for humility, His honor for rejection. Ultimately, Jesus traded His life to become our Savior.

425

Word for the Day

REDEEM

When thinking of *redemption*, we often reflect on Easter—and rightfully so. However, the Christmas story is also a story of *redemption*. Throughout history, women have been marked and carry the stigma of Eve's weakness—being deceived to believe a serpent instead of the Creator. Through Mary, however, the role of the woman has been *redeemed* as salvation comes through her. Joseph serves as a model husband—loving, caring, and protecting his soul mate in the midst of questionable circumstances.

Most importantly, Jesus vacated His royal place in heaven to come live among us. Living in the world He created, Christ was not recognized or honored. He chose to come, knowing the suffering He would face from beginning to end. He came to *redeem* us from sin and the captivity it holds on our souls, minds, and bodies. He came to *redeem*, knowing many would never choose to accept life made available through His death.

Redemption for all—that is the essence of the Christmas story. As the angel proclaimed, "She will bring forth a Son, and you shall call His name JESUS, for He will save His people from their sins" (Matthew 1:21 NKJV).

ROOM

Luke 2 says Mary gave birth, wrapped Jesus in swaddling clothes, and laid Him in a manger. Why a manger? The scripture says there was no *room* for them in the inn. The holidays are filled with festivities—visiting, feasting, giving gifts, and spending time with those we love. I enjoy hearing Andy Williams sing "It's the Most Wonderful Time of the Year." I love most everything about Christmas. However, let me be transparent—the holidays don't always play out the imagery of our dreams.

Christmas time can be stressful, frustrating, and depressing. Some child is going to wake up disappointed. Some parent is going to cry all night because he or she couldn't afford the toy their child wanted. Someone will grieve the loss of their loved one. Some teenager will wake up cold and scared, wishing they could go home.

Jesus's birthday would not top our list of ideal celebrations, but His arrival brought the gift of hope to every man, woman, boy, and girl. If we make *room* in our hearts for Him, the spirit of Christmas will live in us from year to year. If we make *room* in our hearts for Him, we will make *room* for others—not just at Christmastime, but every day of the year. If we make *room* for others, we can change the world!

> "And above all things have fervent love for one another, for 'love will cover a multitude of sins'" (1 Peter 4:8 NKJV).

Word for the Day

BIRTHDAY

Christmas should be about celebrating Jesus's *birthday*. Truly, His *birthday* was less than ideal. He was born in a stench-filled cave and was laid in an animal feeding trough for a bed. His *birthday* was not about what people gave Him, rather what He gave people.

Perhaps you have been shopping for months to get the perfect gifts. The Creator designed us to enjoy giving, but the best gifts may not be available for purchase. The greatest gift may be forgiving someone. The greatest gift may be investing time in others. The greatest gift may be partnering with someone in prayer and encouragement. These gifts are truly priceless and reflect the character of our Father.

As a child, I recall our church giving fruit bags each year at Christmastime. Usually there would be one or two small pieces of candy in it, and that's what I always grabbed first! I will cherish the wonderful memory of the fruit bags, but the fruit of the Spirit is so much better—it's daily living proof of God's character in us (Galatians 5:22).

Father, I desire to share your love, joy, peace, longsuffering, kindness, goodness, and faithfulness to every family member, friend, and stranger. You have placed the greatest gift inside us. Help me to honor Your *birthday* by sharing Your character with whoever You place in my path.

(Merry Christmas, everyone. May you enjoy heaven's blessings this season!)

Special Days

POST-CHRISTMAS

OVER

Today, some will be taking down the Christmas tree, packing up all the decorations, and getting back to routine. Others will hold on a few more days to squeeze out the last bit of Christmas cheer. The shops will begin to fill up again as exchanges are made and after-holiday sales compete for Christmas cash. Some will earmark this holiday as the best one yet while others may label it disappointing, stressful, or just another day. In any case, our mind-set tells us Christmas is *over*.

While we fill the holiday season with traditions and all the busyness that comes with it, the ultimate reason for the season births hope with the coming of a Savior. That, my friend, means Christmas is never *over*!

The most important part of Christmas lives within us, and we are compelled to share it with the world. Whether we feel sad, relieved, or ready to move to the new year, I pray the spirit of Christmas is renewed within us and spills over to our families, friends, and neighbors. "I pray that God, the source of hope, will fill you completely with joy and peace because you trust him. Then you will overflow with confident hope through the power of the Holy Spirit" (Romans 15:13 NLT).

Word for the Day

PRESENCE

If I had all the Christmas presents that get returned, exchanged, re-gifted, or tucked away in a closet, I would have enough inventory to start my own business! Of course, gift giving is about the thoughtfulness behind it, right? Come on, we all need to appreciate the thought; although I admit some of us could invest a little more thought into the giving process. Deadlines can push us into making thoughtless choices. I'm guilty!

I love presents, but my years are teaching me that our greatest gift can simply be our *presence*. The time our kids spend with us is priceless! Certainly, without doubt, the Lord's *presence* makes the holiday and every day, a blessed one. His *presence* connects us, empowers us, and changes us to resemble Him in character. He desires that we enter His *presence* daily. He doesn't push himself on us, nor does He walk away. The door is always open. He is delighted to meet us in the secret place—that place where it's just Him and us.

The *presence* of Christ in us is the best gift we will ever receive. The *presence* of Christ in us will be the best present we can give to the world. "You will show me the way of life, granting me the joy of your presence and the pleasures of living with you forever" (Psalm 16:11 NLT).

Father, thank you for sending Your *presence* to live among us and in us. Teach us how to walk in your *presence* each minute of every day. May Your *presence* in us touch those around us. May Your *presence* light the world!

HAVE

America is blessed! Compared to many countries, we *have* plenty with an abundance to share, yet people are searching for more. The entire Old Testament points to the need for a Savior. The New Testament proclaims the good news: "The Savior—yes, the Messiah, the Lord—has been born today in Bethlehem, the city of David! (Luke 2:11 NLT).

We *have* a Savior! From a cattle stall to the cross, our Savior, Jesus Christ, fulfilled His destiny to provide all that we will ever need. The wails and groans of the Hebrew children cried for the need of a Savior, but our song should be "Joy to the world! The Lord is come!" While the world needs a Savior, we can proclaim we *have* a Savior and point them to the cross.

For those of us who know Him, we must not allow difficult times to rob our understanding of who God is. Psalm 42:5–6 (NLT) says, "Why am I discouraged? Why is my heart so sad? I will put my hope in God! I will praise him again—my Savior and my God!"

Let us remember the good news that brings great joy to all people: We *have* a Savior!

GOODWILL

There are two events that seem to bring out *goodwill* in man: crisis and Christmas. My children are firsthand recipients of *goodwill*. In September 2018, Hurricane Florence destroyed their home and all they had. Restoration was accomplished by the *goodwill* God placed in the hearts of so many who graciously supported them, giving their time, skills, funds, encouragement, and prayers.

The Christmas season often creates *goodwill*. Opportunities to give are on every corner and in every mailbox. Our heavenly Father created us in His image; thus, we are created to show *goodwill*.

Doing what our Creator has designed us to do sends a fresh burst of "God-sized serotonin" that reaches our deepest core! Jesus describes *goodwill* this way: "'Lord, when did we ever see you hungry and feed you? Or thirsty and give you something to drink? Or a stranger and show you hospitality? Or naked and give you clothing? When did we ever see you sick or in prison and visit you?' And the King will say, 'I tell you the truth, when you did it to one of the least of these my brothers and sisters, you were doing it to me!'" (Matthew 25:37–40 NLT).

Goodwill should be our lifestyle, not just a response to crisis or Christmas. What we do for others glorifies our Father. As Paul says in Galatians 6:9–10, "So let's not get tired of doing what is good. At just the right time we will reap a harvest of blessing if we don't give up. Therefore, whenever we have the opportunity, we should do good to everyone—especially to those in the family of faith" (NLT).

WHO

As we celebrate the arrival of a new year, the media will salute the old one. Major events will be replayed, highlighting the good, the bad, and the ugly. Faces and images will most likely flash across our screens, representing those who have made it to the prestigious *"Who's Who"* list: the richest, the most powerful, the most whatever. One thing is for certain: I will not be on the list! I won't personally know those *who* are.

There is a list, however, on which I am included: the Lamb's Book of Life. My name is written in the book! Hallelujah! I know *who* created me and *who* loves me. I gratefully know the one *who* died for my sins. I'm elated to know *who* is coming back to rule and reign. I personally know *who* is in control.

I am a blessed woman! I am included on the most important list of all—not because of *who* I am, but *whose* I am. Are you on the list?

Word for the Day

AHEAD

B eing the last day of the year, many of us spend time looking back, reflecting on the past twelve months. There were good times, and there were bad times. Who knew how this year would unfold? Our Father did! Nothing catches Him by surprise.

Our Creator already knows what the new year holds for each of us. The words He gave to Moses to communicate to the children of Israel are applicable to us. "Do not be afraid or discouraged, for the LORD will personally go ahead of you. He will be with you; He will neither fail you nor abandon you" (Deuteronomy 31:8 NLT).

The Lord has already gone *ahead* of us and is fully aware of each bump in the road—every challenge, the temptations we will incur, the decisions we will face. He has already begun to prepare us. We can't look *ahead* and know what God knows, but we can look *ahead* with peace, knowing our Father's already been there.

Special Days

CRISIS

Word for the Day

CALM

Yesterday carried strong winds and the dread of the unknown. Today brings *calmer* winds and hope of restoration. I am referring to Hurricane Dorian, but crisis may be sitting on your doorstep and you're yet to find the *calm* in your mind-set. Psalm 91:1 (NLT) says, "Those who live in the shelter of the Most High will find rest in the shadow of the Almighty."

Your crisis may be storm-related or it may be life-related. Some things are too big for us to fix, but there is a God—the Most High. Psalm 91 says our God rescues us, protects us, covers us, and shelters us. What the Holy Spirit does on the inside of us opens the door for God-sized miracles.

Ask the Holy Spirit to heal your mind-set. Camp out in the Word to restore hope, strength, and faith. Psalm 91 is a great place to start. Allowing our Father to heal the inside brings a *calm* that spills into our everyday living.

> "The Lord says, 'I will rescue those who love me. I will protect those who trust in my name. When they call on me, I will answer; I will be with them in trouble. I will rescue and honor them. I will reward them with a long life and give them my salvation'" (Psalm 91:14–16 NLT).

Word for the Day

AFFECT

The coronavirus will be etched in 2020's global history. A year ago, I would not have believed a virus would bring America to a slow crawl. Whether we become infected with the virus or not, we are all *affected*.

As believers, however, we have the best news to share: God loves us, and He is in control. This is the time to seek God's mercy, favor, and healing. This is the time to be the church! After all, the church is not a building; it's the body of Christ. The lack of assembling ourselves under one roof leaves us feeling like fish out of water. Our Father is well aware of the situation, and He can restore healing as quickly as the enemy took it. Meanwhile, let's be the church and do what Jesus would do. Let's pray for the sick, pray for protection, and pray for those in authority. Let's become the ones who encourage instead of the ones who criticize. Let's infect our community with good citizenship, love, hope, and compassion.

This is a grand opportunity to reflect the character of Christ. The scriptures say it best: "And because of his glory and excellence, he has given us great and precious promises. These are the promises that enable you to share his divine nature and escape the world's corruption caused by human desires. In view of all this, make every effort to respond to God's promises. Supplement your faith with a generous provision of moral excellence, and moral excellence with knowledge, and knowledge with self-control, and self-control with patient endurance, and patient endurance with godliness, and godliness with brotherly affection, and brotherly affection with love for everyone" (2 Peter 1:4–7 NLT).

Let's infect our communities with the hope of Jesus Christ, who is the only one who can *affect* the whole man—body, soul, and mind.

Word for the Day

DISTANCE

COVID-19 births a new buzz word for 2020: Social *distancing*. Is this hard for most of us? Of course, it is! Our Creator designed us to be sociable. He also created us with the need to connect to Him. I'm grateful we have the technology to stay in touch with family and friends. While it's not the same, we can stay connected at a *distance* until the danger of spreading the virus passes.

Our Father has provided everything we need to stay in relationship with Him. First, He sent His Son to bridge the gap Adam and Eve created when they sinned in the garden. Jesus Christ became the gateway to restore relationship with the Father. He has given us His Word to teach us how to maintain our relationship, and He has given us the Holy Spirit to seal our relationship with constant companionship.

We don't know what it's like to see our Father face-to-face, but we will one day. We will live with Him forever—never to connect at a *distance* again. Yes, it will be a great day when the coronavirus and social *distancing* is history, but an even greater day is coming when we will see our Savior face-to-face! "For the Lord himself will come down from heaven with a commanding shout, with the voice of the archangel, and with the trumpet call of God. First, the believers who have died will rise from their graves. Then, together with them, we who are still alive and remain on the earth will be caught up in the clouds to meet the Lord in the air. Then we will be with the Lord forever" (1 Thessalonians 4:16-17 NLT).

Word for the Day

DOSE

When we find ourselves ailing, we often seek help from our doctors. Thank God for their dedication and skills that help us get better. Sometimes they will prescribe a regimen of medicines or supplements to combat the virus or disease attacking us. Taking the last *dose* is as important as taking the first one. Once we start feeling better, we're often tempted to disregard the doctor's instructions.

The Great Physician reminds me today that He has given us His Word and His Holy Spirit to keep us spiritually, physically, and emotionally well. We need a healthy *dose* everyday—whether we're feeling sick or not! Conventional medicine requires strict adherence to intake instructions. The Great Physician's medicine is simple: take all you can! You'll love the side effects: love, joy, peace, patience, kindness, goodness, faithfulness, knowledge, and wisdom.

With the threat of the coronavirus pandemic, it's imperative we run to the Word and allow the Holy Spirit to anoint us with His peace. A healthy spirit will go a long way in getting us through hard times, so we may need to increase our *dosage* around-the-clock.

When feelings of fear approach, it's time to take a *dose*. (Try reading 2 Chronicles 20 or Psalm 23.) When worry tries to flood our minds, it's time to grab another *dose*. (Try Psalm 61. Need more? Add Psalm 91 or Philippians 4.) And even when we're feeling strong, it's imperative to take a good *dose*. (Check out John 15.)

Remember the Great Physician's instructions: take all you can! He has an unlimited supply, and you can't over*dose*. "The name of the LORD is a strong tower; the righteous run to it and are safe" (Proverbs 18:10 NKJV).

Word for the Day

TRUST

I'm wondering where my next roll is coming from. No, I'm not talking about bread. I'm talking toilet paper! Whoever thought toilet paper would become a hard-to-find commodity? I'm beginning to feel like the man who camped by the pool of Bethesda. He missed one opportunity after another to get into the healing waters, because someone always beat him to it. When it comes to getting my next roll, it seems like I'm a day early or a day late!

All kidding aside, perhaps the Lord is teaching people like me to be content with what we have today and *trust* Him for tomorrow. Jesus gave us a model prayer in Matthew 6. I learned to recite it as a child. You probably did too. Here I am, in my senior years, being enlightened to verse 11 (NKJV) that says, "Give us this day our daily bread." The model prayer teaches us to ask for what we need each day—day by day—no more, no less. My mouth speaks these words, but my comfort level says, "I want it all, and I want it now."

America has lived in abundance. Convenience has become entitlement. Being a new experience for most of us, convenience is being stripped by the coronavirus pandemic. Now we are being called to live wisely, one day at a time. God fed manna to the children of Israel in the wilderness but only provided a day's portion (Exodus 16). When the next day arrived, a new portion was available—no more, no less.

Our Creator already knows what our tomorrow looks like. Certainly, we have an obligation to practice good stewardship, but our Father wants us to recognize Him as Yahweh-Yireh, our Provider. We're always going to worry about tomorrow if we are in control.

Tomorrow is too big—too much for any of us without God! Why not *trust* the one who's already been there?

> "All you who fear the LORD, trust the LORD! He is your helper and your shield" (Psalm 115:11 NLT).

Word for the Day

OTHERS

Being the baby of my family, I never experienced what it was like to be replaced as the youngest. Some might label "us babies" as the spoiled ones. I think many of us are beginning to realize how blessed we are—how America has spoiled us. In the midst of COVID-19, we are waking up to change. Not all of it is bad. We are being called to repentance. We are being called to prayer. We are being called to serve *others*.

Let's put it in perspective. We can whine about the empty shelves. We can fret over a chipped nail or a past-due haircut, or we can look at *others* that are out of a job. Those who are jobless can sit wringing their hands, or they can think about the business owners who've been forced to shut their doors. The business owners can either padlock what they have left or find ways to contribute and become part of a solution. America is waking up to the challenge.

How can we be so insensitive to whine when our neighbor may not survive the day? How can we afford to do nothing when there is something we can do? Ultimately, all of us who are healthy and well can find ways to serve those who aren't. We may be restricted to our homes, but our prayers aren't confined! They are reaching the only one who can forgive and heal our land.

I don't think America is adapting to a new normal—only a temporary one. God is our healer and defender. Second Chronicles 7:14 (NLT) says, "Then if my people who are called by my name will humble themselves and pray and seek my face and turn from their wicked ways, I will hear from heaven and will forgive their sins and restore their land." Father, help me do what I can do, because *others* are depending on it.

LOOK

History (Numbers 21) records how the Israelites forgot God. They no longer remembered Him as their God of deliverance. They were no longer thankful. The miracle manna was no longer appetizing or satisfying. Their hearts were hard, and they no longer revered God. They spoke against Him and His appointed leader, Moses. Consequently, poisonous snakes entered their camp, and many died from the bites. In their moment of crisis, they realized their sin and called on Moses to intercede for them. The Lord instructed Moses to place an image of a snake on a pole. Those who had been bitten were told if they would *look* up at the snake, they would live.

As Hollywood says, "The names have been changed to protect the innocent," but the storyline is strikingly similar. The world has forgotten God. They are no longer thankful, nor do they desire the things of God. His children are ignored, disregarded, and in some places, even persecuted to the extent of death. Sin is everywhere, and sin is destroying people everywhere. The consequences are deadly. We're in crisis!

You and I have the answer—let's point people to the cross. Christ is the Savior of the world. He is our hope, our help, and our healer. Let us *look* up and intercede on behalf of our families, our communities, and our world. Prayer changes everything!

Father, we confess our sins, our weaknesses, and ask You to revive us. We cannot save ourselves, but You can restore all things. We *look* to You for our redemption. Once again, forgive our sins and heal our land. "Turn us again to yourself, O God. Make your face shine down upon us. Only then will we be saved" (Psalm 80:3 NLT).

ABOUT THE AUTHOR

Being a preacher's kid, Kathy Barker grew up playing church and eventually serving in church. If you hear her speak, you will surely detect a southern accent. She has taught Sunday school to kids, teens, and seniors alike; worked in Christian summer camps; and continues to work in music ministry. After retiring from a federal government career, Kathy volunteered with a pregnancy crisis support center where she now serves on staff. Kathy and her husband, JR, have been married for thirty-five years and reside in Smithfield, North Carolina.

CPSIA information can be obtained
at www.ICGtesting.com
Printed in the USA
BVHW030228091221
623619BV00005B/87